TRIUMPH IN THE ATLANTIC

The Naval Struggle Against the Axis

Edited by Fleet Admiral CHESTER W. NIMITZ, u.s.n.,

HENRY H. ADAMS, and E. B. POTTER

PRENTICE-HALL, INC. A SPECTRUM BOOK Englewood Cliffs, N. J.

TRIUMPH IN THE ATLANTIC: The Naval Struggle Against the Axis consists of Chapters 27 through 33, slightly revised and corrected, of *SEA POWER*. It is a companion volume to *TRIUMPH IN THE PACIFIC: The Navy's Struggle Against Japan.*

Library of Congress Catalog Card No.: 64-15310

Printed in the United States of America—C
P 93076

Table of Contents

Preface

Triumph in the Atlantic is the story of the Allied navies against the Axis. It was the sea war that made the land war in Europe and Africa possible. The sea war was fought over the range of the Atlantic and Mediterranean, against the worst hazards men could invent and the worst nature could provide. Through U-boat and surface attack, air threat and minefields, piercing cold and blazing heat, mountainous seas, blinding fog and cutting winds, ships carried out their missions of bringing the troops and supplies to the men and women who needed them.

The authors, while retaining responsibility for errors of fact and interpretation, are grateful to many for their help in this narrative. Among them are Admiral H. Kent Hewitt, USN (Ret.); the late Commander F. Barley, RNVR (Ret.), Commander G. A. Titterton, RN (Ret.), Lieutenant Commander M. G. Saunders, RN (Ret.), and Lieutenant Commander P. K. Kemp, RN (Ret.), of the Historical Section, British Admiralty; Lieutenant Commander D. W. Waters, RN (Ret.), Keeper of the Navigation Section, National Maritime Museum, Greenwich; Vice Admiral Giuseppe Fioravanzo, former Director of the Historical Division of the *Marina Italiana;* Vice Admiral Friedrich Ruge, former Chief of Naval Operations, Federal German Navy; and M. Jacques Mordal, Historical Section, Ministry of the French *Marine.*

The authors wish to acknowledge sources for illustrations appearing on the following pages: page 21, adapted from Antony Martienssen, *Hitler and His Admirals* (New York: E. P. Dutton & Co., 1949); page 32, adapted, with the permission of the Controller of H. M. Stationery Office, from Captain S. W. Roskill, RN, *The War at Sea, 1939-45,* vol. II (London: H. M. Stationery Office, 1956); page 96, adapted from David W. Waters, "The Philosophy and Conduct of Maritime War," *Journal of the Royal Naval Scientific Service,* July 1958; page 107 adapted from Dwight D. Eisenhower, *Crusade in Europe,* copyright 1948 by Doubleday and Company, Inc., by permission of the publisher.

The authors and Admiral Nimitz wish to emphasize that *Triumph in the Atlantic* is in no sense official history. The opinions expressed are the writers' own.

H. H. A.
E. B. P.

1

Atlantic Surface Operations

"It is peace in our time," said Britain's Prime Minister, Neville Chamberlain, when he returned from the Munich conference with Adolf Hitler. Less than a year later, at 0445 on September 1, 1939, Nazi armies hurled themselves against Poland, and the holocaust of World War II began. The danger signs had been unmistakable from the latter part of August, when Hitler signed with Russia a non-aggression pact that freed him from the danger of Soviet intervention. England and France had mutual aid treaties with Poland, but Hitler had no reason to suspect that they would honor them any more than they had fulfilled their Munich-repudiated moral obligations to Czechoslovakia.

The German *Führer* planned a swift campaign that would smash Poland while Britain and France vacillated. He thus would present them with a *fait accompli*. But he failed to consider the change in temper of both leaders and people in the two western countries. This time he would be opposed with force to the utmost, on land, on sea, and in the air. The British presented the Germans an ultimatum during the evening of September 1 and issued a final warning at 0900 on the 3rd. At 1115 on September 3, 1939, in a broadcast to the nation, Prime Minister Chamberlain announced that His Majesty's Government was at war with Germany. France followed suit that afternoon. The same day a round-faced, chubby man of dynamic fighting spirit returned as First Lord of the British Admiralty, an office he had relinquished 24 years earlier. A signal was flashed to the fleet: "Winston is back."

There was little that Britain or France could do to aid Poland. Germany unleashed a new kind of warfare on the Polish plains, a war of rapid movement, heavily mechanized, in which tanks were used to spearhead long lines of advance and to encircle whole armies. Overhead, the *Luftwaffe* swept the ineffectual Polish Air Force from the skies, and then roared in with Stukas and Messerschmitts to wipe out Polish infantry strong points in the way of the onrushing German divisions. In a few weeks all was over on the Polish front. Here the *Blitzkrieg*, or lightning war, tactics had done their work. But all was not over in the West. Though British and French mobilization had come too late to help Poland, Britain and France laid plans to meet any westward thrusts of the German *Wehrmacht*—Britain primarily through the use of her sea power; France by means of her armies sheltered behind the Maginot Line.

Hitler had no wish to face a real war with Britain and France—at that time. He accepted the Russian occupation of half of Poland in an effort to keep the war localized. He hoped that he could persuade Britain and France to accept the situation and agree to peace, thus affording him time to build up his navy for a war in the West in 1944 or 1945. Hence, after the Polish operation had been completed, Hitler refrained from any offensive action on the Western Front, a measure of restraint that brought about what has been called the "Phony War." Through the winter of 1939-40 German troops in the Siegfried Line faced French troops in the Maginot Line with only small skirmishes relieving the monotony.

The War Begins at Sea

Near the end of 1938, Grand Admiral Erich Raeder, *Oberbefehlshaber der Kriegsmarine,* had presented Hitler with a choice of plans. One, based on the assumption that war was imminent, called for most of Germany's naval resources to be devoted to weapons of commerce warfare —U-boats, raiders, minelayers, and coast defense forces. The other, known as PLAN Z, was a long-range program, based on the assumption that war was not to be expected for ten years. Under this plan, Germany would build a surface fleet of ships so superior to those of the Royal Navy that she could wrest mastery of the oceans from Britain.

Hitler informed Raeder that he should proceed on the basis of PLAN Z. The reason for this decision, sorely mistaken in the light of subsequent events, is difficult to fathom. Hitler valued the big ships for their political influence. He also appears to have been seized with a desire to emulate and perhaps outstrip Great Britain, little anticipating that his projects on the Continent would involve him in war with her. When he overreached himself in Poland, he was stunned by the British ultimatum. Not until 1940 did he give up hope of Britain's agreeing to peace.

Whatever the reason for Hitler's decision, it left his navy in no condition for war. By the end of 1939 PLAN Z was well launched, but the fleet would not be combat-ready before 1945. Experiments had yet to be evaluated. Only interim ship types had been completed. Having begun by laying down conventional vessels, the Germans were gradually introducing bolder experiments. To ensure long radius of action they depended heavily on diesel propulsion, but in 1939 some German ships had mixed power plants, using both diesel and steam.

At the outbreak of war, the German navy comprised the following units: two battleships, *Scharnhorst* and *Gneisenau*, completed; two battleships, *Bismarck* and *Tirpitz*, nearing completion; three 10,000-ton, 11-inch "pocket battleships," *Deutschland, Scheer,* and *Graf Spee;* three heavy cruisers, *Hipper, Prinz Eugen,* and *Blücher;* and six light cruisers, *Karlsruhe, Köln, Leipzig, Nürnberg, Emden,* and *Königsberg.* Twenty-six merchant ships had been converted into armed merchant cruisers. A respectable number of destroyers, torpedo boats, minesweepers, and auxiliaries completed the surface fleet. German submarine warfare, which was directed by Admiral Karl Dönitz, began operations with only 56 U-boats. Twenty-one submarines, the *Graf Spee,* and the *Deutschland* were at sea in waiting areas even before the outbreak of war.

The Germans at sea struck hard from the first. The day England entered the war, the British passenger liner *Athenia* was sunk by *U-30,* whose commander could not resist the temptation when he found her in his periscope sights. Dönitz, Raeder, and Hitler all issued denials of German responsibility—in good faith because they could not believe a U-boat commander had disobeyed their orders to spare passenger ships. In less good faith was Propaganda Minister Goebbels' declaration that Churchill had engineered the whole thing himself in the hope of involving the United States in the war.

British naval strategy was necessarily almost the converse of Germany's. The Royal Navy promptly blockaded the German North Sea coast and the exits from the Baltic by means of the Home Fleet based on Scapa Flow. Britain's most vital task however was to ensure that ships bringing more than 40 million tons of cargo a year entered British ports and discharged their cargoes. Oddly enough, pre-war British planning to attain that goal overlooked the lessons of World War I. Reviving the old misconception that convoys are less efficient in delivering goods than independently routed ships, the Admiralty planned to continue independent sailings. The sinking of the *Athenia* however changed Admiralty minds, and convoys were quickly instituted.

The first convoy sailed for Halifax on September 8. Its escort accompanied it for 300 miles, then picked up an inbound convoy and brought it safely to United Kingdom ports. This was the early pattern of convoy operations, because shortage of escorts did not permit protection far beyond the British coast. During the first two years of the war moreover, because of the activity of German surface raiders, the Admiralty considered it necessary to provide each convoy with a heavy escort, a battleship or cruiser if possible, otherwise a converted, armed passenger liner.

That the threat from German surface raiders was real was soon made apparent by the activities of the *Deutschland* and the *Graf Spee.* By the middle of October the *Deutschland* had sunk two merchant ships and committed a first class diplomatic blunder by seizing the American freighter *City of Flint*. Under a prize crew, the *City of Flint* sailed to Murmansk, in North Russia. Later, en route to Germany via Norwegian territorial waters, she was intercepted by the Norwegians and returned to her master. The incident caused much anti-German sentiment in the United States. It was also the first incident to attract Hitler's attention, militarily, to Norway. On her return to Germany, the *Deutschland* was renamed *Lützow* lest home morale suffer should a ship named *Deutschland* be lost.

The Battle of the River Plate, December 13, 1939

The *Graf Spee* operated in the area between Pernambuco and Cape Town, although in November she slipped over into the Indian Ocean south of Madagascar for a brief period. On the way back, she met her supply ship *Altmark*, refueled, transferred prisoners, and then resumed her search for victims. The effectiveness of her cruise, completely apart from the 50,000 tons she sank, is shown in the number of Allied ships assigned to chase her. Out of Freetown, the British naval base on the western bulge of Africa, operated the carrier *Ark Royal* and the battle cruiser *Renown;* from Dakar two French heavy cruisers and the British carrier *Hermes* joined the search. The heavy cruisers *Sussex* and *Shropshire* were poised at the Cape of Good Hope, and up and down the east coast of South America ranged Commodore Sir Henry Harwood's force consisting of the two heavy cruisers *Cumberland* and *Exeter* and the light cruisers *Ajax* and H.M.N.Z.S. *Achilles.*

Commodore Harwood's group, less the *Cumberland,* which was refitting in the Falklands, on December 13 succeeded in intercepting the *Graf Spee* in the approaches to the River Plate. The contact presented Harwood a ticklish tactical problem. The *Graf Spee's* six 11-inch guns outranged the cruiser guns by about 8,000 yards. None of the cruisers could long withstand her fire. Their only opportunity would be to come in from widely diverging angles in order to force the *Graf Spee* to divide her fire. The cruisers would not be able to reply until they had passed through the danger zone from about 30,000 yards, the range of the *Graf Spee's* guns, to about 22,000 yards, the effective limit of the cruisers' main batteries. If the *Graf Spee* had been properly handled, she would have turned directly away from the cruisers, forcing them to a stern chase. Even with their speed advantage of about five knots, it would have taken the cruisers nearly half an hour to pass through the danger zone. Probably they would never have made it. But Captain Hans Langsdorff thought he had a cruiser and two destroyers to deal with. Since they stood between him and the open sea, he ran down to meet

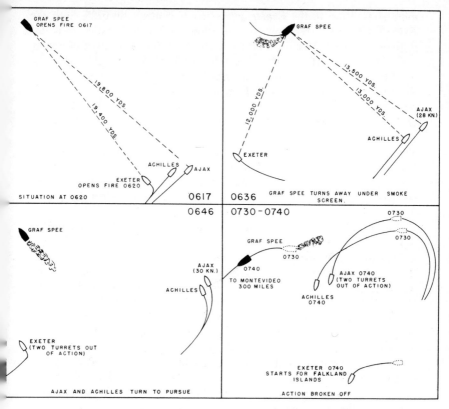

BATTLE OF THE RIVER PLATE, DECEMBER 13, 1939

them and to break his way through to freedom. The three British cruisers were in column, the *Ajax* leading and the *Exeter* in the rear. At 0617 the *Graf Spee* opened fire, whereupon the *Exeter* made a turn to port to engage from the south, while the two light cruisers held their northerly course to engage the enemy's opposite bow. On the completion of her turn, at 0620, the *Exeter* opened fire at a range of 19,400 yards. The *Ajax* and *Achilles* commenced fire a few minutes later, and the 6- and 8-inch shells from all three ships began to hit effectively. The *Graf Spee*'s shells also took their toll. Soon the *Exeter* received a hit that knocked out her "B" turret, destroyed bridge communications, and killed or wounded nearly everyone on the bridge. The German then shifted fire to the two light cruisers and turned away under a smoke screen, apparently to make for the River Plate. As the *Ajax* turned in pursuit, the *Graf Spee* once more shifted fire to the *Exeter,* again under control. By 0725, both the *Exeter*'s forward turrets were out of action, and at 0730 power was lost to the after turret. Meanwhile the *Ajax* had two turrets put out of action, and Commodore Harwood decided to break off until night, when he would have a chance to make a torpedo attack. The *Exeter* started on the long voyage to the Falklands, while the wounded *Graf Spee* set her course for Montevideo, dogged by the *Ajax* and *Achilles.* Occasional exchanges of fire occurred all day, but neither side attempted to renew the battle. A little after midnight, the *Graf Spee* entered Montevideo. There Langsdorff hoped to effect repairs and force his way clear at a later date. He had chosen Montevideo on the advice of his navigator and was not aware of the political situation whereby he would have received a much more sympathetic welcome in Buenos Aires, farther up the river.

Frenzied diplomatic activities on the part of the German consular representatives were unsuccessful in getting permission for the *Graf Spee* to remain in port longer than 72 hours. British propaganda was more successful in giving the impression of a large British fleet just offshore. Actually only the *Cumberland* had joined the battered *Ajax* and *Achilles.* From Berlin Langsdorff received the option of fighting his way out or scuttling his ship. Shortage of ammunition decided him to take the latter course. Having landed wounded, prisoners, and most of his crew, he got underway on the afternoon of December 17. The British cruisers went to action stations, but before they could engage her, the *Graf Spee*'s skeleton crew abandoned her just before she blew up. Langsdorff shot himself shortly afterward. Thereafter for several months the Germans abandoned the use of surface raiders.

Other Operations at Sea

While the *Graf Spee* was still finding victims, other units of the German navy had been active. Most striking was the penetration of Scapa Flow on the night of October 14 by the *U-47* under the command of Lieutenant Günther Prien, who was to become one of Germany's U-boat aces. Prien successfully navigated the tortuous channel and sank the battleship *Royal Oak* with the loss of 786 of her officers and men. In late November the two German battleships *Scharnhorst* and *Gneisenau* passed out into the Atlantic through the North Sea, primarily to cover the return of the *Deutschland* from her mid-Atlantic raiding, and incidentally to see what they could pick up in the way of British merchant shipping. They came upon H.M.S. *Rawalpindi,* a converted passenger liner armed with four old 6-inch guns and carried on the Admiralty List as an armed merchant cruiser. Her commander, thinking he had found the *Deutschland,* was under no illusions about the outcome of such an encounter, but he accepted the odds against him. The *Scharnhorst* opened fire and the *Rawalpindi* replied as best she could. In a few minutes, the British ship was reduced to a helpless wreck. Before she sank, the cruisers *Newcastle* and *Delhi* arrived on the scene, but only to lose contact with the Germans in the darkness and heavy rain. The British Home Fleet sortied from Scapa Flow, but the two Germans, their presence revealed and hence their usefulness lost, headed for home, slipping through the British cordon. The hopeless fight of the *Rawalpindi* had not been in vain, since the two powerful raiders were driven from the sea before they could get into the commerce areas.

The *Altmark* Affair

The German supply ship *Altmark*, which had replenished the *Graf Spee* shortly before her final action off Montevideo, was serving as a floating prison for some 300 British seamen taken by the pocket battleship. The British were anxious to capture the *Altmark*, but she successfully hid in the South Atlantic for nearly two months. Gambling that the search had died down, she attempted to make her way back to Germany. She was favored by the weather and was not sighted until February 14, in Norwegian territorial waters. A flotilla of destroyers under Captain Philip Vian in H.M.S. *Cossack* intercepted her at Jossing Fiord but took no further action pending a directive from the Admiralty. When Vian received his instructions, he sent two destroyers with orders for a boarding party to examine the vessel. Two Norwegian gunboats met the small force and told Vian that the *Altmark* was unarmed, had been examined, and had received permission to proceed to Germany, making use of Norwegian territorial waters. Accordingly the destroyers withdrew for further instructions.

Churchill now sent orders for Vian to board the *Altmark*, using force if necessary in self-defense. While the Norwegian authorities continued their protests, the *Altmark* made the first belligerent move by getting under way and attempting to ram the *Cossack*, which evaded the clumsy attempt and then ran alongside the German ship and sent over a boarding party. After a sharp hand-to-hand fight, the German crew surrendered. Examination revealed that the British prisoners were battened down in storerooms and that the ship had two pompoms and four machine guns.

Although the British action was a violation of Norway's neutrality, Norway's position was by no means clear. The *Altmark* had not, in fact, been searched, claiming immunity by reason of the special service flag which made her a naval auxiliary. The British claimed that she was not on "innocent passage," since she was returning from war operations and had prisoners on board, and that it was up to Norway to enforce her own neutral rights. Yet Norway was in the unhappy position of not daring to enforce her rights against her two powerful belligerent neighbors. Although most of her people were sympathetic with the Allied cause, they feared Germany and her ever-present threat of action. Hence Norway made strong protests to Britain over the *Altmark* affair, hoping, no doubt, thereby to stave off German counter-action.

The Invasion of Norway

Norwegian hopes of being allowed to remain on the sidelines of the war were vain. A glance at the map gives a partial reason; from the Norwegian coast the British naval base at Scapa Flow can be outflanked. If Germany intended to operate either U-boats or surface units in the open Atlantic, she could get them out more easily from Norwegian than from German bases. But another feature, not so readily apparent, made use of Norwegian waters even more vital to Germany. Norway's coast, extending from Egersund to North Cape, offers a 1,000-mile-long sheltered passage between the offshore islands and the mainland. This passage, known as the Leads, has served Norway as a means of communication since Viking times; it also served the Germans in the two world wars. Ignoring Norwegian neutrality, German ships could take advantage of their own air cover in traversing the Skagerrak or Kattegat, make a dash across the narrow seas between the Skaw and Kristiansand or Egersund, and then follow the Leads until they chose to make a break through to the Atlantic.

Yet the use of the Leads by warships was only a small part of the story. The principal reason for the German invasion of Norway can be given in the single word, *iron*. Annually Germany imported 15 million tons of iron ore, and of this total, nearly 75 per cent came from Scandinavia. In summer this ore was carried through the Baltic Sea from the Swedish port of Lulea to Germany, safe from the Royal Navy, which could not penetrate the Skagerrak. But the Baltic freezes in winter, and then the iron ore had to be transported overland to the Norwegian town of Narvik. Forty-one per cent of Scandinavian iron came by this route. Thus Norway was vital to Germany.

Admiral Raeder early brought the Norwegian situation to Hitler's attention, but argued that Norway's neutrality was to the advantage of Germany, provided it was respected by the British. Yet, realizing that Britain would not allow such a gaping hole in her blockade to go unplugged, Raeder ordered the naval staff, the *Seekriegsleitung* (SKL), to prepare plans for the invasion of Norway, should it be necessary. In an attempt to win his goal by peaceable means, he arranged for a meeting between Hitler and the strongly pro-German Vidkun Quisling, who he mistakenly believed could win control of the Storting, the Norwegian

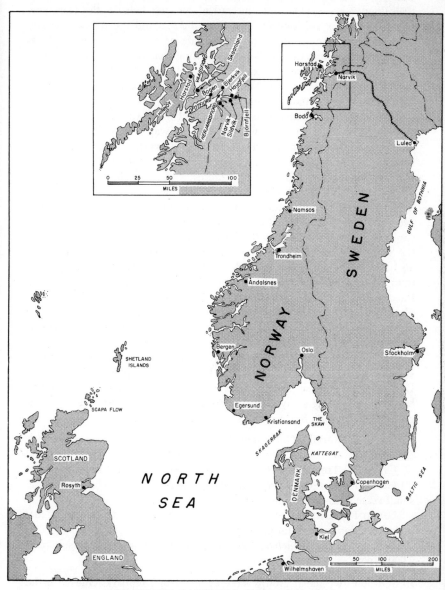

NORWEGIAN CAMPAIGN, APRIL–JUNE 1940

parliament. The winter proved that events would not take the course that Raeder hoped. Quisling, instead of offering help to the Germans, began to ask for aid himself. The *City of Flint* and the *Altmark* affairs indicated that the Leads were not as safe as they had seemed. Then intelligence reports reached Berlin indicating that the British were planning to mine the Leads. The Germans believed that the Norwegians would acquiesce. Hence on March 1, 1940, Hitler issued the order for Operation WESERÜBUNG, the invasion of Norway and Denmark.

The operation violated every principle of naval strategy except one—surprise. The invasion force would make its way across the sea in the face of the power of the foremost navy in the world and would land at several widely separated points, some nearly a thousand miles from German bases. It would have to establish and maintain itself and fend off the inevitable British counterattack. Yet these things had to be done if Norway was to be captured. One feature gave the key to success—the geography of the area. After the initial assault, German supply lines could be maintained through the Kattegat with only a short dash through the Skagerrak from the Skaw to Oslo Fiord. In this area, close to German air bases in the north, the Royal Navy could not operate. To protect this route the Germans decided to occupy Denmark as well as Norway. Thus Raeder and the SKL estimated that if the initial landings could take place without excessive loss, then the positions could be maintained through sea transport to Oslo and by overland transport from Oslo to the various occupied positions.

The Germans committed their entire surface navy and most of their U-boats to the Norwegian operation. Raeder fully expected to lose half. Dönitz, to his intense annoyance, was ordered to provide 25 U-boats to be stationed off Norway. He had to strip the North Atlantic hunting grounds to comply. Surface ships were assigned as follows:

Group I, Narvik: *Gneisenau, Scharnhorst,* and ten destroyers with 2,000 troops.

Group II, Trondheim: *Hipper,* four destroyers, and 1,700 troops.

Group III, Bergen: *Köln, Königsberg,* the old training cruiser *Bremse,* small vessels (E-boats) and 900 troops.

Group IV, Kristiansand and Arendal: *Karlsruhe,* a depot ship, a torpedo boat flotilla, and 1,400 troops.

Group V, Oslo: *Blücher, Lützow, Emden,* a few small vessels, and 2,000 troops.

In addition, two naval groups were assigned to Denmark. One with the old battleship *Schleswig-Holstein* had the responsibility for the Great Belt area, while a smaller group of light craft with 1,000 men undertook the capture of Copenhagen.

All landings were to be carried out simultaneously in the early morning of April 9, 1940. While the German preparations were going forward, the British, in one of the major coincidences of the war, were themselves planning operations in Norway. To attempt to stop the German use of the Leads, the Admiralty planned to lay mine fields off Narvik, announcing their intention to the Norwegian government simultaneously with the act. This operation was scheduled for the night of April 6, and had it been carried out then, it might well have balked the German scheme. Anticipating that the Germans might react vigorously to the mining, even to the extent of an invasion of Norway, the British had a small expeditionary force embarked in ships to proceed with the minelaying forces. However, because of last minute difficulties, the undertaking was postponed for 48 hours, and as intelligence of German activity reached London, the Cabinet decided to disembark the troops until the situation was "clarified." Thus, when the German expedition sailed, the troops so sorely needed for prompt counteraction in Norway were in England.

The opening event of the Norwegian drama took place at sea on April 8 with a chance encounter between a German destroyer and the British destroyer *Glowworm*. Before either ship was seriously damaged, the German heavy cruiser *Hipper* from the Trondheim group appeared on the scene, Gallantly the *Glowworm* attacked the newcomer, making effective use of smoke. At length, in a sinking condition, she rammed her adversary, tearing a hole in the cruiser's side. As the *Glowworm* fell away, she blew up and sank. The Germans rescued some 40 survivors. Her captain was posthumously awarded the Victoria Cross.

The next act took place about 0330 on the morning of April 9, when the battle cruiser *Renown* encountered the *Gneisenau* and *Scharnhorst* in a brief, inconclusive engagement. To the British, the circumstances did not seem to indicate a major German assault on Norway, although the Admiralty believed that these forces might be bound for Narvik. The Norwegians also did not consider the events ominous, nor had they taken warning from the sinking of the German transport *Rio de Janeiro* by a submarine a few hours earlier off Kristiansand. When these warnings were misinterpreted, the situation passed its critical moment. The German gamble was beginning to succeed.

Denmark offered little resistance. A thousand soldiers landed in Copenhagen, and a smaller detachment on the western side of the island quickly seized key positions and communications. Before the Danes realized what was happening, they were under the Nazi heel.

In Oslo the Germans received one of their most serious setbacks. They had to traverse the 70-mile-long Oslo Fiord, where they could not expect to escape observation, even at night. Near the naval base at Horton, some 25 miles south of Oslo, the Fiord narrows to about 200 yards, and here the naval guns were alert. Opening a prompt and effective fire, the Norwegians sank the cruiser *Blücher* at 0623. While the

German naval attaché waited anxiously on the pier at Oslo, the German assault forces landed south of Horton and seized it from the rear. This accomplished, they pressed on. In the meantime Fornebo Airfield at Oslo had been seized by airborne troops, and the city was soon under control of the Germans. The King, however, had removed the government to Hammar, 100 miles to the north.

At most other points the landings were unopposed or met little serious resistance, except that the guns at Bergen heavily damaged and immobilized light cruiser *Königsberg,* allowing British naval aircraft to sink her the next day. At Narvik, far to the north, the German invasion force was opposed only by the Norwegian coastal defense ships *Eidsvold* and *Norge,* which were sunk after a gallant but futile resistance. Then the ten destroyers proceeded up the Fiord to land their troops, while the two battleships carried out their mission of general support.

It seemed that Operation WESERÜBUNG had succeeded beyond the most optimistic expectations of its planners. The losses had been very light and all objectives were in German hands by the end of April 9. It was now up to the Army to exploit the opportunities won for them by the Navy. The Navy still had the tasks of getting its warships out of Norwegian waters and of maintaining the supply lines to Norway.

The first counterattack came at Narvik. The British Admiralty, recognizing the supreme importance of this port, prepared to act as swiftly as possible. Believing that only one destroyer had entered Narvik, they ordered Captain B. A. W. Warburton-Lee, commanding a destroyer flotilla: "Proceed to Narvik and sink or capture enemy ship. It is at your discretion to land forces, if you think you can recapture Narvik from the number of enemy present." Later, learning that the Germans were stronger than had been anticipated, they gave Warburton-Lee the option of canceling the operation if he believed German defenses made it impracticable. His reply was characteristic of the traditions of the Royal Navy: "Going into action."

Accompanied by the destroyers *Hunter, Havock, Hotspur,* and *Hostile,* Captain Warburton-Lee in the *Hardy* entered Ofot Fiord before dawn. In the approach phase, the *Hotspur* and *Hostile* engaged the shore batteries while the other three ships pressed into the port. There they found not one, but five German destroyers and several merchant ships. In the first attack, the *Hardy* torpedoed German destroyer *Wilhelm Heidkamp,* killing the German commodore. Another German destroyer was sunk by gunfire and a third was beached. Recovering from their surprise, the Germans opened fire and straddled but failed to hit the *Havock.* The British ships then retired under a smoke screen. Shortly they returned for a second attack, augmented by the *Hostile* and *Hotspur,* the latter sinking two merchant ships. The British pressed home a third attack, but this time the fortunes changed. Warburton-Lee discovered three fresh

German destroyers coming down on him from Herjangs Fiord. At a range of 10,000 yards he opened fire and turned away. The British ships then commenced a retirement, keeping up a running fire, but ran into an ambush at Ballangen Fiord, where two more destroyers were awaiting them. The *Georg Thiel* engaged the *Hardy*, which shortly afterward took a hit on the bridge that killed Warburton-Lee. The *Hardy* sank a few minutes later. Making a swing to the left, the *Georg Thiel* launched a spread of torpedoes at the *Hunter*, which also sank. The *Hotspur* and *Hostile* were both damaged, but, together with the *Havock*, made their way to the open sea. The damage the Germans had sustained made them helpless to follow or to carry out their planned retirement to Germany. On the way out, the three surviving British destroyers encountered German ammunition ship *Rauenfels*. After a few salvos from their guns, the German blew up in a tremendous explosion.

A few days later, on April 13, a heavy British naval force including battleship *Warspite* and carrier *Furious* finished off the work begun by Warburton-Lee, sinking all eight destroyers that had survived his attack. The lesson of these two battles was plain. Warburton-Lee, much outnumbered, had accepted action in an area where the speed and maneuverability of his ships were restricted and in an area that afforded many chances for ambush. Effecting tactical surprise on his arrival, he did considerable damage, but was surprised himself by being caught between two forces, one of which blocked his way to the open sea. In the second battle, the British properly used overwhelming force to ensure completion of the job.

In general, British reaction to the German operations in Norway was marked by indecision and improvisation. Keenly conscious that the Germans had flouted Britain's sea power, the British eagerly sought a way to hit back at the invaders. The situation called for rapid, decisive countermeasures, for the German forces were the most vulnerable immediately following the landings. Until road and rail communications were opened from Oslo to the several points of German occupation, troops had to live on the materials already provided them. The sea could not serve for supply in face of an alerted British Home Fleet. While the Germans worked feverishly to build internal communications in Norway, the British Cabinet lost critical days in trying to decide where to counterattack. With most of their troops already committed to the French front, there were very few available for operations in Norway, although the French were willing to supplement the British contingent with a brigade of Chasseurs Alpins and two brigades of the Foreign Legion. Where the Allied troops could best be placed was the big strategic problem facing the Cabinet. Two main possibilities offered themselves, Narvik and Trondheim. As has already been noted, Narvik was of supreme importance, since it controlled the export of iron ore from

Norway and Sweden. Also, in view of the success already won there by the naval forces, Narvik appealed to several key officials, including Churchill. On the other hand, Trondheim had its adherents because here Norway narrows to only a few miles and all land communications to the north can be controlled from that city. The Cabinet started to follow up the naval successes in the Narvik area, but when this operation was barely under way, the government shifted the point of the main attack to the Trondheim area.

Narvik

The first detachment of troops sailed for Narvik on April 12, 1940, with troops under the command of Major General Mackesy, while the naval forces in support were under Admiral of the Fleet Lord Cork and Orrery. General Mackesy's instructions contained the following points:

> It is clearly illegal to bombard a populated area in the hope of hitting a legitimate target which is known to be in the area, but which cannot be precisely located and identified.

❖   ❖   ❖

> The object of the force will be to eject the Germans from the Narvik area and establish control of Narvik itself. . . . Your initial task will be to establish your force at Harstad, ensure the cooperation of Norwegian forces that may be there, and obtain the information necessary to enable you to plan further operations. It is not intended that you should land in the face of opposition. . . . The decision whether to land or not will be taken by the senior naval officer in consultation with you. If landing is impossible at Harstad, some other suitable locality should be tried. A landing must be carried out when you have sufficient troops.

The cautious tone of these instructions seems to have impressed itself so deeply upon General Mackesy's mind that he took little account of a more aggressive suggestion in a personal letter from General Ironside, Chief of the Imperial General Staff: "You may have a chance of taking advantage of naval action and should do so if you can. Boldness is required."

The manner in which the Narvik attack was planned clearly reveals British unpreparedness for conducting amphibious operations. Mackesy's instructions emphasized caution, when boldness was needed. Mackesy and Cork were made equal commanders, with no clear-cut definition of their individual or joint responsibilities. Most curious of all was the choice of Harstad for the initial landing. Forces at Harstad could not interdict German supplies to Narvik, the main objective, and to attack Narvik from Harstad would require further amphibious operations.

While the expedition was en route to Harstad, Cork received a dispatch from the Commander in Chief of the Home Fleet suggesting that, in view of the success of the attack by the *Warspite* and *Furious*, a direct assault on Narvik could be carried out. Cork urged Mackesy to make the attempt, but the General refused, pointing to his instructions with regard to bombing civilian areas. Further pressed, Mackesy insisted that the German defenses at Narvik were too strong to be forced by means of naval bombardment. Finally, he admitted that his transports were not combat loaded. In the face of Mackesy's opposition and unpreparedness, Cork had no alternative but to proceed with the original plan.

Next came a dispatch from the Cabinet urging the bolder course on Mackesy:

> Your proposals involve damaging deadlock at Narvik and the neutralisation of one of our best brigades. We cannot send you the Chasseurs Alpins. The *Warspite* will be needed elsewhere in two or three days. Full consideration should, therefore, be given by you to an assault upon Narvik covered by the *Warspite* and the destroyers, which might also operate at Rombaks Fiord. The capture of the port and town would be an important success. We should like to receive from you the reasons why this is not possible, and your estimate of the degree of resistance to be expected on the waterfront. Matter most urgent.

Mackesy remained adamant, and the landing at Harstad proceeded. Once ashore, he announced that he was unable to advance on Narvik until the snow melted and until he had built up his supplies. Thus while the Germans strengthened Narvik, British troops at Harstad suffered attrition from the cold and from *Luftwaffe* attacks that seriously imperiled attempts at supply and reinforcement.

Trondheim

Meanwhile the British cabinet had turned its attention to Trondheim. The plan called for a main assault at Trondheim itself, with subsidiary landings at Namsos, a hundred miles to the north, and at Åndalsnes, a hundred miles to the south. The landing at Namsos took place under heavy German air attack on April 15, and that at Åndalsnes three days later. The main landing at Trondheim was to follow April 22. But on the 18th, the Chiefs of Staff began to have reservations about the Trondheim landing, emphasizing the tremendous risks of the long approach up the Fiord. They recommended instead that the landings at Namsos and Åndalsnes be developed into main drives, to capture Trondheim overland by a double envelopment. At length this view prevailed, in spite of the opposition of Churchill and of Admiral of the Fleet Sir Roger Keyes, who offered to take some older ships into Trondheim himself. The counsel of caution once more carried the day.

The Allied Evacuation From Norway

It soon became evident that the Allies could not maintain their beach-heads at Namsos and Åndalsnes in the face of growing German air power operating from captured Norwegian airfields. British and French cruisers and destroyers could bring in supplies and reinforcements by night, but during the day the *Luftwaffe* ruled the air, bombing the Allied bases into rubble and interdicting Allied communications. British carriers attempted to provide fighter support, but there were not enough carriers to operate aircraft continuously and not enough fighters to provide simultaneous protection for the carriers, other naval forces in the area, and the troops ashore. An attempt by a squadron of fighters from H.M.S. *Glorious* to operate from a frozen lake while the carrier pulled out of German bomber range resulted in the prompt destruction of the fighters. The Allies had no alternative to evacuating their forces in late April and early May, leaving the Germans in possession of all of southern and central Norway.

There remained however the British toehold at Harstad, in the north. On April 20, the Cabinet, exasperated by General Mackesy's repeated delays, appointed Lord Cork to over-all command of the operations against Narvik. Finally, in mid-May, the British made their assault, not directly against Narvik, but against Bjerkvik, to the north, with the intention of building up a force there and then attacking Narvik across Rombaks Fiord. The Bjerkvik operation, supported by planes from the *Ark Royal*, was a complete success. By now airfields had been prepared ashore for use by the R.A.F., and carriers *Glorious* and *Furious* ferried in enough fighters to offset the growing German air power in the area through the next stage in the campaign.

By this time however Germany had invaded the Low Countries and France, and total Allied defeat was imminent on the Western Front. Accordingly fresh instructions went to British forces in the Narvik area: capture the city, destroy the installations, and prepare for evacuation. Narvik fell to the British on May 28, following a successful crossing of Rombaks Fiord the preceding day. The evacuation took place soon afterward, being completed by June 8, in three convoys transporting 24,000 men and quantities of equipment and supplies.

To oppose this evacuation Raeder sent the *Scharnhorst* and the *Gneisenau* to the northern area. Known as Operation JUNO, this sweep had the further purpose of covering the movement of other elements of the German fleet to Trondheim. With the British Home Fleet committed to support of the Narvik evacuation, the German ships reached Trondheim safely. The *Scharnhorst* and *Gneisenau* surprised and sank the *Glorious* before she had a chance to get her planes into the air, together with her two escorting destroyers, which made gallant efforts to save their charge. In addition the Germans sank two merchant ships and an antisubmarine trawler. The remainder of the Allied Expeditionary Force reached England safely.

Thus ended the Norwegian campaign. Brilliantly conceived and executed by the Germans, it showed what could be accomplished by a ruthless nation, willing to take any advantage of friendship and neutrality. Germany's use of the sea routes across areas theoretically commanded by British sea power showed what an inferior naval force can accomplish through surprise. Once the Germans had made good their beachheads they no longer had to rely on surprise, for they could supply and reinforce their forces via the Kattegat, immune to Allied attack, and then overland in Norway.

The British operations in Norway had to be undertaken, if only for political reasons, but they cost Britain more prestige than they gained. The Belgians, the French, and, later, the Greeks remembered Norway when their own days of crisis arrived.

The Fall of France

The disastrous Allied expedition into Norway brought about the fall of the British government. On May 10, 1940, the day that Hitler struck at the Low Countries, Neville Chamberlain yielded the office of Prime Minister to Winston Churchill, who set out to form a National Government with ministers representing all parties, in contrast to the Conservative Government of his predecessor. Under Churchill's leadership the war was pursued with vigor and courage through the darkest hours, when Britain stood alone.

Neither Holland nor Belgium was able to make a significant resistance to the *Blitzkrieg* of the Nazi forces pouring across the Rhine. Hitler, finally abandoning all hopes of a compromise peace with the West, had hurled his armies through the Low Countries, as the Kaiser had done a quarter of a century before. The Allies were forced back at point after point, overwhelmed as the Poles had been by a combination of air power and panzer (armored) divisions. Although the French and British air forces occasionally achieved local superiority, they were never able to stop the onrushing Germans. Despite French protests, the British retained 25 air squadrons for home defense, refusing to commit everything to what was rapidly becoming a lost cause.

By again advancing through Belgium, as in World War I, the Germans simply passed around the left flank of the Maginot Line. Then the panzer divisions, followed up by motorized infantry, drove westward from Sedan to the English Channel, trapping the British Expeditionary Force in Belgium and Northern France. As early as May 20, the Admiralty, recognizing that a supreme effort was now needed to save the army, began to organize shipping for an evacuation from Dunkirk, on the French coast near the Belgian border. British private boat owners spontaneously aided naval efforts, volunteering themselves and their craft for service. The Lords of Admiralty accepted these gladly, but there was hard naval planning as well. They hoped to rescue about 45,000 men in two days.

Hitler, believing that the *Luftwaffe* would render escape impossible, ordered his panzer forces to stop short of Dunkirk—partly in fear that he was over-extended and partly to give Air Marshal Hermann Goering's planes the glory of wiping out the would-be evacuees. Goering intended to paralyze the troops on the beach by repeated bombing and to sink the rescue ships as fast as they appeared. He reckoned however without three factors. First, bombing of the troops was ineffective, the soft sand absorbing much of the force of the explosions. Second, the Royal Air Force was fully committed to protecting the Dunkirk beachhead; even the British Metropolitan Air Force, the last reserve that had been withheld from the defense of France, entered the battle. Third, the presence of evacuation ships and craft in such large numbers provided simply too many targets. Pleasure boats, fishing craft, destroyers, mine-sweepers, trawlers—ships and boats of all types—shuttled from Dunkirk beach to English ports and then back to reload. When the operation was completed, 338,226 men had been safely delivered to England by 861 vessels, with a total loss of 243 vessels sunk and many damaged. Less spectacularly, nearly half a million British and French, soldiers and civilians, were lifted from other French ports during the last hours of France's freedom.

On June 11, in order to participate in the German victory, Italy declared war on France and Britain, and Italian troops crossed the French border. Paris fell to the Germans on June 14, and the next day Premier Paul Reynaud requested the British government to release France from her pledge not to make separate terms with Germany. The British agreed on the condition that the French fleet would not fall into the hands of the common enemy. Determined to fight on, Britain urged France to continue the battle from her colonies in North Africa and from overseas. Churchill even went the length of offering France union with England, the two people to share common citizenship. The French Assembly rejected this appeal and could see no way to comply with Britain's requests for continuation of the war. Churchill and Reynaud advised General Weygand to surrender in the field, as this would not tie the hands of the French government. Weygand refused. He would not surrender, said he, unless an armistice were negotiated by the na-tional government. Such a national armistice would of course be bind-ing on all French armed forces, not simply on the army as Churchill and Reynaud desired. For the French navy to continue the war from overseas would be a violation of the armistice terms, and Germany would be able to undertake whatever measures she saw fit in retaliation. Weygand of course was imposing his desires on the political level, but Premier Reynaud did not relieve him. Reynaud was in fact in no position to take any action, for the next day, June 16, he was forced to resign, being succeeded by Marshal Philippe Pétain, who immediately appealed for an armistice. The Germans put the capstone on French humiliation by conducting the armistice proceedings in the same railroad car that had been used for the German Armistice in 1918. France was divided into two zones: occupied France, the Atlantic front and all of the northern part including Paris; and unoccupied France, with a government under Pétain but dominated by the Nazi sympathizer Pierre Laval and his associates.

Meanwhile Admiral François Darlan, Commander in Chief of the French navy, who had pledged his word of honor that the French fleet would not fall intact into the hands of the Germans, sent all ships the following message in code:

> I refer to the clauses of the armistice now being telegraphed in plain language by other channels. I am taking advantage of the last coded messages I can send in order to make known my views on this matter.
>
> First—The demobilized warships are to stay French, under the French flag, with reduced French crews, remaining in French metropolitan or colonial ports.
>
> Second—Secret preparations for auto-sabotage are to be made in order that an enemy or foreigner seizing a vessel by force shall not be able to make use of it.
>
> Third—Should the Armistice Commission charged with interpreting the text come to a decision different from that in paragraph one, warships are without further orders to be dispatched to the United States or, alternatively, scuttled, provided that no other action is possible to preserve them from the enemy. Under no circumstances are they to fall into enemy hands intact.
>
> Fourth—Ships that seek refuge abroad are not to be used in operations against Germany or Italy without prior orders from the Commander in Chief.

The armistice terms as finally announced provided that French ships were to be assembled in ports to be specified, either in France or in French colonies under German or Italian control. Germany solemnly declared it her intention not to make use of the French ships herself or to claim them at the conclusion of peace. On the other hand, the armistice provided that French Atlantic bases must be placed completely at the disposal of the Germans for U-boat operations. Italian terms were almost identical with the German. The armistice with both Germany and Italy became effective at 0035 on June 25, 1940.

Despite French assurances and despite their knowledge of the general provisions concerning the French fleet, the British felt far from satisfied that the French navy would in fact be kept from Axis hands. Some French ships were already in British ports—two battleships, four light cruisers, a few submarines, eight destroyers, and about 200 mine-sweepers and antisubmarine vessels. But a large number of vessels were in French national or colonial ports, where the Germans might gain control of them.

The situation confronted the British with a dilemma. Hourly expecting invasion, hard put to fulfill existing naval commitments, they were in no shape to cope with a fleet the size of that remaining to France. Having no knowledge of Darlan's orders of June 24, the British felt that they could not stake their national security on the word of their enemies. Noting that the ships would be under Axis control and that the armistice could be voided at any time by Germany on grounds of "noncompliance," the British War Cabinet reluctantly decided to take whatever measures were necessary to see that the French fleet did not fall into Axis hands, accepting the risk that their action might bring France into the war against them. On July 3, 1940, all French ships at Plymouth and Portsmouth were seized. Some of the French sailors volunteered to man their former vessels and serve under the Free French flag, taking as their commander General Charles de Gaulle, who had established himself as head of the Free French Government in Exile in opposition to the German-dominated Vichy government of Marshal Pétain.

The resolution of the problem of the French fleet in the Mediterranean brought tragedy, as will be recounted in the next chapter. To immobilize the French battleship *Richelieu* at Dakar, on the western bulge of Africa, the British carrier *Hermes* approached and sent in six torpedo-bombers which attacked the battleship, doing enough damage to keep her off the seas for a year. Two French cruisers and a carrier in the West Indies were neutralized through the diplomatic efforts of President Roosevelt. Thus, while attaining only partial success, the British were able to preserve their tenuous command of the sea, but at a cost of embittering their former French allies. This unfortunate by-product of their operations was to exact its toll at the time of Operation TORCH, the invasion of North Africa in late 1942.

German Plans for the Invasion of England: Operation Sea Lion

Jubilant over his swift conquest of France and confident that Britain would capitulate in a few weeks, Hitler at first paid scant attention to any idea of invading England. In this belief he was encouraged by *Luftwaffe* commander Hermann Goering. Admiral Raeder however feared the situation was such that Hitler might suddenly order a cross-

Channel attack. Raeder regarded Britain as the chief foe, but had little confidence in the success of an invasion, since he felt that he had inadequate time and resources to stage it. Although his exploratory soundings got no response, Raeder went ahead with preliminary planning in order not to be caught off guard when it became obvious even to Hitler and Goering that Britain had no intention of surrendering. Raeder understood the difficulties far better than the army commanders, who commenced to show an interest in invading England, for they had millions of victorious troops on hand and no place to go with them. They eyed the English Channel and thought that crossing it would present no more problems than crossing a very wide river. Encouraged by the army, Hitler on July 16, 1940, issued a directive for the invasion of England, Operation SEA LION.

This directive, drawn up by the army, showed little grasp of the naval problems involved. It ordered that the landing be made on a broad front extending from Ramsgate to a point near the Isle of Wight, a front of approximately 200 miles, and that it be ready to jump off by August 13. Patiently Raeder explained that landing on such a scale would require many harbors for preparation of the invasion fleet, that the French ones were too damaged for use, that the concentration of shipping in these harbors would infallibly reveal the plan to the British, and that in any

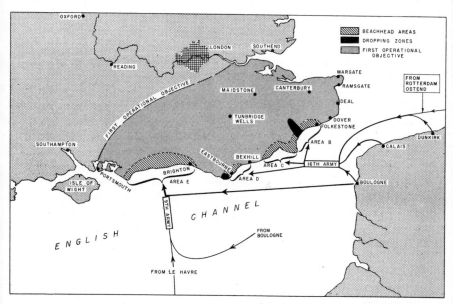

GERMAN PLANS FOR INVADING ENGLAND, SUMMER 1940

event Germany did not have anything like the number of ships the operation would require. Raeder emphasized that the assault must be on a narrow front where there could be a reasonable hope of maintaining a supply line across the Channel. From his point of view the only possible landing sites lay between Dover and Beachy Head. On hearing this proposal, the Chief of the Army General Staff retorted, "I might just as well put the troops that have landed straight through a sausage machine." The Naval Chief of Staff replied that he wanted to put the troops ashore and not at the bottom of the sea.

Hitler finally had to intervene personally to resolve the conflict. The plan, as finally worked out, was for landings in four main areas: Folkstone-Dungeness, Dungeness-Cliffs End, Bexhill-Beachy Head, and Brighton-Selsey Bill. This compromise pleased no one, but both the army and the navy proceeded to draw up their plans in accordance with it.

In the meantime, everything depended on the *Luftwaffe*. All agreed that command of the air was an absolute prerequisite to an invasion attempt. The *Luftwaffe* unleashed heavy attacks against air installations in the south of England and other points to gain superiority over the R.A.F. The air effort was also intended to force Britain to sue for peace. The hope of sweeping the R.A.F. from the skies was vain. The British refusal to commit the 25 home defense squadrons to the Battle of France now paid off in the air "Battle of Britain." The British pilots shot down nearly two planes to each loss of their own. During the early critical period of the air war, the month of August 1940, the *Luftwaffe* was never able to whittle the R.A.F. strength down to an acceptable level for risking Operation SEA LION.

The day of decision for SEA LION was September 14, 1940. At a meeting of the Grand Council, after hearing reports from his commanders in chief, Hitler decided against giving the order to launch the invasion, scheduled for September 28. This decision meant that there was little prospect that SEA LION could be staged that year, since suitable tide and moon conditions could not be expected until October 24. Then bad weather could be expected to interfere.

On October 12, 1940 Hitler postponed the cross-Channel attack indefinitely, but continued preparations for invasion in order to maintain pressure on the British. On December 18 he, in effect, canceled Operation SEA LION altogether by issuing an alert for Operation BARBAROSSA: "The *Wehrmacht* must be prepared, even before the end of the war against England, to overthrow Russia in a quick campaign."

Before Hitler could launch his attack on the Soviet Union, he was obliged to divert forces to North Africa and to Greece. He planned the campaign against Russia in order to remove a potential enemy and to capture a new source of materials and manpower. He moved forces to the Mediterranean theater in order to rescue defeated Italian troops and to shore up the Axis position there. But he also saw both operations as means toward ultimately bringing Britain to terms. In this context, his attack on Russia was intended to eliminate a possible British ally. His North African campaign grew into a drive against the Suez Canal via Egypt, to be followed by a drive against India via Iran. As Hitler thus strategically faced east, an undefeated and defiant Britain behind his back obliged him to retain 49 divisions in western Europe to guard the Atlantic Coast. This overextending of her military strength was at length to prove fatal to Germany.

The point especially to be noted is that Hitler was attempting *simultaneously* to duplicate Napoleon's campaigns of 1798 and 1812, and for much of the same reasons. Both of Napoleon's campaigns had ultimately ended in failure. An additional factor in the strategic picture of 1941 was that Great Britain could look to the United States for support. Hitler's armies marched into Russia on June 22. The United States immediately extended Lend-Lease aid to the Soviet Union. Six months later, as the Russian winter stalled the German drive, the United States was in the war on the side of Britain and Russia. What Churchill called "the Grand Alliance" was complete.

We must now backtrack to consider the continuing war at sea and on the Atlantic front.

Dakar

Repulsed from the Continent, Britain reverted to her traditional peripheral strategy, using her sea-conferred mobility to probe for soft spots. Despite the immobilization of the battleship *Richelieu,* the British Cabinet remained uneasy with Dakar in the hands of the Vichy French government. For Dakar, on the westernmost point of Africa, commands the narrows of the Atlantic. Should it be taken over by the Germans for use as a base for submarines and surface raiders, Dakar could pose a real threat to British commerce and to British military transport around Africa to Egypt. Accordingly the Cabinet ordered an offensive operation to "liberate" Dakar into the hands of the Free French. The landing, which presumably would not be seriously resisted, was to be carried out by 4,200 British and 2,700 Free French troops, the latter under the direct command of General de Gaulle. The landing operation was to be supported by a naval force of two battleships, a carrier, and several cruisers and destroyers under Vice Admiral J. H. D. Cunningham. Transports and support in early September 1940 proceeded toward the British port of Freetown, southeast of Dakar, which was to be the advanced base of operations.

Through coincidence and mismanagement the Dakar operation came to naught. The coincidence was that just at this time a Vichy force of three cruisers and three destroyers set out from Toulon for Libreville, French Equatorial Africa. Through diplomatic sources the British Admiralty learned of this departure, and a British destroyer sighted and briefly shadowed the Vichy force in the Straits of Gibraltar. Yet nothing immediately was done to prevent the arrival of these reinforcements in the vicinity of Dakar. The significance of the movement was not immediately perceived at the Admiralty. Admiral Sir James Somerville, commanding naval Force H, and Sir Dudley North, Commander North Atlantic Station, both at Gibraltar, each assumed that the other had orders from the Admiralty to intercept the Vichy ships. When at last the Admiralty awakened to the situation, the ships were far down the African coast. Somerville, belatedly alerted, succeeded only in chasing two of the cruisers into the port of Dakar, where they added to the defense force, though Dakar had not been their destination.

On September 23, 1940, Cunningham at last stood off Dakar. Instead of finding a ready welcome for de Gaulle and his troops, he was met by determined resistance. A landing attempt was repulsed. British bombardment of the harbor on the 24th and 25th achieved little. On the contrary, the immobilized *Richelieu* and the two Vichy cruisers, firing through a smoke screen laid by a destroyer, made most of the hits. On the 25th, the British battleship *Resolution,* already battered by four shells, was heavily damaged by a torpedo fired from a Vichy submarine. On receiving news of this, the Admiralty ordered the action broken off. The operation seemed to the world to be a prime example of confusion, delay, and muddle.

Although the Dakar attack failed, the flexibility of the War Cabinet enabled Britain to retrieve something from the operation. By landing de Gaulle and his Free French forces at Douala in Cameroons, the British barred the Vichy French from a proposed penetration into French Equatorial Africa—thus removing a threat to Freetown and providing the British with an important air base in Central Africa.

German Surface Raiders in 1940

The pocket battleship *Scheer* made her debut into Atlantic waters in October 1940, followed a month later by the heavy cruiser *Hipper.* Both cruised the North Atlantic in an effort to break up the convoys from Halifax to the British Isles.

On November 5 the *Scheer* encountered the independently-routed British merchantman *Mopan,* which she sank after taking off the crew. As the *Mopan* was going down, the masts of Convoy HX-84, consisting of 37 ships, loomed over the horizon. The requirements of the Mediterranean theater at that time were such that Convoy HX-84 was being escorted by only one vessel, the armed merchant cruiser *Jervis Bay.*

Here was a situation made to order for the *Scheer.* With her speed and firepower she was apparently in a position to sink the greater part of the convoy. Two things balked her: the lateness of the hour and the fight put up by the *Jervis Bay*. While the convoy scattered, making smoke, the escort radioed an alarm and closed the pocket battleship at top speed. The 6-inch guns of the *Jervis Bay* were of course no match for the 11-inch guns of her opponent, but the hour it took the *Scheer* to finish her off saved most of the convoy. The pocket battleship was able to overtake and sink only five of the 37 vessels before nightfall ended the chase. After dark the *Scheer* fled the area to elude the British forces which the Germans knew would be converging from all directions in response to the *Jervis Bay*'s radio warning. Evidently ships in convoy, even when poorly escorted, were safer than ships sailing out of convoy. The *Scheer* steamed rapidly south, refueled from a supply ship, made a brief appearance in the West Indies, and then disappeared into the South Atlantic and Indian Oceans, returning to Kiel in April 1941, having sunk 16 ships totaling 99,000 tons.

The *Hipper* achieved little. She attacked a convoy near the Azores, only to find it escorted by four British cruisers. After a brief action, the *Hipper* managed to shake off pursuit and make her way back home.

The *Bismarck* Breaks Out

In the spring of 1941, the *Hipper, Scharnhorst,* and *Gneisenau* again made brief sweeps into the Atlantic, sinking more than 20,000 tons in two months of operation. The *Hipper* returned to Germany, but in late March the two battleships were at Brest, a strategically located port from which to launch further raiding operations.

Admiral Raeder had now conceived the most ambitious raider operation of the Atlantic war. In the Baltic lay the great battleship *Bismarck,* newly completed, and the heavy cruiser *Prinz Eugen*. Raeder planned to send these vessels out into the Atlantic, where they would be joined by the *Scharnhorst* and *Gneisenau*. The powerful squadron thus formed, supplemented with a stepped-up U-boat campaign, could be counted on to paralyze British shipping. In preparation for this operation, supply ships and tankers were dispatched ahead to prearranged rendezvous areas far from shipping areas, and German merchantmen disguised as neutrals combed the convoy routes in search of information.

But damage suffered by the *Scharnhorst* on her last cruise could not be repaired in time, and in April the *Gneisenau* was put out of action by a torpedo from a British aircraft. Yet, not to delay the operation, for which extensive preparations had been made, Raeder ordered the *Bismarck* and the *Prinz Eugen* to Bergen, Norway. Here they were to await thick weather and then break out into the Atlantic, the long way around north of Iceland. The *Scharnhorst* was to join them as soon as her damages were repaired.

The *Bismarck* and the *Prinz Eugen*, while passing through the Kattegat, were sighted by a Swedish cruiser. Sweden passed the word to England, and British reconnaissance aircraft got a look at the two raiders as they neared Bergen. The British Admiralty correctly estimated the German intention and made plans to forestall it. Eleven convoys, including one troop convoy, were in the Atlantic or about to sail. A concentration of German naval strength against them would have been calamitous.

The Admiralty was particularly concerned about the *Bismarck*. In the spring of 1941 she was the most powerful battleship in commission. Mounting eight 15-inch guns in her main battery, she had a secondary battery of twelve 5.9's and an antiaircraft battery of sixteen 4.1's. Her armor was the most advanced on any capital ship, amounting to 16,000 tons dead weight. She had skillfully designed compartmentation to prevent flooding. All the available resources of the Royal Navy were required to track her down and sink her.

The weather closed down on the Norwegian coast as the *Bismarck* and the *Prinz Eugen* reached Bergen. On May 22 a British aircraft in a daring reconnaissance ascertained that the raiders had departed. Admiral Sir John Tovey, Commander in Chief of the British Home Fleet, who was anxiously awaiting news of their movements, immediately took steps to intercept. The Admiralty placed at his disposal all the heavy ships that could be spared. Tovey had with him at Scapa Flow the battleships *King George V*, flagship, and *Prince of Wales* and the battle cruiser *Hood* in addition to destroyers and cruisers. In England were the carrier *Victorious*, which had not yet had her working-up cruise, and the battle cruiser *Repulse*. At Gibraltar, under the command of Admiral Sir James Somerville, were the battle cruiser *Renown* and the carrier *Ark Royal*. The battleships *Rodney* and *Ramillies* were on duty escorting convoys in the Atlantic, and the battleship *Revenge* was at Halifax. All these ships played some part in tracking down and sinking the *Bismarck*.

In order to keep the various routes available to the *Bismarck* under observation and to have a force capable of striking at any of them, Tovey had to divide his force to cover all possible contingencies. Bad weather hampered his efforts. Because he had to keep the least likely passages under the lightest observation, he covered the passage between the Orkneys and the Faroes only by air search. He stationed a cruiser force in the passage between the Faroes and Iceland and headed thither himself in the *King George V* with the *Victorious* and *Repulse*. The heavy cruisers *Suffolk* and *Norfolk* patrolled the Denmark Strait, between Iceland and Greenland, supported by the *Prince of Wales* and *Hood*, en route at high speed from Scapa Flow, under the command of Vice Admiral L. E. Holland in the *Hood*.

First contact with the raiders was made in the early evening of May 23 in the Denmark Strait by the *Norfolk* and *Suffolk* under the command of Rear Admiral Wake-Walker. The *Suffolk*, which made the sighting,

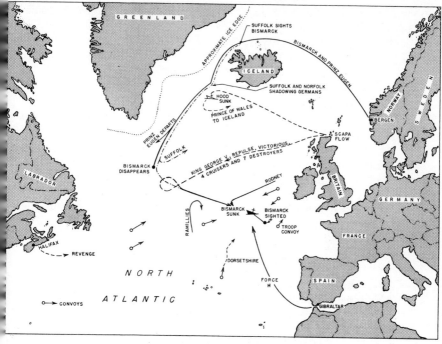

THE CHASE OF THE *BISMARCK*

immediately took refuge in a fog bank and began tracking the Germans by radar. All night the two cruisers hung on to the German warships, broadcasting information that would enable the big ships to bring them into action.

On board the battle cruiser *Hood*, Admiral Holland calculated his intercept course and prepared for action at any time after 0140, May 24. Contact was not made until 0535, whereupon the *Hood* and the new battleship *Prince of Wales* advanced into action. Admiral Holland, maneuvering both his ships together, ordered a head-on approach which denied him the use of their after guns. The Germans opened fire, concentrating on the *Hood*. To confuse their aim and to bring his after turrets to bear, Holland ordered a 20-degree turn to port, but scarcely had the ships begun to swing in response to the signal when the *Hood* disintegrated, hit in the magazine by a shell from the *Bismarck*. The *Prince of Wales* had to swing hard a-starboard to avoid the floating wreckage of the *Hood*. The situation had dramatically reversed. Tactical superiority had passed to the Germans. To make matters worse, the *Prince of Wales*, too new to have the mechanical difficulties worked out of her, was able to fire only about three guns a salvo.

Rear Admiral Wake-Walker, who had been enjoying a ringside seat from the bridge of the *Norfolk*, now found himself senior British officer present with the full responsibility for the *Bismarck* on his shoulders. In view of the loss of the *Hood*, the inefficiency of and battle damage to the *Prince of Wales*, and the comparative weakness of his cruisers, he decided to resume shadowing tactics in hopes of enabling Tovey's force to arrive on the scene.

The loss of the *Hood* can be blamed in large measure on British lack of readiness to spend money on conversion of older ships during the lean years of peacetime budgets. She was known to be vulnerable to plunging fire, but during the pre-war years nothing had been done to strengthen her. When war came it was too late; as long as she could operate, she could not be spared.

The *Bismarck* Disappears

"*Hood* has blown up."

The signal stunned the Admiralty. Nearly every officer on duty in the War Room had served in the *Hood* and remembered her as the pride of the Royal Navy, the backbone of Britain's sea defenses. Now she was gone. With saddened hearts but redoubled determination they plotted the *Bismarck*'s death. Already they had ordered Admiral Somerville's Force H to sea from Gibraltar to participate in running the Germans down. Now they summoned the battleships *Rodney* and *Ramillies* to break off from convoys and join in the chase. The battleship *Revenge* raised steam and proceeded with all possible speed from Halifax.

After being dogged all day by the *Norfolk*, *Suffolk*, and *Prince of Wales*, the *Bismarck* suddenly turned on the *Suffolk*, which opened range rapidly. This move was made to cover the departure of the *Prinz Eugen*, which escaped to the south and entered Brest ten days later. Once again the game of shadowing went on. Since the ships were by this time entering known U-boat waters, all British vessels were zigzagging. On the outward leg of one of these zigzags, the *Suffolk* lost radar contact and failed to regain it. Once more the *Bismarck* was loose. Three courses of action seemed to be open to her. She was known to be trailing oil from the encounter with the *Hood* and *Prince of Wales*. She might be in need of repairs. If so, she would head for Germany or for one of two French ports, Brest or St. Nazaire. Alternately, she might be heading for a rendezvous with a supply ship and then on to operations in whatever quarter of the globe she chose. When radio-direction-finder signals led Tovey to believe that she was heading for the North Sea and Germany, he steamed north for several hours to attempt an interception. Both he and the Admiralty had begun to have misgivings about this course of action, when a recomputation of the direction-finder bearings aboard the *King George V* revealed a strong probability that the *Bismarck* was heading for a French port. A new dispatch from the Admiralty plotted the German battleship as being within a 50-mile radius of the position lat. 55° 15′ N, long. 32° 00′ W, about 600 miles southeast of Cape Farewell on the southern tip of Greenland. Tovey accordingly turned to attempt to intercept the *Bismarck*'s probable course toward Brest, but his cruisers and the carrier *Victorious* held for home, being too short of fuel to continue. Tovey also ordered the damaged *Prince of Wales* to proceed to England. Convoys were diverted to get them out of the probable danger area. The *Rodney*'s course toward the North Sea was not immediately corrected, and she crossed ahead of the *Bismarck* on the afternoon of May 25. If she had been alerted, she could easily have made an interception. As it was, Somerville's Force H, consisting of carrier *Ark Royal*, battle cruiser *Renown*, and escorting ships, was now the only British force in position to do so.

Realizing that the shortage of fuel for the smaller ships would soon leave the larger vessels exposed to submarine attack, the Admiralty decided that five destroyers could be spared from the Convoy WS-8B and one from the Irish Sea Patrol and sent them under Captain Vian of the *Altmark* affair to rendezvous with Tovey. During the night all forces raced toward the *Bismarck*'s most probable position.

Bismarckdämmerung

By the morning of May 26, the pursuers began to lose hope. The wind had increased during the night, forcing Somerville's ships to slow from 25 to 17 knots. The flight deck of the *Ark Royal* was pitching between 53 and 55 feet, but in spite of the difficulties and dangers of air operations, a search patrol set out from the carrier at 0835. Still no word of the *Bismarck*. Suddenly at 1030, a Catalina flying patrol from the Coastal Air Command broadcast a sighting of a battleship in position lat. 49° 33′ N, long. 21° 50′ W, approximately 750 miles west of Brest, steering course 150 at 20 knots. On all ships, plotting officers hurried with their work. It was no British battleship. The *Bismarck* was found.

On receipt of the news, Captain Vian in destroyer *Cossack* decided to disregard his instructions to rendezvous with Admiral Tovey and turned with his five destroyers to intercept the *Bismarck*. Swordfish aircraft from the *Ark Royal* took over shadowing the German, but her position was too far ahead of any of the forces to make interception likely. Only an air strike from the *Ark Royal* could hope to slow her down until the heavy ships could come up. The strike preparations began immediately, while the cruiser *Sheffield* darted away at high speed to take up a station shadowing the Nazi battleship. Then came near-tragedy. The pilots, improperly briefed, attacked the *Sheffield,* which had accompanied them from Gibraltar, under the impression that she was the *Bismarck.* Only highly skilled shiphandling and a belated radio warning averted a calamity. The next two strikes found the *Bismarck,* for the *Sheffield* had gone ahead and already located her. The pilots of these strikes had been briefed to fly to the *Sheffield* and take their departure from her. She would coach them on the target, which she did with alacrity. The results of this strike were at first uncertain, and early reports led Tovey to believe that no significant damage had been done. However, he eventually learned that the *Bismarck* was heading in a northerly direction. Since this course was directly into the teeth of her enemies, the conclusion could only be that either the ship was having rudder difficulties or that damage was forcing her to take the heavy seas on her bow. In fact, both conjectures were true. The *Bismarck* had been hit in her steering engine compartment, and her rudders were jammed full over. Only by maneuvering with her engines could she avoid circling. Also a following sea would threaten further flooding because of the weakened bulkheads of the steering engine compartment. There was no choice. The *Bismarck* had to head into the sea. She was obliged at last to face her gathering enemies.

Darkness fell, and with it came Captain Vian and his destroyers to assist the *Sheffield* in shadowing. Vian saw no objection to attempting to put a few torpedoes into her as well. His first concerted attack the *Bismarck* drove off without damage either to herself or the destroyers. Captain Vian then stationed one destroyer on each bow and one on each quarter and himself took position astern. During the night each destroyer made several torpedo attacks on the *Bismarck* but made no hits because each time fire from the battleship forced the attacking destroyer to break off the action before it could get to effective torpedo launching position.

Raeder had been making every effort to save the *Bismarck.* He summoned all available submarines to the area, but those closest had already expended all their torpedoes and could only watch impotently. By an odd chance, one U-boat passed within 400 yards of the *Ark Royal,* but having fired her last torpedo the previous day, was powerless to harm the British carrier.

By morning the heavy British ships reached the scene of action. At 0847 the battleships *Rodney* and *King George V* exchanged the first salvos with the *Bismarck* at a range of 25,000 yards. The *Bismarck,* although badly crippled, still had magnificent endurance and splendid fire control. Her third salvo straddled the *Rodney,* but soon the weight of British firepower began to tell, hitting the *Bismarck's* main battery director early in the action so that the accuracy of her fire diminished appreciably. Soon the *Bismarck* was a helpless wreck, rolling sluggishly in the trough of the sea. But she refused to sink. At length Admiral Tovey, with barely enough fuel to get home, had to break off. The cruiser *Dorsetshire* requested permission to expend her last three torpedoes on the *Bismarck* before leaving, and as her third torpedo hit, the *Bismarck* slowly rolled over and disappeared beneath the waves. The *Hood* had been avenged.

The loss of the *Bismarck* put an end to German use of major combat ships for attack on transoceanic commerce. Raeder's standing with Hitler took a decided drop. German commerce warfare on the high seas thereafter was left to Dönitz' U-boats and a few disguised merchant raiders.

The Channel Dash

British pride in the Royal Navy's achievement in hunting down and destroying the mighty *Bismarck* was somewhat quenched early the following year when the Germans brought home the last of their big surface raiders under the very noses of the Admiralty. After the *Bismarck* episode, the *Scharnhorst, Gneisenau,* and *Prinz Eugen* had remained at Brest. Despite damaging air attacks staged from Britain, all three were repaired and ready for operations by February 1942. Noting this, the British Admiralty anticipated that they would soon put to sea in an effort to regain home ports.

Hitler, convinced that the Allies were about to attack Norway, desired to concentrate all his naval strength there. Hence he ordered the three ships at Brest to make a break for home. They were not to proceed by way of the open Atlantic, which had proved a grave for the *Bismarck,* but use the shortest route, through the English Channel. Coming this way they would at least have strong land-based fighter support.

The Germans estimated that if they could maintain complete secrecy and leave Brest after dark, they would be through the most dangerous waters before the British could organize their defenses. With the Home Fleet far away at Scapa Flow, the German ships could expect opposition only from light surface forces, air attacks, and mine fields. Carefully sweeping the Channel route, the Germans prepared to give maximum air cover and provided the big ships with an escort of six destroyers and three torpedo boats. Eighteen more torpedo boats would join the escort as the force swept past Le Havre.

The *Scharnhorst, Gneisenau,* and *Prinz Eugen,* under command of Vice Admiral Ciliax, left Brest after dark on February 11, 1942. The night departure ran contrary to British estimates, for the Admiralty had assumed that the Germans would leave Brest during the day in order to pass through the Straits of Dover in darkness. The Royal Air Force had night reconnaissance planes over the Brest area, but radar failed to function in the only two planes that might have detected the German departure. Worse, R.A.F. headquarters failed to notify the Admiralty of the

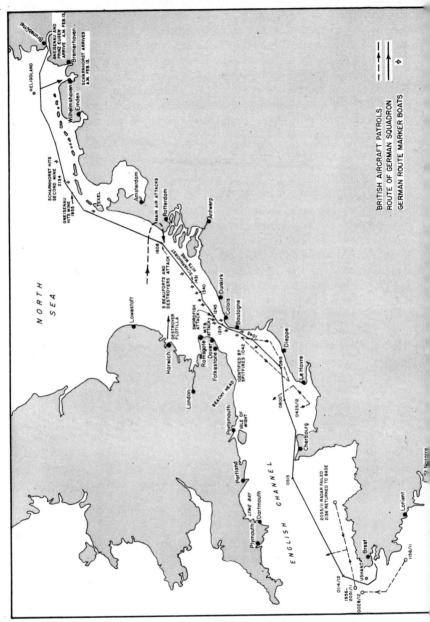

THE CHANNEL DASH

breakdown. Finally, at 1100 on the 12th, an R.A.F. plane made radar contact through thickening weather with the German force, but even this contact was incorrectly evaluated. By the time a corrected report of the contact reached the Admiralty, the German ships had already passed through the Straits into the North Sea. The British attacked with coastal guns, torpedo boats, and with hundreds of aircraft without slowing down the fleeing Germans in the least. Tempestuous weather defeated a British destroyer attack. Unscathed, the three big German vessels reached waters off the Dutch coast. Here at last they ran into trouble: both the *Scharnhorst* and the *Gneisenau* hit British-laid mines. While the damage to the *Gneisenau* was minor, the *Scharnhorst* was out of action for months.

The failure to stop the Germans aroused great indignation in Britain. "Vice-Admiral Ciliax has succeeded where the Duke of Medina Sidonia failed," thundered the London *Times,* referring to the ill-fated Spanish Armada of 1588. "Nothing more mortifying to the pride of sea power has happened in Home waters since the 17th century." Nevertheless there were compensating advantages. The threat from Brest to Atlantic convoys had been eliminated. More important, the ineffectiveness of the Royal Navy's air striking power had been so clearly revealed that the Navy at long last began to receive its share of up-to-date aircraft, formerly exclusively the prerogative of the R.A.F.

St. Nazaire

The month following the German Channel dash, the Royal Navy recovered much of its lost prestige by a raid on St. Nazaire. The port was an important U-boat base and contained a lock that could be used as a drydock, the only one outside Germany capable of receiving the battleship *Tirpitz.* To destroy this lock and to damage U-boat installations, the British readied one of their former American destroyers, H.M.S. *Campbeltown* (ex-U.S.S. *Buchanan*), as an explosive blockship to ram and destroy the lock gates. To support the operation and to destroy harbor facilities, a group of motor launches carried a raiding force of Commandos. Entering the Loire late at night on March 27, 1942, the group under Commander R. E. D. Ryder made recognition signals, thereby gaining four valuable minutes during the final approach. When the *Campbeltown* had only 1,000 yards to go, all German batteries opened fire. Her captain increased to full speed and rammed the lock squarely, bringing her time-set explosive charge into perfect position. The crew was taken off in motor launches. Meanwhile the Commandos had fought their way ashore with great difficulty and set about blowing up port and lock machinery. With the main objective achieved, Ryder gave the recall signal, and the survivors made good their escape with the loss of three motor launches on the way home. The next morning, while a group of senior German naval officers were inspecting the *Campbeltown* to plan her removal, the demolition charges blew up, wrecking the lock gate and wiping out the inspection party.

Dieppe

A raid on Dieppe conducted on August 19, 1942 was intended not only to inflict damage but also to test amphibious techniques. Some 5,000 Canadian troops participated. Counting heavily on surprise, the army refused naval gunfire support; hence only eight destroyers with 4-inch guns accompanied the troops. Through a chance encounter with a small German coastal convoy, the raiders on one flank lost surprise and were repulsed with heavy losses, the few men who got ashore being quickly killed or captured. The other flank met with success, but the main assault on Dieppe itself also failed. The presence of a battleship would, in the opinion of the Naval Force Commander, have "probably turned the tide in our favour." The Canadians lost some 3,350 men, or 67 per cent of the troops involved. The raid, while discouraging to ideas of cross-Channel operations in 1942 and 1943, did reveal many weaknesses in amphibious planning which had to be rectified before the forthcoming major landings in Africa and Europe.

Reorganization of the German Navy

The German surface ships were gradually transferred to bases in Norway, where they could repel the invasion Hitler feared and where they would be in a position to strike at Arctic convoys to North Russia. In the early morning hours of December 31, 1942, a German raiding force composed of the pocket battleship *Lützow*, the heavy cruiser *Hipper*, and six destroyers made contact with a convoy meagerly protected by five destroyers, two corvettes, and one trawler. The Germans split up, the *Hipper* with two destroyers attacking the escort, the *Lützow* and four destroyers making for the helpless convoy. Then ensued one of the most amazing actions of the war. Captain R. S. V. Sherbrooke managed his tiny escort force so brilliantly and so aggressively that the entire German force had to turn to deal with him. For more than an hour he held the attention of the Germans, losing only one destroyer, while the convoy escaped into the fog. On the arrival of the British cruisers *Sheffield* and *Jamaica*, the Germans obeyed their standing order to avoid engaging major forces and retired. The convoy reached Russia without the loss of a ship. The Germans lost a destroyer and sustained heavy damage to the *Hipper*. The most important damage however was not to the ships but to the German navy, for this action caused a major reorganization in the German naval high command.

When word of the action reached Hitler, he stormed and raged. He would have all the heavy ships scrapped, he declared, so that their steel could be used by the army and the *Luftwaffe* and their personnel could be sent to man the submarines, which were the only naval forces carrying on a useful fight. He ordered Admiral Raeder to report to him to receive the scrapping order in person, but Raeder managed to get the meeting postponed until January 6. As he waited for Hitler to cool off, he prepared for him a kind of child's guide to sea power, pointing out the importance of the German heavy ships in tying down the British navy. But in the meantime, Goering had got Hitler's ear. Goering had always been intensely jealous of Raeder and sought any method of encompassing his ruin. A braggart, a schemer, and an unscrupulous liar, Goering proposed to win the war with his *Luftwaffe* alone. He had promised to reduce Britain by air attack, and he had failed. He had promised to reduce Russia by air attack, and he had failed. He had promised to keep the German forces in Russia supplied, and he had failed. He had promised to keep German forces in North Africa supplied, and he had failed. He had promised to destroy Allied shipping to Britain, and he had failed. He had promised to himself that he would scuttle Raeder, and he succeeded. Goering promised that his *Luftwaffe* could do, and do better, all that the surface ships could do, and Raeder was out. He resigned on January 30, 1943 and was succeeded by Dönitz. The contrast between the two men was great. Dönitz was an ardent Nazi; Raeder a professional naval officer, generally aloof from politics. Dönitz was a man of action; Raeder, something of a naval philosopher and historian.

When Dönitz took command of the German navy, he was convinced that Hitler's position was sound. This conviction lasted only a few months. When he began to see the war as a whole in contrast to the limited view he had had as U-boat admiral, he realized that Raeder was right; there was more to sea power than submarines. He succeeded in persuading Hitler to reverse the order, so that no ships were scrapped. The rescued ships however were not immediately used significantly. Nearly a year passed before the next major use of a surface ship occurred, once more against the North Russian convoys.

The *Scharnhorst's* Last Cruise

On Christmas Day of 1943, the *Scharnhorst* set out from Norway to intercept a convoy bound for North Russia. But the convoy had been diverted to the northward, and the battleship met instead a cruiser scouting force of the British Home Fleet. In the morning of December 26, H.M.S. *Belfast* made radar contact with the German and opened fire, joined by the *Sheffield* and the *Norfolk*, but foul weather so reduced the speed of the British cruisers that they soon lost contact. Vice Admiral Robert Burnett, judging that the *Scharnhorst* would make for the convoy,

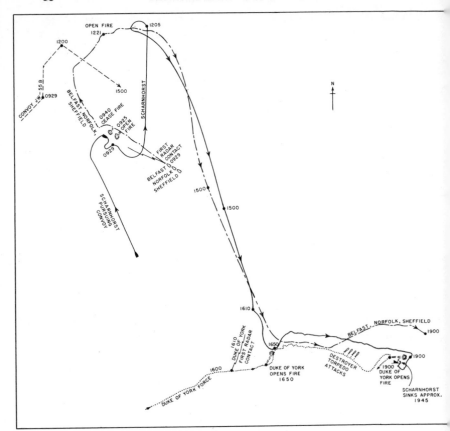

THE SINKING OF THE *SCHARNHORST*, DECEMBER 26, 1943

headed to intercept and again made radar contact a little after noon. Destroyers which Burnett now sent in to attack with torpedoes were defeated by high seas, but the threat was enough to make the battleship head for Norway. This suited Burnett exactly, for the German line of retirement provided a perfect intercept course for the battleship *Duke of York* and the cruiser *Jamaica*, under command of Admiral Sir Bruce Fraser, who had relieved Sir John Tovey as Commander in Chief of the British Home Fleet. The *Belfast, Sheffield,* and *Norfolk* made no further attempt to engage, contenting themselves with shadowing the German. By late afternoon the two British forces were both in the area of expected contact. Because in those latitudes it was already pitch dark, Burnett illuminated with starshell, whereupon the *Duke of York* and the *Jamaica* sighted the *Scharnhorst* and immediately engaged at 12,000 yards. A high-speed eastward chase developed until the 14-inch shells of the British battleship began to take effect, and the *Scharnhorst* lost speed. British destroyers then further slowed her with torpedo attacks. Ordered to sink her with torpedoes, the *Belfast* and the *Jamaica* attacked in concert with destroyers and sent the *Scharnhorst* down off North Cape a little before 2000.

That the *Scharnhorst* was mishandled is evident. She was superior to the three British cruisers which first engaged her and stood a good chance of fighting it out with them to a successful conclusion. If she had done so and then continued toward the convoy, interception by the *Duke of York* would have been impossible, at least until after the *Scharnhorst* had wreaked havoc among the freighters. Her running to the south to regain the Norwegian ports meant that she was running toward the most likely route for the approach of British reinforcements. In running for safety, the *Scharnhorst* adopted the course that offered the least probability of inflicting damage to the British and offered the greatest risk to herself. She had been sent out with a specific task, that of inflicting the maximum damage to the convoy. Her abandonment of her task meant that she was expended uselessly, with no gain to compensate for her loss.

The End of the *Tirpitz*

The chief remaining German surface ship was the huge battleship *Tirpitz* at anchor in Kaa Fiord, an inlet of Alten Fiord far in the north of Norway. Here she was a particular threat to the North Russian convoys. On the night of September 19–20, 1943, three months before the *Scharnhorst* was sunk, the *Tirpitz* had been attacked by British midget submarines. Four midgets, known as X-craft, survivors of six that had been towed across the North Sea by fleet submarines, penetrated the outer fiord. There the *X-10*, beset with misfortunes, turned back. The other three pressed on. One was never heard from again. The other two, *X-6*, commanded by Lieutenant D. Cameron RNR, and *X-7*, Lieutenant B. C. G. Place RN, placed time charges beneath the keel of the *Tirpitz*. Although the Germans discovered and captured the crews of these two midgets, they were unable to move the *Tirpitz* sufficiently to avoid the consequences of the explosion, which unseated her main engine and did heavy damage to her rudders and steering engine.

Following the sinking of the *Scharnhorst*, and when Allied intelligence reports revealed that the Germans had nearly completed repairs to the *Tirpitz*, the British determined to hit her again lest she attack North Russian convoys or make a break for the open Atlantic as the *Bismarck* had done. This time the Admiralty decided to employ carriers.

After receiving special training, flyers from H.M. carriers *Victorious, Furious, Pursuer, Searcher,* and *Emperor* prepared to launch their attack. Sailing from England on March 30, 1944, in order to coordinate with a convoy bound for Russia, they attacked in the early morning of April 3. The *Victorious* and the *Furious* carried bombers, while the other three carriers provided the fighter escort. Attacking in two waves, the planes scored 15 hits, doing extensive damage without however impairing the ability of the *Tirpitz* to steam, for the bombs could not penetrate the eight inches of steel that formed her armor deck.

After the worst of the damage had been repaired, the ship was still not completely seaworthy, and as the dockyards in Germany were too battered to repair her, the Germans decided to move her to Tromsö, north of Narvik, where she might be employed as a floating battery. Tromsö was within range of the R.A.F. long-range bombers. On November 12, 1944, Lancasters capsized her by direct hits with six-ton bombs. This time there was no question of repair. The *Tirpitz* was gone.

2

The Struggle for the Mediterranean

As war approached in 1939, Britain and France, recognizing the vital importance of the Mediterranean theater, laid joint plans to exploit its strategic opportunities and to deny them to the Axis. Britain traditionally considered the Mediterranean her lifeline to the Suez Canal and the Far East, while France considered it the main high road to her colonies in Algeria, Tunisia, and French Morocco. To a great extent the safety of British and French commerce and installations depended on the role Italy would assume in the war. On the assumption that Italy would be an active participant, the Anglo-French allies agreed that British naval forces would assume responsibility for the eastern half and French naval forces the western half of the Mediterranean. At the outbreak of war, the British had a strong Mediterranean Fleet. In addition to their major base at Alexandria, they had secondary establishments at Malta and Gibraltar. The French had three battleships, eleven cruisers, 33 destroyers, and 45 submarines disposed at Toulon, Oran, Mers-el-Kebir, Bizerte, Morocco, and Dakar.

Ever since the Italian invasion of Ethiopia in 1935, the Italian navy had been operating on a quasi-war footing. When the Italians went into Albania in April 1939, the British, not having anticipated the move, hurriedly concentrated their Mediterranean Fleet at Alexandria. In May Hitler and Mussolini proclaimed a Pact of Steel, promising to aid each other in any military action. This dramatic public announcement was secretly modified by the Cavallero Memorandum in which Mussolini informed Hitler that he would not be ready for war for three years and asked him to postpone military action until 1942. Although Hitler agreed in principle, on August 11 the German foreign minister informed his Italian opposite number that Germany was about to attack Poland. Mussolini, mindful of his obligations under the Pact of Steel, sent a lengthy request for raw materials for Germany to supply to Italy. Hitler refused the requested items and informed Mussolini that he would not be

THE MEDITERRANEAN THEATER

requested to enter the war. Consequently, when Germany invaded Poland on September 1, 1939, Mussolini proclaimed Italy's nonbelligerence.

In the face of this unexpected development, the British, urgently requiring ships in other theaters, left the Mediterranean largely on a caretaker basis. Withdrawing most of their ships for service elsewhere, they depended on the French to keep order and to assist the few remaining British ships in enforcing Allied Shipping Control measures. Meanwhile the British bent every effort toward strengthening their positions in the Middle East. In Egypt they had, in addition to the naval base at Alexandria, a body of troops and a Royal Air Force command, stationed there in accordance with the Anglo-Egyptian Treaty of 1936. Because the Egyptian government had done little to build up its armed forces and facilities, the British made great efforts during the winter of 1939–40 to make good the deficiencies.

By spring of 1940 Mussolini was chafing under Allied shipping restrictions and was anxious to extend Italian influence and territory. For years he had dreamed of restoring a Roman Empire in the Mediterranean; his conquests of Ethiopia and of Albania had been moves in this direction. Now he dreamed of an Empire which would challenge in splendor that of the Caesars. He sought means of expelling the two great powers he saw as standing in his way—Britain and France. Meeting Hitler at the Brenner Pass in March 1940, he promised to intervene on the German side at the appropriate time. Soon thereafter he announced to the King and to his military leaders his concept of a "parallel war," which would assist Germany indirectly but which would be designed primarily to further Italian interests. As he watched the rapid success of the Germans in Norway and France, Mussolini made hurried plans to join the war before it should be too late. "To participate in the peace," he proclaimed, "one must participate in the war."

As the British began to see signs that Italy's nonbelligerency might soon shift to outright war, they reviewed their earlier policy of non-provocation of Italy, proposing to substitute a show of force. But Mussolini had already made up his mind. On April 17 he was restrained from a declaration of war only by the strong protests of Marshal Badoglio, chief of the Italian armed forces, on the grounds of unreadiness. Unobtrusively the British began to return strength to the Mediterranean. They resumed responsibility for the eastern Mediterranean, and on April 29, 1940 issued an order that Allied merchant ships bound to or from India or elsewhere in the East would be routed around the Cape of Good Hope. Simultaneously reinforcements for all three services began to appear at British bases in and around the Mediterranean. On the arrival at the end of May of four battleships and the aircraft carrier *Eagle*, Sir Andrew B. Cunningham, Commander in Chief Mediterranean Fleet, shifted his flag from Malta to the *Warspite* and his base of operations to Alexandria. In

June seven cruisers and a force of destroyers arrived. Also under Admiral Cunningham at Alexandria was a French force commanded by Vice Admiral René Godfroy, consisting of battleship *Lorraine*, three heavy cruisers, one light cruiser, three destroyers, and six submarines.

Italy Enters the War

Marshal Badoglio had been right when he told Mussolini that the Italian armed forces were not ready for war. The army was not fully mobilized and was in a poor state of training, while the Italian air force, although strong on paper, had little operational experience. The navy was feeling the consequences of insufficient maintenance and insufficient replacement of ships. The Italian armed forces were inefficiently organized for naval war in the Mediterranean. The three service commands, *Superesercito* (army), *Superareo* (air force), and *Supermarina* (navy), were co-equal but subordinated to the supreme headquarters, *Comando Supremo*. The officers in *Comando Supremo* tended to hold the continental viewpoint of the army and the strategic bombing concepts of the air force; hence they had little sympathy for naval problems and little appreciation of naval opportunities. When the Italian air force was organized in 1923, the navy had been directed to give up all of its aviation to the new service. The navy thus had no control over the aircraft it needed to carry out its missions. Nor did it have any aircraft carriers, for both *Comando Supremo* and Mussolini considered Italy itself to be a gigantic aircraft carrier. Since planes operating from Italian air bases would be able to cover the central Mediterranean, *Comando Supremo* argued that the air force could perfectly well perform all the tasks usually allotted to naval aviation. Air force pilots however were not trained for naval tasks, and the air force, like the *Luftwaffe* and all other major air forces in the war, wished to conduct the fighting in accordance with its own strategic concepts. Thus, when the navy requested aircraft for support of naval operations, the planes were all too frequently allocated elsewhere. The navy controlled only units for naval reconnaissance, and even these planes were flown by air force pilots.

The Italian navy at the outbreak of war consisted of six battleships (of which only two, the *Cavour* and the *Giulio Cesare*, were actually in service), seven heavy and twelve light cruisers, and some 50 destroyers. In addition Italy had 108 submarines, nearly double Germany's total. Two older battleships, the *Duilio* and *Doria*, were being modernized and would join the fleet shortly, while four fast new battleships, the *Littorio*, *Vittorio Veneto*, *Roma*, and *Impero*, were in various stages of construction. The first two of these were nearly ready for service, but the others would require several years to complete. In the Red Sea at Massawa the Italians had a small force of seven destroyers and eight submarines which would be able to pose a threat to Britain's shipping to and from the Suez Canal. Class for class, the Italian ships were more lightly armored but faster than their Allied counterparts. These high-speed characteristics and comparatively small fuel capacity gave them a severely restricted combat radius.

The chief Italian naval base at Taranto was supplemented by others at Naples, Brindisi, and Spezia in Italy; Augusta and Palermo in Sicily; Cagliari in Sardinia; and Tripoli and Benghazi in Libya. The Italian navy saw its strategy in war as defensive in the eastern and western Mediterranean, while in the central Mediterranean it must at all costs protect shipping between Italy and her armies in Libya. Italian naval doctrine prescribed weakening the Allied fleets by raids and by submarine and frogman attack while avoiding encounters with superior forces.

As May wore on, the British recognized that France might be forced from the war and anticipated that Mussolini would wish to join the attack on France so that he might have a place at the victors' feast. In addition to building up the Mediterranean Fleet, the War Cabinet understood that Britain might have to assume responsibility for the western Mediterranean as well as the eastern and took steps to provide a naval force to be based on Gibraltar. Also abandoning the non-provocation policy, the British on May 23 ordered that all Italian merchant ships should be stopped for contraband-control searches. On June 6, Mussolini announced that all waters within twelve miles of Italian territory were dangerous to navigation. Forewarned by this announcement, Admiral Cunningham had most of the Mediterranean Fleet at sea when Italy's declaration of war against Britain and France became effective at one minute after midnight on June 11, 1940.

Cunningham's initial sweep, by which he hoped to surprise units of the Italian navy, met with no success, while an Italian submarine sank the British cruiser *Calypso*. The first two days of the war however cost Italy 130,000 tons of merchant shipping through capture, scuttling, or internment. On June 14, a force of French cruisers bombarded Genoa, the French cooperating in the war against Italy for 15 days until their own surrender to Germany took place.

With France's surrender, as told in the preceding chapter, Britain's concern over the French fleet became acute. The British situation in the Mediterranean in a short month had gone from overwhelming superiority to nearly hopeless inferiority. Instead of having two powerful forces watching a non-belligerent, the British now had the care of the entire Inland Sea with a hostile Italy and the strong possibility that the powerful French ships would be used against them. The War Cabinet therefore ordered its commanders in the Mediterranean to take action.

In anticipation of having to assume responsibility for the western Mediterranean, the Admiralty had already assembled a force at Gibraltar designated as Force H, including the battleships *Valiant* and *Resolution,* the battle cruiser *Hood,* the aircraft carrier *Ark Royal,* two cruisers, and eleven destroyers. Vice Admiral Sir James F. Somerville, its commander, received orders from the War Cabinet to present to the commander of the French detachment at Mers-el-Kebir, the naval anchorage of Oran, the following proposals:

> A. Sail with us and continue to fight for victory against the Germans and Italians.
> B. Sail with reduced crews under our control to a British port. . . .
> C. Alternatively, if you feel bound to stipulate that your ships should not be used against Germans or Italians, since this would break the Armistice, then sail them with us with reduced crews to some French port in the West Indies—Martinique, for instance, where they can be demilitarised to our satisfaction, or perhaps be entrusted to the United States of America, and remain safely until the end of the war, the crews being repatriated.
>
> If you refuse these fair offers, I must with profound regret require you to sink your ships within six hours. Finally, failing the above, I have the orders of His Majesty's Government to use whatever force may be necessary to prevent your ships from falling into German or Italian hands.

On Admiralty orders, Somerville took his entire force to Mers-el-Kebir, arriving early on the morning of July 3, 1940. Sending Captain C. S. Holland, former British naval attaché in Paris, and a personal friend of the French commander, Admiral Marcel Gensoul, to deliver his note, Somerville waited off shore. Sensing an ultimatum, Gensoul refused to receive Holland, but sent his flag lieutenant to represent him. In reply to the British note, Gensoul wrote that previous French assurances still held good, that under no circumstances would French ships be allowed to fall into Axis hands, and that French ships would defend themselves by force. Gensoul felt that he could accept none of the alternatives offered him without breaking the armistice; accordingly he informed his government only that he had been offered an ultimatum. As Admiral Darlan was not available, his chief of staff ordered forces at Toulon and Algiers to Mers-el-Kebir. Meanwhile all participants attempted to find a solution. In the afternoon Gensoul received Holland, proposing a gentleman's agreement, but Somerville, alerted to the coming of French reinforcements, set a final deadline. Unable to accept any of the French counterproposals, Holland withdrew and at 1756 Somerville opened fire, the first shots fired by the British against the French since Waterloo.

The French fleet at Mers-el-Kebir had, during the negotiations, seized the opportunity to prepare for battle. It included four battleships and six super destroyers, as well as a seaplane tender. During the brief action, which included a carrier air strike, three French battleships were either sunk or beached, while the battleship *Strasbourg* made good her escape and reached Toulon undamaged.

At Alexandria the personal friendship between Admirals Cunningham and Godfroy averted tragedy. Cunningham had an advantage over Somerville in that he did not have to fear the arrival of reinforcements, and he was in a position to demand more latitude from his government than Somerville had had. On July 5, the two commanders worked out a gentleman's agreement by which Godfroy would discharge fuel, remove firing mechanisms from his guns, and make no attempt to break out to sea. Cunningham, for his part, agreed to undertake no measures to seize the French ships by force as had been done in England. Thus there remained under Vichy control in the Mediterranean one battleship, one aircraft carrier, four heavy and eight light cruisers, 30 destroyers, and 70 submarines.

Enraged by this attack by their former allies, the French Vichy government ordered reprisal measures against the British. On July 5 French planes attacked Gibraltar, but the bombs all fell harmlessly in the harbor. On July 8 the Vichy government severed diplomatic relations with Britain but did not declare war.

Thus at terrific cost the British had ensured themselves against a significant part of the French fleet. The risk had been great; the full cost would not be known for years.

Britain Against Italy in the Mediterranean

The entry of Italy into the war created serious doubt in the minds of the British on whether they could hold Malta. Its defenses were pitifully weak, promised guns and aircraft having been sent elsewhere to meet desperate needs of the moment. Its proximity to Italy made it of negligible value as a naval base. It could however prove of inestimable value as an air base from which to attack Italian shipping to Libya. Italy lost no time in attempting to knock Malta out altogether, sending 36 raids against the island during June. As a result the submarines which had been based there were forced to leave, and women and children were evacuated. During the next two and a half years, Malta remained under siege, but always a menace to Axis shipping in the Mediterranean.

While covering the evacuation convoys, the British Mediterranean Fleet had its first action with the Italian fleet off Calabria, the toe of the Italian boot. Disposed in three groups, the British had a scouting unit of five light cruisers in the van, followed by the battleship *Warspite*, Cunningham's flagship, screened by five destroyers. Some miles astern were the older battleships *Malaya* and *Royal Sovereign* with the carrier *Eagle*, carrying 19 planes, and escorted by ten more destroyers. As a diversion, Force H made a sweep of the western Mediterranean.

The Italian force, heading northward toward Italy after escorting a convoy to Benghazi, consisted of battleships *Giulio Cesare* and *Cavour*, six heavy cruisers, twelve light cruisers, and destroyers—under command of Admiral Angelo Campioni, Commander in Chief of the Italian Fleet. This force had been especially strengthened in expectation of battle on the return trip.

A strike launched from the *Eagle* failed to find the battleships and expended its torpedoes fruitlessly against the cruisers. The course of the Italians suggested to Cunningham that they were covering movements to Libya; accordingly he maneuvered to get between the Italian force and its base at Taranto. In the afternoon the British light cruisers came upon the Italian cruisers. Heavily outnumbered and outranged, the British fought on until the *Warspite* came to the rescue. Soon thereafter the *Warspite* sighted the two Italian battleships and engaged them at 26,000 yards. After a few rounds, the Italian flagship *Giulio Cesare* received a hit at the base of the forward funnel. Campioni then sent his destroyers in for a torpedo attack and retired behind a smoke screen, to head for Messina. Firing now became general and the battle more confused as the British attempted to cut off the Italian retreat. By 1700 superiority in speed enabled the Italians to make good their escape, and Cunningham, unwilling to risk running into a submarine ambush within 25 miles of the Italian coast, broke off pursuit. Meanwhile two convoys to Alexandria had sailed from Malta, taking advantage of the diversion caused by the battle. Cunningham's force covered their passage, absorbing air attacks which otherwise would have been directed against the merchant ships.

The action off Calabria seemed to prove the soundness of Cunningham's aggressive policy. Although the Italian battleships mounted lighter main battery guns than the British battleships, they had more of them, and the two Italian battleships could have engaged the British flagship closely before the two slower British battleships could have got into action. The Italian force was greatly superior in cruisers. Yet Campioni did not press his advantage. Although the British had a carrier within striking range, it had played an ineffective role. Italian land-based air, on the other hand, had been poorly coordinated, arriving after the battle and then attacking the Italian instead of the British fleet. Happily for the Italians, their airmen's bombing was as inaccurate as their recognition, and no ship was hit.

Italian reluctance to engage approximately equal forces was displayed again on July 19 in the Battle of Cape Spada, when three British destroyers on an antisubmarine sweep northwest of Crete ran into two Italian light cruisers. The destroyers fell back upon the support of the Australian light cruiser *Sydney* and another destroyer, which were to the northward of them. When the Italians sighted the *Sydney* they retired to the southwest, although they had superiority in 6-inch guns and only a slight inferiority in smaller calibers. In the pursuit the *Sydney* sank the cruiser *Bartolomeo Colleoni;* her damaged consort, the *Bande Neri,* managed to reach Tobruk.

After these actions the Admiralty and Cunningham effected a redefinition of the responsibilities for the Mediterranean. Since the Italians had many interests in the eastern half of the area and since the British forces in Egypt and the Middle East required constant support, the eastern fleet was made stronger, while Force H at Gibraltar would be a raiding force, available for operations in the Mediterranean and, under Admiralty control, in the Atlantic. The Flag Officer Commanding North Atlantic, Admiral Sir Dudley North at Gibraltar, could also call upon Force H for assistance in preventing enemy ships from passing the Straits. Cunningham desired to rid himself of his two slow *Royal Sovereigns* and wanted instead a total force of three or four faster *Queen Elizabeths,* including the *Valiant,* which had radar. He also requested an increased number of heavy cruisers to enable him to cope with the Italian preponderance in that type of ship. He particularly desired the carrier *Illustrious* to supplement the inadequate *Eagle.* The redistribution of strength, called Operation HATS, took place in late August and early September unopposed except by moderate air attacks. Cunningham took advantage of the operation to send a small convoy into Malta.

The Italian Offensive in Libya

On September 7, 1940, Mussolini ordered Marshal Graziani, commander of the Italian army in Libya, to begin a land offensive against Egypt. On September 14 the Italians captured the important port city of Sidi Barrani but were unable to go farther because the British navy began to harass their sea-borne supply routes by attacks on Benghazi, Sollum, Bardia, and Sidi Barrani itself. British submarines had met with little success because Italian ships clung as far as possible to shallow coastal waters, where it was difficult for British submarines to operate successfully. Nor was there adequate air strength on Malta. Until December the Italians lost no ships on the Italy-Libya run either from submarine or air attack while they delivered 692,403 tons to Libya during the year. Until Malta could be built up, the British were helpless to interdict this traffic.

Italy Invades Greece

Against the advice of his naval officers, Mussolini on October 15, 1940, at a meeting with army and political leaders, issued orders for the invasion of Greece. He kept his intention to attack a secret from Hitler, who he knew would not approve.

The Greeks had long feared an Italian invasion of their country, but were determined to avoid giving a pretext. Hence they refused to allow the British to send aid ahead of time, to send military advisers, or even to be informed of the Greek strategy of defense. Thus on October 28, when Italian troops crossed the Greek frontier, the British, with slender resources, were faced with a difficult decision. To maintain their position with neutrals in the Middle East, they were obliged to support Greece in her struggle. Any troops that might be sent to Greece would have to be drawn from General Archibald Wavell's forces in Egypt. The problem of air support was equally difficult. The entire British position in the Middle East might be lost if the defenses of Egypt were weakened.

In view of these considerations, the British War Cabinet agreed to sent munitions and money and an R.A.F. contingent. Also by arrangement with the Greek government, the British established a naval fueling base on Crete. The Greeks as it turned out did not at the time need troop assistance, for the Italian offensive stalled on November 8, and a few days later a Greek counteroffensive pushed the invaders back to the Albanian border. Thus in both his North African venture and in his Greek invasion, Mussolini, because of inadequate planning and inadequate support, failed in his attempt to make political expediency promote military success. Instead of winning glory, Mussolini became a laughingstock.

The Carrier Raid on Taranto

In view of the reluctance of the Italian navy to accept decisive action at sea, Cunningham sought to attack their ships at their Taranto base. Originally scheduled for October 21, Trafalgar Day, the operation was twice postponed because of other urgent commitments and because of damage to the *Illustrious.* The delays proved to be fortunate for the British, for when the raid finally took place late at night on November 11, all six of the Italian battleships were in port.

At the last moment the *Eagle* developed defects and had to be left behind. Five of her Swordfish planes were transferred to the *Illustrious,* which arrived at the launching point with 21 aircraft. The latest reconnaissance photographs, flown aboard the carrier on the afternoon of November 11, revealed the position of every Italian unit. As the first wave of twelve planes neared its target, four bombers split off to make a diversion in the inner harbor, and two other planes broke away to drop flares to the east in order to silhouette the battleships for the six torpedo planes. The first attack worked perfectly, the flares showing the targets clearly to the torpedo-plane pilots, who scored hits on the *Cavour* and *Littorio,* at the cost of one plane. A second wave of eight planes an hour later used identical tactics. This wave scored a hit on the *Duilio* and two more on the *Littorio.* This wave also lost one aircraft.

The attack reduced the Italian fleet to three available battleships, the *Giulio Cesare, Vittorio Veneto,* and *Doria.* The *Cavour* never went to sea again, while the *Littorio* and *Duilio* were out of action for some months. The surviving Italian major ships abandoned Taranto as a fleet base, moving to Naples immediately after the attack. Italian air reconnaissance had completely failed to spot the British forces moving up for the attack or the Malta convoy which took advantage of the diversion caused by fleet movements for the Taranto raid. The British gained an additional dividend from the operation, for a light force wiped out a small convoy of four ships bound for Brindisi.

Germany to the Rescue

As a result of the Greek success in repelling the Italian invaders and of their own success in the Taranto operation, the British found their Mediterranean situation much improved. On December 9, General Wavell opened an offensive out of Egypt, capturing Sollum on the 16th, Bardia and Tobruk in January, and reaching Benghazi on February 1. By February 9 the entire bulge of Cyrenaica was in British hands, and Wavell's forces stood before El Agheila at the threshold of Tripolitania.

Throughout the winter of 1940–41, the Mediterranean Fleet had assumed the task of moving supplies from Egypt to Wavell's advancing army. An Inshore Squadron carried the brunt of this labor, its small ships suffering heavy losses to aircraft based in Sicily. Its operations were a brilliant example of the flexibility of sea power in bringing essential materials to an army advancing along a seacoast. The supplies needed were difficult if not impossible of transport along the sand trails and inadequate roads of the Western Desert.

In the face of repeated Italian setbacks, in Greece, in North Africa, and at sea, the OKW (*Oberkommando der Wehrmacht*—the German High Command) held a series of meetings to consider what could be done to retrieve the situation. As early as November 12, 1940, Hitler had decided that it would be necessary to extricate Italy from the consequences of her "regrettable blunder" in Greece. But at the same time, Germany was busy with other commitments, including exploratory staff discussions for Operation BARBAROSSA, the invasion of Russia. Once the officers of the OKW turned their attention to the Mediterranean, they proposed to do what was necessary to make the Inland Sea an Axis lake. First, they planned to give direct troop support to Italy in Greece and Albania, coming down through Romania and Bulgaria in order to insure that the output of the Romanian oil fields would come to Germany. The second part of the plan, Operation FELIX, envisioned having Spain enter the war against Britain. If Spain would not take this step, diplomatic arrangements would be made to allow German troops free passage of Spanish soil in order to capture Gibraltar. A part of this operation was the capture of the Canary and Cape Verde Islands in order to control the entrances to the Mediterranean. If France objected to the passage of German troops for this purpose, all France was to be occupied. Third, Germany planned to send a *Luftwaffe* corps to Italy to cooperate with the Italian air force. Finally, they would send mechanized infantry to Africa, to be designated the *Afrika Korps,* under command of General Erwin Rommel.

During December and January, German *Fliegerkorps X* (Tenth Air Fleet) of some 500 planes, especially trained in attack on ships, moved from Norway to airfields in Calabria and Sicily. Its tasks were to protect Axis shipping with North Africa, prevent the passage of British convoys through the central Mediterranean, and neutralize Malta by air attack.

After a part of the German air reinforcements had already arrived, a British convoy of four cargo ships escorted by two battleships, one aircraft carrier, four cruisers, and destroyers of Force H passed Gibraltar January 6 en route to Malta and Greece. About the same time the battleships *Warspite* and *Valiant,* the carrier *Illustrious,* and seven destroyers of the Mediterranean Fleet sailed from Alexandria to meet the convoy and cover other convoy movements between Malta and Alexandria. In support of the operation Malta-based aircraft attacked the Italian fleet at Naples on the 8th, damaging the battleship *Giulio Cesare* and forcing her and the *Vittorio Veneto* to move to the small base at Spezia well away from the strategic area. This attack left the *Vittorio Veneto* the only serviceable Italian battleship. On the evening of the 9th, after daylight attacks by Italian aircraft from Sardinia, the Gibraltar force turned back undamaged, leaving the convoy with three cruisers and several destroyers to proceed to Malta. That night the cruisers drove off an attack by Italian destroyers, sinking one of them, but a British destroyer struck a mine and had to be towed to Malta. The next day an Italian force from Spezia searched the western Mediterranean for Force H, which had long since passed out of reach.

Around noon on January 10 the Alexandria force, which had joined the convoy from Gibraltar during the night, was attacked west of Malta by about 50 Stuka dive bombers from Sicily. Unlike the Italian pilots, who attacked from high level, the Germans pressed home their attacks with great skill through very heavy antiaircraft fire. Concentrating on the *Illustrious,* they hit the carrier several times. Steering with her engines, the *Illustrious* headed for Malta, and despite an afternoon attack which started large fires, managed to make port that evening. Next day, en route to Alexandria, the cruisers *Gloucester* and *Southampton* were damaged by air attack, the latter so badly that she had to be sunk by her own force.

At Malta the *Illustrious* became the target of numerous air attacks. Nevertheless, the naval constructors succeeded in making temporary repairs to her, and on the night of January 23 she slipped out of the harbor and reached Alexandria without further damage. Since the *Illus-*

trious had to go to the United States for permanent repairs and the *Eagle* was unserviceable, the Mediterranean Fleet would be without a carrier until the arrival of the *Formidable,* which the Admiralty had immediately ordered transferred from the South Atlantic.

While maintaining air attacks on Malta at the rate of three or four a day, the *Luftwaffe* did not neglect the eastern end of the Mediterranean. At the end of January German aircraft from the Dodecanese Islands began dropping magnetic mines in the Suez Canal in such numbers that it had to be closed intermittently throughout the month of February. Thus in the brief space of one month the intervention of the German air force had dramatically reversed the situation in the Mediterranean.

To send ships through the Mediterranean was to subject them to extreme peril. The only feasible route to maintain supply for Britain's Middle Eastern army was the long one around the Cape of Good Hope, through the Red Sea and the Suez Canal. Regular Cape convoys designated WS (for Winston's Specials) brought men, stores, tanks, and ammunition to the Middle East Command. Yet this route was by no means secure. In addition to the obvious threat from the Germans in the Atlantic, the Italians had substantial forces southeast of Suez, with seven destroyers, two motor torpedo boats, and eight submarines based at Kisimayo on the Indian Ocean and at Massawa on the Red Sea. In January 1941 British forces from Kenya and the Sudan began a campaign with fleet support to drive the Italians out of East Africa. In February the Italians abandoned the port of Kisimayo, and in early April British forces took Massawa while torpedo planes from the *Eagle* sank two Italian destroyers and drove one ashore. The remaining Italian naval forces in East Africa scuttled themselves or fled the area. As a result, the President of the United States was able under the Neutrality Act to proclaim the Red Sea open to American shipping, and British convoys had security from attack near their destinations.

In the next few months the British Mediterranean Fleet endured its most severe trial. When the Germans intervened in Greece, the Greek government accepted the active participation of British troops and air forces in the mainland fighting. Although reinforcement of Greece meant that General Wavell's drive had to be stopped short of the Tripolitan border, the War Cabinet felt that the political reasons for aiding Greece outweighed all other considerations. The Mediterranean Fleet, shouldering the responsibilities for transport and protection of three divisions and an armored brigade with their supplies, had to commit so much of its strength to the Aegean that it could spare little attention for Italian convoys to Libya. The result was nearly fatal to the British position in North Africa, for during the month of March, Italian ships carried General Rommel's *Afrika Korps* across the Mediterranean.

The first British convoy sailed for Piraeus March 5, others following every three days. Italian explosive motor boats sank a British cruiser in Suda Bay on the night of March 26, and a few days later an Italian submarine sank another. During a period of about six weeks however the fleet carried 58,000 troops with their equipment and supplies to Greece without loss.

The Battle of Cape Matapan, March 28–29, 1941

Pressed by the Germans, the Italian navy planned to employ their last operational battleship, the *Vittorio Veneto,* with eight cruisers and a number of destroyers to strike at British convoys to Greece. Commanded by Admiral Angelo Iachino, the force sailed under the misapprehension that the British could oppose them with only one battleship, for *Fliegerkorps X* claimed to have put the *Warspite* and *Barham* out of action.

During the morning of March 27 air search and cover by the German and Italian landbased air forces proved ineffective, and about noon the Italian naval force was shadowed by a British flying boat about 80 miles east of Sicily. Worried by these developments, the Italian naval command ordered a cruiser group to the north to join the main body before it could make its assigned sweep. On the morning of March 28 the *Vittorio Veneto,* screened by destroyers, was south of the west end of Crete steering southeast with a division of three cruisers and destroyers seven miles in the van and a northern group of five cruisers and destroyers 25 miles to eastward.

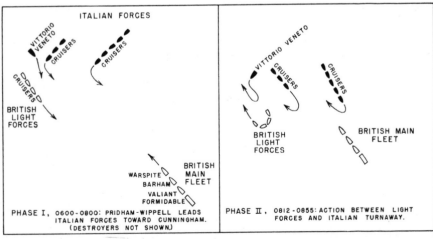

BATTLE OF CAPE MATAPAN, MARCH 28, 1941

Warned by the British intelligence service in Italy, Admiral Cunningham had taken measures to counter the Italian thrust. Clearing convoys from the way, he ordered Vice Admiral H. D. Pridham-Wippell to leave Greece with his cruiser-destroyer force and rendezvous with him south of Crete on the morning of March 28. Cunningham himself sortied from Alexandria in the *Warspite* with the *Valiant,* the *Barham,* the recently arrived carrier *Formidable,* and nine destroyers after dark on the 27th.

At dawn on the 28th search planes from the *Formidable* sighted the Italian cruiser group and almost simultaneously a scout plane from the *Vittorio Veneto* spotted Pridham-Wippell's light forces. A few moments later, Pridham-Wippell sighted another Italian light force. As at the Battle of Jutland, neither commander knew of the presence of heavy forces nearby. Also, as Beatty had done at Jutland, Pridham-Wippell turned to lead the group he had just sighted toward Cunningham's battleships, a running fight continuing for nearly an hour, with no hits on either side. At 0855 Iachino directed his light forces to break off the action, as they were nearing the range of British shore-based air. Pridham-Wippell followed their retirement in order to keep in touch. To prevent his light forces from running into a trap, Cunningham ordered the *Formidable* to make a torpedo strike on the unengaged group of Italian cruisers. The planes however had so far to go that before they arrived on the scene the next dramatic development occurred. At 1100 a lookout in the *Orion,* Pridham-Wippell's flagship, spotted the *Vittorio Veneto,* which immediately opened accurate fire with her 15-inch guns. Caught between the *Vittorio Veneto* and the cruisers, Pridham-Wippell turned south behind a smoke screen. At this point the *Formidable*'s torpedo planes arrived and attacked the Italian battleship. Although they scored no hits, they caused Iachino to break off the chase and set a course for home at 25 knots, with the British in pursuit.

For the next few hours the *Formidable* made repeated strikes in an effort to slow the Italian force so that the British battleships could come up. At 1520 a torpedo hit stopped the *Vittorio Veneto* temporarily, but an hour and a half later she was making 19 knots. Cunningham meanwhile had ordered Pridham-Wippell to press on at 30 knots with his cruisers and attempt to make visual contact with the fleeing Italian force. The battle fleet followed at its top speed of 24 knots. Because the British underestimated the speed of the *Vittorio Veneto* by four knots, their intercept courses were wide of the mark. Against just such a contingency Cunningham ordered another strike by the *Formidable*'s planes, which stopped the cruiser *Pola,* the Italian main body continuing its run for home.

After these events the battle lost form. Misjudging the course and speed of the enemy, Pridham-Wippell failed to maintain contact after passing the crippled *Pola.* The battleships coming up later first mistook as British an Italian cruiser force returning to the aid of their helpless sister. Quickly rectifying that error, the battle fleet engaged the Italian group, sinking three cruisers, including the *Pola*, and two destroyers. The remainder of the Italian force made its way safely to port.

The British had achieved a considerable tactical victory at almost no cost to themselves. Although the *Vittorio Veneto* escaped them, they had sunk three Italian cruisers and two destroyers. One British cruiser had been slightly damaged, and one plane and pilot were lost. Belated air attacks by the *Luftwaffe* failed to do any additional damage to the British force.

The disproportionate victory provided a much needed lift to the morale of the Alexandria fleet and the British public at a time when the Mediterranean situation seemed dark. It had the important strategic consequence that the Italian fleet did not venture from the safety of its ports to interfere with British naval operations in the waters around Greece and Crete.

The Loss of Greece and Crete

British troops did not remain long in Greece. From Bulgaria the German army had invaded southern Yugoslavia and Greece on April 6. To the 800 supporting aircraft of *Fliegerkorps IV*, the Royal Air Force could oppose only 80 operational planes plus two long-ranged bomber squadrons flying night missions from Egypt. Outflanked and outnumbered, the Greek and Yugoslav armies retreated. Yugoslavia capitulated on April 17. The Greeks had already decided that their cause was lost. The Greek King informally suggested that, to spare the country the ravages of further fighting, the British send no more troops and evacuate those already there. The War Cabinet immediately agreed to evacuate the mainland, and all British troops began to fall back on embarkation ports. On April 24 the Greeks surrendered. On the same night the British evacuation began.

For this task, even more difficult than Dunkirk, the Mediterranean Fleet had available seven cruisers, 20 destroyers, 21 transports, and a number of small craft. The port of Piraeus having been destroyed by the explosion of an ammunition

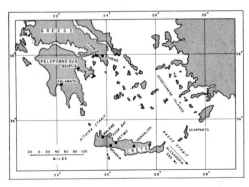

SOUTHERN GREECE AND CRETE

ship early in April, the evacuation had to be managed from three beaches in the Athens area and three in the Peloponnesus. To avoid air attack, the evacuating ships were ordered not to approach the beaches until one hour after dark and to leave by 0300. For six days the operation continued, with no air cover, with embarkation ports widely separated, and with less effective organization than at Dunkirk. Ship losses were heavy. Yet at the end over 50,000 British troops were saved. In addition, one cruiser, six destroyers, and four submarines of the Greek navy escaped to Alexandria.

Although the British had been forced out of Greece, they determined to save Crete. Its strategic position for controlling shipping in the eastern Mediterranean made the War Cabinet take the decision to hold it at all costs. A large number of troops evacuated from Greece served to stiffen the island's defenses, although loss of replacement parts caused the evacuation of all planes except for those the fleet might be able to provide. On the other hand, Crete lay within easy reach—60 miles—of the newly established German airfields in Greece and of an Italian strip on Scarpanto, only 45 miles to the east.

At dawn on May 20 the expected German assault came. The primary attack was made by 16,000 airborne troops of *Fliegerkorps XI* transported in 530 planes and 100 gliders, while following up were 7,000 reserve troops to be transported by sea. At 0800 gliders towed by transport planes landed troops west of Maleme airfield, and 15 minutes later parachute troops began to drop to the east. By the end of the day 5,000 airborne troops of the Seventh Airborne Division had landed, and Maleme field, though still under British artillery fire, was partly in German hands. Retimo and Heraklion fields had also been attacked, but less strongly, and the British forces there had held. Next day the Germans used Maleme airfield to build up their forces, even though many of their aircraft had to crash-land on the shell-pocked field.

For the sea defense of Crete Admiral Cunningham divided his forces into three groups. To the east and west of Crete two cruiser-destroyer forces were stationed during daylight hours with orders to carry out sweeps north of the island at night or when enemy forces were known to be at sea. The main body, including the *Valiant*, the *Warspite*, a cruiser, and eight destroyers, provided general support. On the night of May 21, a cruiser force which swept around the west end of the island met a German invasion flotilla of small craft 20 miles to the northward and sank about 15 of them, drowning some 4,000 troops. Low on ammunition, the cruisers withdrew to the westward to join the battleship force. Meanwhile another British cruiser force sweeping to the northwest sank several small vessels of another German convoy and drove it off.

Since it was now daylight and the British ships were low on ammunition and already under heavy air attack, their commander, satisfied that the convoy was retiring, did not pursue it but instead retired to the southwest and asked for support from the battleship force. Before the forces could join, two cruisers were damaged, and at 1330 the battleship *Warspite* was hit and a destroyer was sunk by Axis planes. Of two cruisers sent to help the stricken destroyer, one was sunk by air attack in Kithira Strait at 1550. About an hour later another British battleship was damaged, and in the next two and one half hours another cruiser was hit twice and finally sunk. During this night and day of wild activity, no German soldier reached Crete. Yet, although the Mediterranean Fleet had prevented the seaborne invasion of the island, on May 22 German airborne forces made Maleme airfield operational and began landing 20 troop-carrying planes and towed gliders an hour.

During the next few days the British forces fared badly on sea and land. On May 23 two destroyers en route to Alexandria were sunk by air attack. On the 26th while making an air strike against Scarpanto airfield, the carrier *Formidable* and a destroyer were badly damaged. Ashore, German troops broke through to Suda Bay, and the British troops there began to retire across the mountains to Sphakia on the south coast. Late that night the British decided to evacuate their forces from Crete. Next morning the *Barham* was damaged while covering the retirement of lighter forces from Suda Bay.

Like the withdrawal from Greece, the evacuation of Crete had to be carried out during darkness. On May 28 three cruisers and six destroyers manned by exhausted crews sailed from Alexandria for the Heraklion area in response to Cunningham's signal "Stick it out, we must never let the Army down." Although one cruiser was hit and forced to retire during the approach, the rest of the force embarked 4,000 troops that night. Homeward bound a damaged destroyer lost steering control and had to be abandoned, and air attacks sank a destroyer and damaged another and two cruisers. A bomb that exploded on the crowded mess deck of cruiser *Orion* killed or wounded 540 troops. In the whole force a total of 800 troops were killed, wounded, or captured.

Evacuation from Sphakia on the south coast was naturally less costly. During the night of May 29 four cruisers, a fast transport, and three destroyers picked up 7,000 troops and got away with damage to only one cruiser. Meanwhile the British forces in the Retimo area had surrendered. The next night 4,000 more troops were evacuated from Sphakia with the loss of still another cruiser.

In all the Royal Navy saved about 17,000 troops from Crete, at a cost to itself of three cruisers and six destroyers sunk; one aircraft carrier, three battleships, six cruisers, and seven destroyers damaged, and just over 2,000 caualties. Although the British had suffered about 13,000 casualties, their stubborn defense had cost the Germans 400 planes and

15,000 to 20,000 troops, including 5,000 men of their only airborne division. The British defense of Crete actually saved Malta, for after their Cretan experience the Germans had no airborne force available for further operations.

But the post-Crete situation of the Mediterranean Fleet was not a happy one. Despite the arrival of reinforcements consisting of a battleship, two cruisers, and six new destroyers in early May, at the beginning of June only two battleships, three cruisers, and 17 destroyers were operational. The British supply line from Alexandria to Malta was now flanked to the northward by German air forces based on Crete. As Malta grew weaker from lack of supplies, the Axis supply line to North Africa would become more secure.

Another threat to the eastern flank of the British army in Egypt and the fuel supply of the Royal Navy had developed meanwhile in the Middle East. In early April the pro-Axis Rashid Ali seized control of the government of Iraq. On the 18th, British naval forces under the Commander in Chief India supported a landing at Basra which quickly forced Rashid Ali to flee to Iran. By mutual agreement British and Russian forces moved into Iran in August to prevent its seizure by the Germans.

In Syria German agents, encouraged by the anti-British feelings of the Vichy-minded French colonial government, had been active. Here the French had a small naval force of two super destroyers armed with five 5.5-inch guns and capable of 40 knots, three submarines, a sloop, and a patrol vessel. To oppose these the British Mediterranean Fleet sent two cruisers and four destroyers to Haifa, Palestine. In early June a fast attack transport supported by another cruiser and two more destroyers landed British troops in Syria while other British and Free French forces advanced from Palestine. Three days later an armistice was signed. Before the fighting ended at sea, however, one of the French super destroyers heavily damaged a British destroyer, and French aircraft severely damaged two others. Reinforced by two more cruisers, British ships and naval aircraft sank a super destroyer en route to Syria with arms for the French and damaged the two that were already there. They also sank a submarine and two merchant ships.

Rommel Takes the Offensive

While the British vainly attempted to save Greece and Crete, disaster loomed on the Egyptian border. Although the *Afrika Korps* had arrived during March, 1941, at first Rommel was concerned only with halting Wavell's drive toward Tripoli. Rommel himself had arrived in February and had devoted himself to stiffening the Italian defenses. Establishing a base at Tripoli, Rommel organized a group of small coasting ships to transport supplies from Tripoli to the port of Sirte, and later Ras el Ali some 250 miles to the east, a move necessitated by the fact that the Italians had never built a railway along the coast. Field Marshal Walther von Brauschitsch, Commander in Chief of the German army, had informed Rommel that there was to be no question of a major German offensive in North Africa and that he could expect no reinforcements. Rommel realized however that limited objectives could not be held in the desert, and that if he were to carry out his instructions to take Benghazi, he could not hold it, but must take all of Cyrenaica in order to obtain a position where he could secure his flanks.

Although Rommel's orders were not to begin even a limited offensive until the end of May, he feared that the delay would enable the British to strengthen the El Agheila-Bir es Sueva position, so he launched his attack on April 2. Wavell, who had sent part of his forces to Greece, and who had been forced to relieve his most experienced troops in Libya with inexperienced units fresh from home, could not withstand the precision of Rommel's advance and gave permission to fall back to Benghazi, or farther if necessary.

Agedabia fell to the Germans on the first day of their offensive, and reports came to Rommel that Benghazi had been evacuated. At this point, the Italian Commander in Chief, General Graziani, attempted to assert his authority and stop Rommel's advance as exceeding instructions from Rome and as impossible of support in the precarious supply situation. Rommel refused to consider wasting his opportunity. While the two men argued, Rommel received a dispatch from the OKW giving him complete freedom of action. After this, the *Afrika Korps* moved rapidly, seizing Benghazi the following day. Cutting across the bulge of Cyrenaica, Rommel reached Derna on April 8, capturing the city and some 800 men.

Immediately Rommel drove on toward Tobruk, which the British were busily reinforcing by sea through the efforts of the Inshore Squadron. After several unsuccessful attacks on Tobruk, thwarted by stubborn British resistance, the necessity for using inexperienced Italian troops, and the preoccupation of the *Luftwaffe* with strategic bombing rather than tactical support, Rommel decided to by-pass Tobruk and drive for Sollum, just over the Egyptian border where he expected to stabilize his front. By the end of May the *Afrika Korps* had established a strong position in the Sollum-Halfaya-Sidi Omar triangle, where it sought to build supplies for an offensive into Egypt.

The arrival in May of a special convoy, code-named Tiger, laden with 238 tanks, the first successful passage in several months of merchant ships from Gibraltar to Alexandria, made it possible for General Wavell to mount a counteroffensive against Rommel's position. Covered by maximum tactical air support, the drive, Operation BATTLEAXE, opened June 15. After heavy fighting, the attack failed, and General Wavell was replaced as Commander in Chief of the British Armies in the Middle East by General Sir Claude Auchinleck. The North African front thereupon stabilized for some months, neither the British nor the Germans having sufficient strength to mount an offensive. Further, while Tobruk remained in British hands Rommel could not advance to the important outpost of Mersa Matruh, whose airstrip would have enabled him to strike at Alexandria, Cairo, and the Suez Canal.

Off North Africa the Inshore Squadron kept up the supply of beleaguered Tobruk throughout the spring and summer. In August the overworked ships of the Tobruk Run were further burdened by the task of removing from Tobruk and replacing with others 19,000 Australian troops which the Dominion Government desired at home for defense against the Japanese threat. By the end of October the Inshore Squadron had completed the exchange and at the same time had delivered about 8,000 tons of stores for the garrison. Finally in November Auchinleck launched an offensive that raised the siege of Tobruk on December 10 and reached Benghazi two weeks later. In the 242 days of the Tobruk siege, the Inshore Squadron had brought in some 33,000 troops, 92 guns, 72 tanks, and 34,000 tons of supplies. During the same period its ships had removed 34,000 troops, 7,500 wounded, and 7,000 prisoners. The entire support operation had cost two destroyers, one minelayer, 24 small naval vessels, and six merchant ships sunk, with damage to seven destroyers, one attack transport, 19 smaller naval vessels, and seven merchant ships.

The Battle of Supplies

During the summer of 1941, both sides in North Africa undertook to build up strength. The Germans, consolidating their gains in Greece, Crete, and Cyrenaica, used the maximum of Axis shipping capacity to send troops and supplies to North Africa. To oppose this flow of goods to Rommel, the British had to depend on Malta.

Situated almost at the mid-point of the Mediterranean, Malta not only served as a way station for ships passing between Gibraltar and Alexandria; it also sat squarely athwart the normal sea routes between Italy and Libya. Fighter planes and bombers based on Malta forced Axis shipping to make wide detours beyond the range of air strikes, effectively cutting down the efficiency of transport to North Africa. As a fleet base, Malta could threaten Italian and German convoys, forcing the Italian fleet to provide heavy escorts and to accept action under unfavorable conditions of air cover. When Malta was strong, nearly two fifths of Axis shipping for North Africa went to the bottom; when the island was weak, over 95 per cent arrived safely. The chart on page 62 shows this story graphically.

To keep Malta supplied, the British decided to send strongly escorted

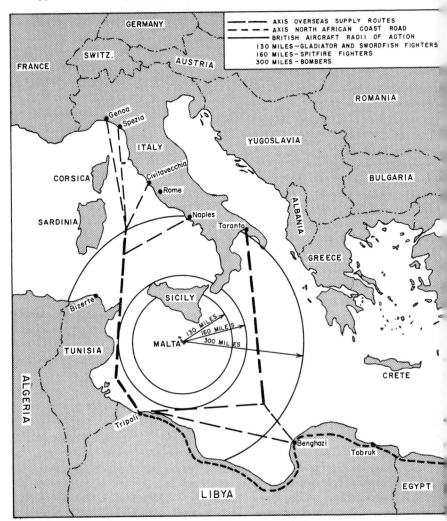

AXIS OVERSEAS SUPPLY ROUTES
AXIS NORTH AFRICAN COAST ROAD
BRITISH AIRCRAFT RADII OF ACTION
130 MILES – GLADIATOR AND SWORDFISH FIGHTERS
160 MILES – SPITFIRE FIGHTERS
300 MILES – BOMBERS

THE IMPORTANCE OF MALTA

convoys approximately once a month. They had to provide heavy cover in view of heavy attacks to be expected from the Italian and German air forces and because of the danger of opposition by the Italian fleet. As a rule two convoys were run simultaneously, one from Gibraltar and one from Alexandria. Force H would escort the Gibraltar convoy as far as the Sicilian Channel, while the Mediterranean Fleet gave the Alexandria convoy protection right through to Malta. Despite all the British could do, convoys often were unable to win through under the blistering attacks from the skies.

As a result of the losses incurred in the Greek campaign, no surface ships could be spared for Malta during the late spring and summer, but in other respects the Malta situation greatly improved, largely because of the transfer in June of *Fliegerkorps X* from Sicily to Greece to replace half of *Fliegerkorps IV*, which was being transferred to Russia. Meanwhile British submarines and aircraft kept up the work of interdicting Axis communications to North Africa. In the first six months of 1940, the Axis shipped some 2,372,000 tons of material, losing not quite 80,000 tons for a loss rate of 3.4 per cent. In the second half of the year, while shipping only some 1,750,000 tons, they lost nearly 400,000 for a loss rate of 22.7 per cent.

To strengthen Malta's offensive capability, in October 1941 two cruisers and two destroyers dispatched from England were based on the island and designated Force K. On the night of November 8 they intercepted a Tripoli-bound convoy of seven German supply ships protected by two Italian cruisers and six destroyers, sinking all seven supply ships and one of the escorting destroyers. A British submarine sank another of the Italian destroyers the next day. About two weeks later a cruiser and a destroyer of Force K found two tankers escorted by two destroyers and sank both tankers while the escort escaped. At the end of November Force K was reinforced by two more cruisers and destroyers. In the middle of December four destroyers of Force K caught two Italian cruisers in the desperate expedient of rushing gasoline to Tripoli and turned them into blazing torches.

On November 18, 1941, the British Eighth Army began another offensive, advancing rapidly to Benghazi. Because of heavy losses in Axis shipping and lack of reinforcements, Rommel was forced to retreat after a masterly stand. He pulled all the way back to Agedabia before increased strength enabled him to resume the offensive.

The success of Force K and other Malta forces and the loss of Cyrenaica caused the German High Command to take a renewed look at the Mediterranean problem. Although Hitler was bemused with his campaign in Russia, others, especially Raeder, were fully aware of the strategic importance of the Mediterranean. The SKL (German naval staff) urged measures to strengthen Italy's use of her fleet to protect the shipping to North Africa. But when these matters came to Hitler's attention in August 1941, he ordered instead that U-boats be sent to the Mediterranean, against the advice of Raeder and Dönitz, who wished to maintain the Atlantic attack at full strength. The first two waves of boats made the passage of the Straits of Gibraltar in September and November

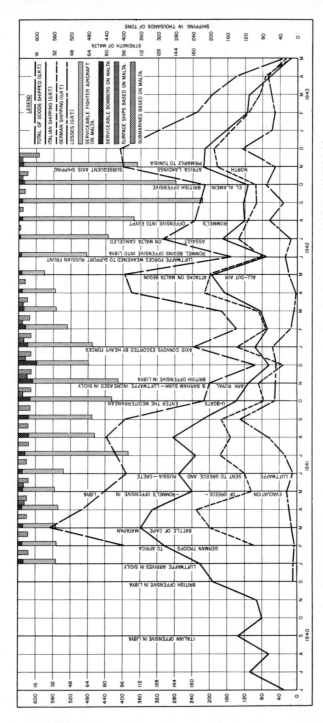

EFFECT OF THE STRENGTH OF MALTA ON AXIS TRANS-MEDITERRANEAN SHIPPING

1941, and soon thereafter made their presence felt dramatically. On November 11, *U-81* sank the *Ark Royal,* and twelve days later *U-331* sent the *Barham* to the bottom. In maneuvering to escape after the attack, the U-boat lost control and went to a depth of 820 feet safely, 490 feet deeper than her designed depth.

Other German efforts to stiffen the Mediterranean Theater followed. In December Hitler sent Field Marshal Albert Kesselring to Italy as Commander in Chief South with orders to gain and hold sea and air supremacy in the Sicilian Channel. At the same time Hitler sent *Flieger-korps II* to Sicily.

To hold up their end of the struggle, the Italians agreed to provide heavy ship support for vital convoys and to attempt further attacks on British harbors. On December 19, 1941, Italian submarine *Scire* launched three two-man torpedoes (midget submarines with detachable warheads) in Alexandria which severely damaged the British battleships *Queen Elizabeth* and *Valiant.* About the same time *U-81,* the killer of the *Ark Royal,* damaged the *Malaya,* leaving the Mediterranean Fleet without a single serviceable heavy ship. Nor could replacements be provided, for Japan had entered the war, and her planes had sent the *Prince of Wales* and the *Repulse* to the bottom only a few days before.

To make matters worse, on December 19, three cruisers and four destroyers of Force K ran into a mine field off Tripoli which sank one destroyer and one cruiser and damaged two other cruisers. As a result of this disaster a big Axis convoy reached Tripoli safely.

Because of these increased Axis measures and severe British losses, the Axis shipping picture in the central Mediterranean improved enormously, enabling Rommel to resume the offensive in North Africa and recapture Cyrenaica during the first two months of 1942. Simultaneously the Axis intensified the air assault on Malta.

Despite the arrival of additional fighters for the defense of the island on November 11, the scale of attack more than doubled to 175 raids in December. In the first four months of 1942, as German air reinforcements poured into Sicily, the monthly total of raids ranged between two and three hundred. At the end of March British carrier *Eagle,* which had been flying in twelve Spitfires at a time, was laid up for repairs. Early in April, at the personal request of Churchill, President Roosevelt made the United States carrier *Wasp* available to fly in its much larger capacity of about 60 Spitfires, but these were all destroyed within a few days. That month the tonnage of bombs dropped on Malta reached a high of 6,700, and the British were forced to withdraw the surface ships that were still operational. Submarines ran in fuel and ammunition, but in early May the last Malta-based submarines retired to Alexandria. A second *Wasp* trip delivered 60 more Spitfires on May 9, just in time for a series of costly air battles on that day and the next.

At the end of these battles, Marshal Kesselring considered that his task of neutralizing Malta had been accomplished.

In March 1942 the supply situation at Malta became so desperate that all British North African forces concerted their efforts to get a convoy through. The Eighth Army made diversionary attacks upon Axis airfields near Tobruk. The Royal Air Force attacked airfields in Cyrenaica and Crete, carried out air reconnaissance and strikes from Libya and Malta, and provided air cover for the convoy to the limit of its endurance. Royal Air Force planes and a naval air squadron bombed the Libyan port of Derna on the nights of March 20 and 21. The weakened Mediterranean Fleet could provide only three cruisers and ten destroyers for cover and an antiaircraft cruiser and six destroyers for escort of the four-ship convoy. Six other destroyers made an antisubmarine sweep along the North African coast, in the course of which one destroyer was sunk; the remaining five, together with a cruiser and destroyer from Malta, reinforced the covering group.

During the morning of March 22 the convoy suffered intermittent air attacks without damage. In the afternoon an Italian force under Admiral Iachino consisting of the battleship *Littorio,* three cruisers, and four destroyers intercepted the British force north of Sirte. By adroit maneuvering, the use of smoke screens, and threatening destroyer attacks, the British admiral was able to keep between his convoy and the Italian force and hold off the superior enemy until sundown, when again Iachino retired to avoid a night action. Two of the four supply ships arived safely at Malta. Yet there was more honor than profit in the victory, for subsequent heavy air attacks upon the harbor sank the other two ships at their moorings after only 5,000 of their 26,000 tons of cargo had been landed.

In June, with Malta reduced to near starvation, the Admiralty made another desperate effort to send in two convoys, one each from Alexandria and Gibraltar. The first, of eleven ships, was escorted by seven cruisers and 26 destroyers with several smaller warships and the ancient, unarmed battleship *Centurion* pretending to be a capital ship. Nine submarines took station to the north of the convoy track to intercept the Italian fleet if it should leave port. Maximum air support covered the convoy as it advanced.

In spite of aircraft and submarines, the Italian fleet came on, losing one cruiser to a submarine, and suffering damage to the *Littorio* from an aircraft torpedo. Although the Italian fleet never made contact, Admiral Sir Philip Vian had to order the convoy to return to Alexandria since his ships had exhausted their ammunition fighting off air attacks.

The eastbound convoy, from Gibraltar, had better luck. Once it reached the Sardinian Narrows it came under heavy air attack, and then in the Sicilian Narrows it encountered a force of Italian destroyers. But, after heavy fighting, two of the six merchant ships won through, bringing temporary respite to Malta.

The Axis Plan to Seize Malta

In the spring of 1942 German and Italian leaders agreed that for their North African ventures to succeed in winning through to Suez and making possible the acquisition of Iranian oil fields, they must first neutralize or capture Malta. Forces based there still exacted a toll of Axis shipping. Accordingly Hitler and Mussolini, meeting at Berchtesgaden late in April, agreed to launch an assault on Malta in July, after Rommel's forthcoming offensive. Rommel was to stop at the Egyptian border so that the *Luftwaffe* planes could be employed for the Malta operation. The plan provided for newly trained German airborne troops to be supported by Italian naval forces and seaborne troops. Hitler, never wholly supporting this operation, constantly sought an excuse to avoid it. He hoped that Rommel would be able to capture Tobruk, which the Axis might then use as a supply port for ships routed via Crete, beyond attack radius of aircraft based on Malta.

On May 26, Rommel resumed his offensive. His forces reached Tobruk on June 19 and broke through the defense perimeter the next day. On June 21, Tobruk fell. For this accomplishment Hitler promoted Rommel to field marshal. Rommel remarked, "I would rather he had given me one more division." The Germans in seizing Tobruk captured vast quantities of stores. In view of this unexpected windfall and with the port of Tobruk now available, Rommel requested permission to take advantage of his momentum and drive into Egypt. Hitler, seeing a chance to avoid the assault on Malta, wrote Mussolini a letter in which he described the Egyptian opportunities in glowing terms and urged him to agree to allow Rommel to attempt to capture Suez. Mussolini acquiesced. Shortly thereafter the Malta operation was postponed until September and then canceled.

Rommel drove hard, seizing Mersa Matruh and its important air base. Then an incredible thing happened. Hitler diverted reinforcements scheduled for Africa to the Russian front. Of the 60,000 tons of supply Rommel had requested for June, only 3,000 were sent. He was able to keep going only by seizing British materials. At one point 85 per cent of his transport consisted of captured British vehicles. He was obliged to call a halt at El Alamein, only 60 miles from Alexandria.

The Turn of the Tide

Once again the supply race was on. While the Axis had to undertake only a three-day voyage to send material to North Africa, the British had to depend on the three-month voyage around the Cape of Good Hope.

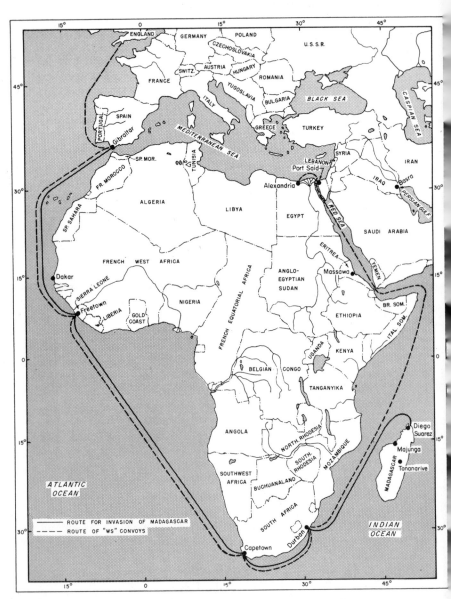

THE MADAGASCAR OPERATION, MAY 1942

Rommel chiefly required food, fuel, and light vehicles, while the British desperately needed tanks. When Tobruk fell, the United States sent 300 brand-new Sherman tanks and 100 self-propelled 105 mm. guns.

Ever since Japan had entered the war and begun operations in the Indian Ocean, the British had been haunted by fears of an Axis base being established at Diego Suarez on Madagascar. From this base German or Japanese naval or air forces could not only threaten India but operate against the vital WS convoys to Egypt. Madagascar belonged to France, but the British had little faith in the Vichy Government, especially after reports of Admiral Darlan's visit to Germany at the beginning of the year and after Vichy's virtual cession of French Indo-China to Japan. Vichy clearly wished to be aligned with the winning side and still believed in an ultimate Axis triumph.

Heavy ships for Operation IRONCLAD, the capture of Madagascar, came from Force H, and included two aircraft carriers, the *Illustrious* and *Indomitable*, as well as the battleship *Ramillies*, two cruisers, eleven destroyers, with smaller craft, and 15 transports and assault vessels. Force H was replaced at Gibraltar by ships from the Home Fleet, which was in turn reinforced by American heavy ships temporarily transferred to Scapa Flow.

The assault on Diego Suarez took place at 0430 on May 5, 1942. After an uncertain start, a flanking attack by 50 marines turned the edge of the defenses, and within a few hours Diego Suarez was in British hands. A few weeks later the British also took Majunga and Tananarive. Once the Vichy officials had been supplanted, the people of the island generally supported the Allied cause.

With the danger to the Cape route cleared up, reinforcement of the British Middle Eastern position proceeded rapidly. In Egypt the British had approximately 630,000 men, and Churchill became impatient for a desert offensive. Shortly after the fall of Tobruk, he made up his mind to go to Cairo to see for himself why General Auchinleck delayed his scheduled attack on Rommel. He found Auchinleck so concerned with his responsibilities for the entire Middle Eastern area that he had not recognized the full importance of North Africa. After many discussions, Churchill decided to split the Middle East command in two, to relieve Auchinleck, and to give the new Near East Command to General Sir Harold Alexander and the Eighth Army to General Sir Bernard L. Montgomery. The latter, immediately on taking over on August 13, began to reorganize and retrain his forces to meet the expected German attack on the El Alamein position and for an eventual offensive. Montgomery planned not merely to roll the Germans back on their supply lines as previous British offensives had done but to destroy them as a fighting force so that they could not be turned against the forthcoming Anglo-American landings in North Africa.

Meanwhile the air reinforcement of Malta continued. Serviceable aircraft on hand rose from a low of 23 in May to 169 in September. Even more important than the increase in numbers was the greatly extended range of the new torpedo planes being delivered. In 1939 the effective attack radius of Malta-based torpedo planes had been only 100 miles; in 1942 it had increased to 400 miles. Now it was impossible for Axis shipping to avoid attacks, even by the most circuitous routing. Even in the harbors of Bardia, Tobruk, and Mersa Matruh, ships suffered heavy attack. Axis coastal shipping also met heavy losses. Thus while Rommel attempted to build up stores for resuming his offensive before September, the supplies he received barely covered his daily requirements for his infantry forces, and not half of what he needed for the Panzer Army. Only captured British supplies alleviated the situation.

Rommel knew that if he was to win a break-through at El Alamein, he would have to attack before the expected British heavy reinforcements could arrive in September. The Italian *Comando Supremo* promised heavy shipments of oil and gasoline, and Kesselring agreed to fly in 500 tons of gasoline a day throughout the offensive. Accepting these promises, Rommel took the risk and on the night of August 30–31, 1942, hurled an attack at the ridge of Alam el Halfa, hoping to outflank the El Alamein defenses. Montgomery refused to be drawn out and contented himself with allowing Rommel's drive to spend itself against his strong defensive positions while the R.A.F. made punishing attacks on the German armor. None of Rommel's promised fuel oil or gasoline arrived, and on September 2, Rommel called off the attack.

"With the failure of this offensive," wrote Rommel, "our last chance of gaining the Suez Canal had gone. We could now expect that the full production of British industry and, more important, the enormous industrial potential of America . . . would finally turn the tide against us."

When Rommel withdrew on September 3, Montgomery did not pursue him. With his own supply line to the eastward secure, Montgomery continued to build up his forces for a massive offensive which began at El Alamein on October 23, 1942. After eleven days of furious fighting, the Eighth Army finally broke through and rolled on to the westward. Tobruk was in British hands again on November 13 and Benghazi on the 24th. On December 15 the Eighth Army reached El Agheila, and Rommel was in retreat toward Tunisia. Far to the westward British and American forces that had landed in Morocco and Algeria were advancing upon his rear. The tide of war in the Mediterranean had turned for the last time.

3

The Battle of the Atlantic

"The only thing that ever really frightened me during the war was the U-boat peril." So wrote Winston Churchill after the victory. From the Allied point of view, the Battle of the Atlantic was being won when nothing was happening. Every time a convoy arrived in port, the battle was that much nearer victory. When a dramatic action took place at sea, the Allied cause came that much nearer defeat. Victory was won by many people, by merchant seamen who sailed in the freighters and tankers, by stevedores who loaded and unloaded them, by seamen, ratings, and officers who manned the escorting vessels and aircraft, by shipyard workers who built both merchant ships and escorts, and by thousands of people on both sides of the Atlantic who plotted U-boat positions, routed convoys, organized sailing lists, experimented with new devices, and analyzed the results of previous actions.

The most curious thing about the Battle of the Atlantic is that neither side really prepared for it. Although the Anglo-German Naval Treaty of 1935 allowed Germany under certain conditions to build her U-boat arm up to parity with that of Great Britain, the Germans constructed few boats because their building yards were fully occupied in preparing surface ships under PLAN Z. Thus Germany began the war with only 56 operational U-boats, of which only 22 were suitable for Atlantic service; of the remainder, ten had not completed operational readiness tests, and 24 were 250-ton boats of short radius, suitable only for North Sea operations.

Britain had allowed preparations for antisubmarine warfare to lapse into the status of a minor activity. The Admiralty had abolished its Mine Sweeping, Antisubmarine, and Trade Divisions. Britain built few small ships for antisubmarine work, for the Admiralty set forth the policy that in the event of another war "the convoy system will only be introduced when the balance of advantage is in its favour and when sinkings are so great that the country no longer feels justified in allowing ships to sail by themselves but feels that, for the protection of their crews, the convoy system is necessary. . . . It is simply a matter of expediency . . . [that] as convoy will not be needed immediately on the outbreak of war it will give us time to improvise protection, while orders are given to build the sloops which we shall eventually require." Because efficient convoy escorts could not be improvised, most of the escorts early in the war were hurriedly adapted from fishing trawlers and other small craft, ill-suited for the rigorous duties they had to undertake. Fortunately with asdic, and the parallel development of sonar in the United States, both the British and the Americans had a reliable underwater detector which, in the hands of an experienced operator, showed the direction and also the range of a submerged submarine out to approximately 1,500 yards. However the U-boats were later to adopt night surfaced attacks, thereby largely nullifying the advantage of asdic. In 1937 the Admiralty had regained full control of the Fleet Air Arm. Although this move had been made for the sake of fleet carrier operations, the Royal Navy could now integrate the Fleet Air Arm efforts into its antisubmarine warfare operations. At the same time the navy also attained close cooperation with the R.A.F. Coastal Command in matters pertaining to the protection of shipping. This harmonious partnership proved a decisive factor in the Atlantic struggle.

Phase I: U-Boat Operations Until the Fall of France

When hostilities began in September 1939, Dönitz was obliged to operate with only a handful of boats rather than the 300 he considered a minimum. Yet one of this handful, *U-30*, by torpedoing the *Athenia* on the opening day of the war, provided an apparent indication of German intentions regarding the resumption of unrestricted U-boat warfare and abruptly dispelled the British Admiralty's hesitation in adopting the convoy system. On August 26, the Admiralty had assumed control of all British merchant shipping, and immediately after the *Athenia* sinking ordered convoys to be established over the principal routes for ships of speeds between nine and 14.9 knots. Ships outside these limits sailed independently. Later in the war, slower ships were included in slow convoys of about six to seven knots. Escort endurance precluded close support beyond 15° W or beyond 47° N for Gibraltar and Sierra Leone convoys. East Coast convoys operated successfully throughout the war with a loss rate of one tenth of one per cent. In October convoys between Britain and Norway began and continued with no losses until the invasion of Norway. Meanwhile a Dover mine barrage closed the Strait to German U-boats.

The success of these measures contrasts sharply with so-called "offensive" operations against U-boats. H.M. aircraft carrier *Ark Royal* on antisubmarine patrol narrowly avoided torpedoes on September 14; three days later *U-29* sank the 22,500-ton carrier *Courageous* patrolling with an inadequate screen off the Irish coast. Remembering the mythical success of the North Sea Mine Barrage of World War I, the British planned a similar barrage in World War II. After the fall of Norway, it was laid between Iceland and Scotland. It destroyed one U-boat, but otherwise did not affect U-boat movements at all.

The Germans too resorted to minelaying on a large scale, employing the *Luftwaffe*, surface vessels, and U-boats to sow their offensive mine fields in harbor entrances, estuaries, and shallows of the English Channel and the North Sea. These mines were of a magnetic impulse type, impossible to sweep by normal methods. On November 23, 1939, the British recovered a German magnetic mine which a plane had dropped in the mud flats in the Thames Estuary. Examination disclosed the operating principle, and the British were able partly to counter the magnetic impulse feature by means of an electrically charged cable running horizontally around each ship. This device, known as a "degaussing cable," cut to some extent into the effectiveness of the German minelaying campaign. Nonetheless, in the first four months of the war, German mines caused serious dislocations to coastal shipping and sank 79 merchant ships totaling 262,697 Gross Register Tons, almost all sailing independently.*

Meanwhile the convoys came through. U-boats sank 153,879 tons of Allied and neutral shipping in September, yet not one of their 41 victims was sailing under escort. By the end of 1939 the Royal Navy had escorted 5,756 vessels with the loss of only twelve ships, four being claimed by U-boats; during the same period 102 independently routed merchant vessels had been lost. Dönitz had lost nine U-boats, nearly a sixth of his strength. As he later revealed in his postwar *Essay on the Conduct of the War at Sea*, "U-boats at sea in operational areas during the winter 1939–40 never exceeded ten in number and at times fell as low as two."

Because of wide fluctuations in escort availability, screening dispositions changed frequently. Theoretically the best defense against U-boat assault was a formation that completely enclosed the merchant ships. These were disposed on a broad front with short flanks, a formation which reduced the U-boat's opportunities for beam attacks. To protect a convoy with a perimeter of seven miles (e.g. ten columns of four ships, columns 600 yards apart, ships in column 400 yards apart, as was the practice in 1939–40) escort commanders initially adopted the box screen of World War I, stationing an escort on each corner of the merchant

---

* Gross Register Ton, abbreviated G.R.T., is an internationally accepted measure of the carrying capacity of a cargo ship, computed on the basis of 100 cubic feet of cargo space per ton. Warship tonnage is measured in displacement tons. A freighter of 3,000 G.R.T. would have about 5,000 tons displacement.

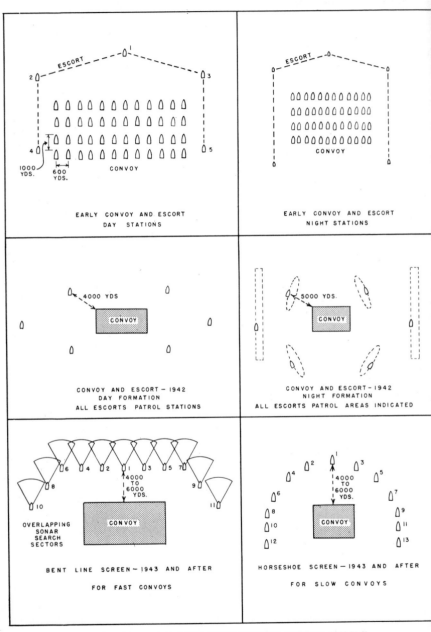

EARLY CONVOY AND ESCORT
DAY STATIONS

EARLY CONVOY AND ESCORT
NIGHT STATIONS

CONVOY AND ESCORT — 1942
DAY FORMATION
ALL ESCORTS PATROL STATIONS

CONVOY AND ESCORT — 1942
NIGHT FORMATION
ALL ESCORTS PATROL AREAS INDICATED

BENT LINE SCREEN — 1943 AND AFTER
FOR FAST CONVOYS

HORSESHOE SCREEN — 1943 AND AFTER
FOR SLOW CONVOYS

PRINCIPAL CONVOY FORMATIONS, WORLD WAR II

formation and ordering any additional units into the arc directly ahead. Early in World War II it was customary to employ cruisers or battleships in the escort, but when the threat of surface raiders diminished, the practice was abandoned as too dangerous to the large ships.

A typical early transatlantic convoy was made up of 30 to 40 merchant ships steaming in from nine to twelve columns. The customary rectangular formation with a broad front was adopted for several reasons. First, it reduced a U-boat's opportunities to attack from the advantageous beam positions; second, it was the most convenient one for inter-ship visual communication; third, it reduced the tendency of ships in the rear of a long column to surge up on the ships ahead; and fourth, it was the best compromise formation for controlling, with few escorts, the largest number of ships with the least risk of collision. Furthermore, it gave the escorts the most favorable opportunities both to deter U-boats from attacking and for attacking the threatening U-boats. Grouping of ships does, obviously, bunch targets, but a "browning shot," one fired in the general direction of a convoy, is unlikely to find a target if the ships are adequately spaced. Also the risk that a U-boat might slip through the defenses submerged by day or surfaced by night and sink a number of ships with a single salvo can likewise be reduced by appropriate inter-ship spacing.

Early British doctrine called for a prompt "hold-down" on an attacking U-boat. Such tactics, though successful in limiting convoy losses before the advent of wolf pack operations, seldom produced a kill, because there were so few escorts with each convoy, and most of these were of such relatively low speed that they were obliged to rejoin their convoy before they could gain the opportunity of delivering a *coup de grâce*. Thus a U-boat that had evaded its attackers could often resume stalking the same convoy. Dönitz' submariners favored night surfaced attacks from 45 degrees on either bow of the convoy, ensuring a short torpedo run that afforded the merchantmen little time for evasive action. Evolving British escort doctrine called for heavier bow defenses, ultimately producing in 1942 the "bent-line" screen, which provided strong protection on the bows while deploying additional warships directly ahead to intercept "down-the-throat" approaches. The problem of how to frustrate browning shots bedeviled escort commanders until 1942, when, using shipboard radar and H/F D/F (high frequency radio direction finder), they were able to extend their screens to ranges of 4,000 to 6,000 yards from the main body. At the same time the interval between columns was increased from 600 to 1,000 yards, a measure which reduced by about 50 per cent the probability of a browning shot hitting a ship, while increasing the perimeter of the convoy by less than 8 per cent.

U-boat mining operations in British waters during the first quarter of

1940 offered little indication of the intensified campaign that Admiral Dönitz was soon to unleash. Continuing their concentration in the Southwestern Approaches, German U-boats sank 85 ships aggregating 280,829 tons during January and February; only seven of their victims were in convoy, and these sinkings from convoy were achieved only at the cost of three U-boats. In the next three months, merchant ship losses declined as a result of a major redeployment of Dönitz' flotillas for the invasion of Norway, to which some 25 boats were committed.

In the ultimate success of the Norwegian invasion the U-boats played no part, being frustrated by widespread torpedo failures. Off Narvik, Günther Prien launched repeated attacks on anchored transports and cruisers, only to have all his magnetic torpedoes run deep. An exhaustive analysis of such unsuccessful attacks convinced the SKL (German naval staff) that torpedo failures had prevented U-boats from claiming one or more battleships, seven cruisers, and a number of destroyers and transports. Subsequent investigations, which resulted in a shakeup of the German Torpedo Inspectorate, revealed that the magnetic torpedo had an unreliable detonator as well as a tendency to run well below the selected depth settings. These were virtually the same by-products of inadequate testing that were soon to plague American submariners in the Pacific. Unfortunately for the Allies, the Germans rectified their deficiencies much more promptly than the Americans did.

Humiliating as the northern operations proved for BdU (*Befehlshaber der U-Boote*—Commander Submarines), the spring of 1940 laid substantial foundations for Dönitz' subsequent months of triumph in the Atlantic. The acquisition of Norway's entire coastline and the subsequent conquest of the Low Countries and France gave to Hitler the means of turning Britain's maritime flanks. While secondary U-boat havens were being established in Norway, Dönitz personally supervised the creation of heavily fortified bases on the French Atlantic coast at Brest, Lorient, St. Nazaire, La Rochelle, and Bordeaux. Possession of these French bases meant a reduction of over 50 per cent in the transit time of U-boats to their Atlantic hunting grounds. Unfortunately for Britain, the R.A.F. was so heavily engaged over the Channel that it was unable to disrupt the construction of massive concrete "pens" in these Biscay ports, with the result that they were strengthened to the point of invulnerability. Late in July *Luftwaffe* support added to the strategic effectiveness of these French bases.

Phase II: The Mid-Atlantic Offensive Based on French Ports

In July 1940 U-boats began operating from French bases. The reduction in cruising time to patrol stations had the effect of increasing the number of U-boats available in the operating areas. Thus Dönitz was able to make an attack on convoys by the tactical innovation of *Rudel-taktik,* or wolf pack operations. Still preferring to attack independent shipping, the U-boats nevertheless now had a means of forcing their way through the escorts to the body of the convoy. The toll of Allied shipping mounted ominously, exceeding 500,000 tons in June; U-boats accounted for 58 merchantmen of 284,113 tons, largely in the vulnerable Southwestern Approaches. These June sinkings were but a prelude to the French-based "Golden Age," of the *U-Waffe,* a four-month campaign in which Dönitz' wolf packs, abetted by the *Luftwaffe,* unleashed their first crippling assaults on North Atlantic convoys. Midway in July BdU concentrated his strength in the waters off Rockall Bank, 260 miles west of Scotland, and for the first time employed wolf pack tactics. When a U-boat made contact with a convoy it would not attack immediately, but would trail, decks awash, well behind the target, while it reported the convoy's course, speed, and composition to BdU headquarters in France. BdU would then assume tactical command, ordering the other boats of the pack to make contact with the shadower. On the scene, the senior commander would then take over, attempting to coordinate a night surfaced attack that would swamp the escort and then annihilate the convoy. Dönitz, soon concluding that effective control of pack attacks was impossible on the scene, began directing the operations by radio from U-boat command headquarters.

In order to assist in the new campaign, Italy dispatched some 27 submarines to the Atlantic to cooperate with the Germans against merchant shipping. With German assistance, the Italians established a submarine base at Bordeaux, from which the Italian boats operated under German strategic command. At first the Germans attempted to integrate the Italians into pack warfare, but because the Mediterranean boats were slow and unhandy, the results were less than ideal. At length the Italians were allocated the waters south of 45° N as their operating area. Because most Allied traffic operated north of this parallel, the Italians found few targets.

The British were hard pressed to meet the new threats. Casualties to destroyers and other escorts during the Norwegian campaign and the Dunkirk evacuation had been heavy. Since at that time there was a daily average of 2,000 British merchant ships at sea, the need for escorts was desperate. Additional destroyers were ordered and two new types were authorized—corvettes and frigates. The former were vessels of less than 1,000 tons, mounting one or two 4-inch guns, equipped with depth charges and asdic. Corvettes were unsuited for operations in the North Atlantic, yet they had to be used there because nothing else could be provided in time. The new frigates, appearing considerably later, were much larger and had better sea-keeping qualities than the corvettes. These two types, assisted by trawlers, luggers, and other small vessels, bore the brunt of escort work in the North Atlantic for half the war. To tide them over the difficult times ahead, Churchill as early as May 1940 requested the loan of some 50 American destroyers for convoy work.

In July 1940 the British extended the limits of close escort of convoy from 15° W to 17° W for transatlantic convoys, a move that served to nullify a part of the gain of the U-boats' time on station. On the other hand, escorts of ocean convoys were severely weakened by withdrawal of larger escort ships to be used in anti-invasion patrol during the summer of 1940. Some convoys sailed protected by a single escort. Sinkings naturally mounted as summer wore on. The following table for seven months in 1940 shows the results of pack operations and of weakening convoy escorts. The sinking figures are losses in tons from all causes.

March	April	May	June
107,009	158,218	288,461	585,496

July	August	September
386,913	397,229	448,621

In October, to try to cut down the slaughter, the Admiralty again extended the westward limits of ocean convoy escort, this time to 19° W. This advantage, however, was largely offset by a War Cabinet decision made in November at the recommendation of an economic council despite Admiralty protests. Until then only ships making at least 15 knots were permitted to sail independently; by the new decision those making 13 knots or better were released from convoy, which sailed at 11 knots or less. This change, intended to increase amounts of much-needed cargo reaching Britain, actually had the reverse effect. For, as the Admiralty had predicted, increased sinkings of the independently sailed vessels soon canceled out the advantage of swifter individual voyages. Although the economic experts insisted on counting stragglers from convoys as sailing in convoy, losses among individually sailed vessels were by their count still twice those of ships under escort. In June 1941 the lower speed limit of unescorted vessels was again raised to 15 knots. Once this change became effective, the number of sinkings of the faster ships which were once more restored to convoys dropped, as the Admiralty antisubmarine experts had predicted it would.

U-boats preferred to enjoy the easy kills of independent ships rather than employ wolf pack tactics to tangle with convoys, however inadequately they might be escorted. For a five-week period in late 1940, not a single ocean convoy was molested, yet independent losses soared. In the mid-Atlantic, not only were ships unescorted, but also the U-boats had immunity from air attack. In spite of long-range air patrols from Britain and from Canada, there remained a broad stretch of the central

North Atlantic which land-based aircraft simply could not reach. In this "Black Pit" the U-boats reaped a rich harvest among ships sailing independently. As convoy escort was extended westward, the U-boats perforce had to make pack attacks on escorted convoys. Most heavily hit was eastbound SC-7, a slow 34-ship convoy intercepted some 250 miles northwest of Bloody Foreland, north Ireland. Attacking at dusk, Lieutenant Commander Otto Kretschmer in *U-99* with six other experienced boats penetrated the four-ship screen, sinking 17 merchantmen in a midnight melee. Scarcely had this "Night of the Long Knives" ended, when weakly escorted HX-79, a fast 49-ship convoy, ran afoul of Günther Prien's *U-47* and five others which again swamped the defense and claimed an additional 14 victims. Several boats had already exhausted their torpedoes and had begun homeward passage when eastbound HX-79A entered these same waters, at the cost of seven more merchantmen.

These one-sided encounters climaxed Dönitz' first determined foray into the Northwestern Approaches, the "Happy Time" in which his U-boats sank 217 merchant vessels, totaling over 1,100,000 tons, at the cost of only six boats. Such success firmly convinced BdU of the bright prospects of wolf pack operations, yet, because of the limited number of boats available and their need for replenishment, they could not maintain this attrition rate. Less than half a dozen U-boats patrolled off Rockall during the last two months of 1940, and heavy weather frustrated efforts to locate the increasingly evasive British convoys. Allied merchant tonnage losses from U-boat attack declined to an average of some 180,000 tons during November and December. By Christmas 1940 only one U-boat lurked in the Northwestern Approaches, and when Dönitz reckoned accounts at the end of the year, he discovered that construction had barely made good the loss of 31 boats since the war's outbreak.

In the spring of 1941, the *U-Waffe* achieved increased success. Late in February, Dönitz dispatched several of his most experienced commanders to conduct an all-out blitz in the Northwestern Approaches where, on the evening of March 6, four boats located westbound Convoy OB-293, which they attacked for 24 hours. At dusk on the 7th, Prien in *U-47*, seeking to increase his bag of some 160,000 tons, attempted to penetrate the screen under the cover of a rain squall. H.M.S. *Wolverine* spotted Prien's submarine through the gloom and dispatched the killer of the *Royal Oak* with a barrage of depth charges. Eight days later the remainder of the group located HX-112. Although Schepke in the *U-100* promptly sank a 10,000-ton tanker, the U-boats achieved no further sinkings until the night of the 16th when the *U-99's* commander, Otto Kretschmer, slipped through the screen and, racing up and down the columns, torpedoed four tankers and two freighters before disappearing astern of the main body. At midnight the escort commander, Commander Donald Macintyre in H.M.S. *Walker*, detected *U-100* approaching on the surface. Crash diving, Schepke escaped, but a determined joint attack by two destroyers forced him to the surface where he was fatally rammed by H.M.S. *Vanoc*. Minutes later the *Walker* blasted *U-99* to the surface with an accurate pattern of depth charges. Most of the crew, including Kretschmer, were subsequently rescued by Macintyre. Thus the British captured the *U-Waffe's* most brilliant tactician, whose score of 266,629 tons sunk was unequalled during the war.

The loss of their three outstanding aces within little more than a week produced profound depression at BdU headquarters at Lorient. With other losses, the Germans were suddenly confronted with an attrition rate of nearly 20 per cent in the Northwestern Approaches. As foul weather continued to frustrate *Luftwaffe* reconnaissance over the North Channel, between Ireland and Scotland, Dönitz reluctantly shifted his wolf pack operations some 200 miles to the west, beyond the range of Coastal Command bombers based on Northern Ireland. This move provided the first indication of his "tonnage warfare," the strategic corollary of wolf-pack tactics. Tonnage warfare was founded on the concept of concentrating U-boat activity in areas where the most Allied merchant tonnage might be sunk at least cost to the *U-Waffe*. Thus, when defenses became strong in one area, Dönitz would shift his boats to another in order to capitalize on remaining "soft spots," even though vital Allied cargoes might meanwhile be delivered to crucial areas. As a result, during several critical periods in the war the North Atlantic was almost completely uncontested.

On April 1, 1941, the British Admiralty received operational control of Coastal Command aircraft and hence was able to integrate air activities directly with convoy movements. Beginning in April, long-range aircraft were based on Iceland, whence they were able to cut drastically the size of the Black Pit, which now came to be known as the Greenland Air Gap. With these changes came increased fuel capacity in the newer escorts, which enabled escort to be provided as far as 35° W. The increasing strength of the Royal Canadian Navy permitted the Canadians to undertake escort in the western Atlantic and to establish a link with the British. On May 27, 1941, there sailed from Halifax Convoy HX-129, the first North Atlantic convoy to be escorted all the way across the ocean.

This sailing marked the end of the second phase of the Battle of the Atlantic. Since the beginning of the war, the U-boats had sunk some 650 ships, yet only ten per cent of these had been lost from escorted convoys, and none had been sunk when air escort supplemented surface escorts. On the other hand, 60 per cent of all U-boats lost had been sunk while attacking convoys. Now, the Germans would be obliged to attack convoys, accepting an increased loss rate of U-boats if they were to maintain their rate of sinkings.

Phase III: "All Aid to Britain Short of War"

From the earliest days of the war the United States had watched the events in Europe apprehensively, and most Americans desired to remain on the sidelines. The U.S. Navy had studied the Battle of the Atlantic, but America's primary naval efforts were directed at keeping the belligerents out of the Western Hemisphere. On September 5, 1939, in an effort to avoid involvement, President Roosevelt had established a Neutrality Patrol. Early in October, the Pan-American republics had announced a neutrality zone extending some 300 miles out into the Atlantic. Both of these measures were designed to keep the war localized. Strong anti-war sentiment had resulted in the American Neutrality Act of 1937, which abandoned many of the neutral rights the United States had fought for in World War I and established the "cash-and-carry" principle that belligerents could trade with the United States only if they bought goods with cash and carried them in their own ships. The Act prohibited trade in munitions, but rising pro-Allied sentiment in November 1939 brought about a change to permit munitions to be sold on the same basis. Although by language the cash-and-carry policy was strictly neutral, actually it favored the British, for their blockade allowed no German shipping in the North Atlantic.

The end of the period of "Phony War" awakened the American Congress to the threat from abroad. Swiftly it passed legislation providing for a two-ocean navy and for the first peacetime draft in United States history. Events however were moving faster than legislation. Great Britain's desperate need for destroyers grew more evident every day. On the other hand, considerable doubt existed, in Washington as elsewhere, that Britain could survive the German onslaught. The prospect that the Royal Navy might be turned over to Germany made it necessary for the United States to conserve ships and to build new ones as rapidly as possible. Accordingly, President Roosevelt sought assurance from Churchill that the British fleet would never be surrendered to Germany. Churchill refused to make an unequivocal promise. The most he would say was that *he* would never do it; in the event of a British defeat, his government might be turned out of office and another group might use the fleet as bargaining chips at the surrender table.

Although this assurance was somewhat less than satisfactory, Roosevelt decided to take a calculated risk and transfer 50 American destroyers to the British flag. There was of course a danger that Germany would declare war on the United States, but Hitler had no desire to involve himself with America until the situation in Europe was settled.

Lord Lothian, British Ambassador to the United States, concluded arrangements in late July 1940 for a deal whereby the United States would give 50 "obsolete" destroyers to Great Britain in return for 99-year leases on a series of bases running from Newfoundland to Trinidad. Final agreement was signed in September. By mid-April of the following year, the 50 destroyers had been delivered, as well as ten *Lake*-class Coast Guard cutters well equipped for antisubmarine duty.

The American destroyers alone were not enough to solve Britain's problems of supply. In response to the destroyers-bases deal, Hitler on September 6, 1940 removed the last restrictions on U-boat warfare against British ships and accepted the possibility that some American ships might accidentally be sunk. He even toyed with the idea of seizing some of the Atlantic islands, but Raeder warned him that the German navy was in no position to mount such operations.

In an effort to give further assistance to Great Britain in her struggle against Nazi Germany, President Roosevelt in December 1940 proposed the idea of Lend-Lease. British ships would still have to pick up the goods; only the "cash" part of the "cash-and-carry" policy was to be changed. This proposal, unlike the destroyers-bases deal, required Congressional approval, which took place in March 1941 after extended hearings. Once again Hitler did not declare war.

The change from the Neutrality Act to Lend-Lease was another step in the President's "all aid short of war" policy. In order to see how America's efforts could best be directed to the common cause, Roosevelt sent military representatives to England in August 1940 for "exploratory talks." These discussions led to plans for cooperation in the Atlantic war in the event of American participation. This conference was followed by another in Washington in late January 1941, which resulted in the "ABC-1 Staff Agreement," which spelled out, first, America's "short of war" contribution and, second, the action to be taken by the United States in the event she was forced into the war. Fundamental to this doctrine was the basic concept that in event of war with Japan, Britain and the United States would devote their primary effort to defeating Germany first. Germany was considered the more dangerous because of her industrial development, the achievements of her scientists, her proximity to Britain and Russia, and her military achievements thus far. This strategic decision was never changed during the war, even though it later became possible to take the offensive in both oceans at the same time. The United States agreed that in the near future the U.S. Navy would assist in escorting convoys in the North Atlantic.

To prepare for these new responsibilities, the Navy Department reorganized the Neutrality Patrol and gave it the more appropriate title of United States Atlantic Fleet. On February 1, 1941 Admiral Ernest J. King hoisted his flag as its commander. By mid-June plans for American escort of transatlantic convoys were made whereby the U.S. Navy was to concentrate on the segment from Argentia, Newfoundland to Iceland, where British escorts would take over. The acquisition of terminal bases for these operations posed a difficult problem, one whose solution was suggested early in March when Hitler publicly extended his U-boats' war zone right up to Greenland's three-mile limit. Under strong British persuasion, the government of Iceland on July 7 permitted an American naval force to land the First Marine Brigade at Reykjavik as an advance element in the relief of Britain's garrison already there. Within two months, United States naval patrol squadrons were flying convoy coverage from Reykjavik, while surface escorts refueled at nearby Hvalfjordur.

While the Atlantic Fleet's short-of-war operations provided badly needed protection for Allied and neutral shipping that joined American-escorted convoys, these operations were, for political reasons, initially declared to be independent of the North Atlantic convoy pattern that Britain had developed between Nova Scotia and the British Isles. By July the Anglo-Canadian system had achieved at least minimum anti-submarine surface escort for both slow (6½-knot) and fast (9-knot) convoys all the way across the North Atlantic. Canadian escorts normally shepherded these "Halifax" convoys as far east as a Mid-Ocean Meeting Point (MOMP) at the 35th meridian, where British warships based in Iceland took charge, proceeding with little air cover to the EASTOMP, about the 18th meridian, before turning the convoy over to Western Approaches forces for the final run to the North Channel. A heavy attack on Convoy HX-126, which lost nine ships off Cape Farewell, Greenland, during May, underscored the pressing need for continuous air escort for North Atlantic convoys, but two grim years lay ahead before such coverage could be extended to the Greenland Air Gap.

Three events in the Spring of 1941 evoked further American action despite dangers of involvement in the war. First was the sinking by a German surface raider of the Egyptian ship Zamzam carrying 135 American passengers. The second was the sinking in late May of the South Africa-bound American freighter Robin Moor by a U-boat which left without making any provisions for the safety of the crew. The third was the appearance of the Bismarck, which shocked American as well as British public opinion by her sinking of the Hood. On May 27, the very day the Bismarck was sunk, President Roosevelt declared an Unlimited National Emergency and announced to the country that more vigorous steps would be taken to keep the Germans from American waters.

The United States Navy found itself as ill-prepared for antisubmarine

war as the British had been in 1939. The obvious need was for an escort
vessel smaller than a destroyer and especially designed for convoy work,
a vessel which could be built more rapidly than a destroyer and at
lower cost. While in many ways a destroyer is an ideal escort ship, her
high speed and versatile offensive power are largely wasted in escort-
of-convoy work. The answer was found in the destroyer escort, a smaller
version of the destroyer, slower, and especially designed for antisubmarine operations. The British and Canadian navies began building
steam versions of these vesels at the rate of about eight a month, and
in July 1941 American shipyards started construction of them for the
British at the rate of ten a month. American models included both steam
and diesel-electric types.

The German invasion of Russia in June 1941 added considerably to
the problems of supply, for the Russians were also afforded Lend-Lease
aid and had few ships in which to transport the goods. To discuss this
problem and others, Churchill and Roosevelt met at Argentia, Newfoundland in August. This meeting enabled the Chiefs of Staff of the
two countries to discuss plans for American escort of convoys, and it
produced the Atlantic Charter, a statement of the war aims of England
and the United States.

For a considerable period American warships on Atlantic patrol had
broadcast to the British the location of U-boats detected, although the
Americans had refrained from attacking. After Admiral King had described such U-boats as "potentially hostile," there was some doubt as
to what action an American naval vessel should take if it should encounter a U-boat in the American zone of responsibility. That question
was answered by the affair of the *Greer*. This U.S. destroyer was about
200 miles southwest of Iceland when on September 4, 1941 she received
a signal from a British plane that a U-boat was about ten miles ahead
of her. The *Greer* made sound contact with *U-652*, keeping the contact
for over three hours, but not attacking. At length, the U-boat fired a
torpedo at the *Greer*, which evaded, and then counterattacked with
depth charges. Thus the first shots were exchanged in the undeclared
war between German and American naval forces. President Roosevelt
issued a statement declaring, "From now on, if German or Italian vessels
of war enter the waters, the protection of which is necessary for American defense, they do so at their own risk."

By this time Dönitz had an increased and rapidly growing number
of U-boats and was responding to Allied end-to-end convoys by strong
wolf pack attacks. The *U-Waffe* however had been frustrated by fog
and inadequate air reconnaissance, claiming only 377,339 tons of shipping during the third quarter of 1941. In mid-October BdU succeeded in
staging a major attack against North Atlantic convoys. On that occasion,
American escorts dispatched to the relief of Convoy SC-48 learned a

number of hard lessons, including the futility of indiscriminate depth charging and the need for aggressive night patrolling. Assaulted some 400 miles south of Iceland, this 50-ship convoy had already lost three vessels when five U.S. destroyers and two British escorts reached the scene. Their close screening tactics failed to prevent the U-boats from sinking six more ships with relative impunity, and shortly thereafter they torpedoed but failed to sink the American destroyer *Kearny* as she was silhouetted by one of the burning freighters. The Atlantic Fleet had scarcely digested the lessons of this encounter when it sustained its first loss, U.S.S. *Reuben James*, on October 31 as she and four other American destroyers were escorting HX-156 some 600 miles west of Ireland.

Notwithstanding these early disasters, British naval officials keenly appreciated the growing United States commitment in the North Atlantic, and by mid-October 1941, following American agreement to extend convoy coverage east to within 400 miles of Ireland, the Commander in Chief, Western Approaches (Cincwa) found it possible to shift three escort groups from the Northwestern Approaches to supplement the escorts of hard-pressed convoys bound for Gibraltar and West African ports. This strategic redeployment proved highly opportune for the Admiralty, now confronted with reports of U-boat activity in several new maritime theaters. Heavy weather weakened Dönitz' North Atlantic campaign during the last quarter of 1941, a period in which U-boats sank only 342,820 tons of Allied shipping, yet these same months saw increasing concentrations of U-boats all the way from North Cape to the African Gold Coast. Long-range 1,100-ton (Type IX-B) U-boats had launched operations off Freetown, West Africa in May 1941, highlighted by the record success of *U-107*, which sank some 87,000 tons of shipping in a single patrol and obliged the Admiralty to divert convoys well west of the Canaries. German plans for a mid-winter blitz off Capetown were temporarily frustrated by British success in sinking two German supply ships, but it was evident that South African antisubmarine defenses would soon be strained to the utmost.

In spite of Allied air bases in Iceland, there still remained the Greenland Air Gap, where U-boats ranged freely in the continued absence of aircraft and where convoys still sailed with inadequate numbers of surface escorts. To assign fleet carriers to the convoys for air protection was out of the question, for the fleet had too few for its other needs. Yet something had to be done not only to afford protection in the Greenland Air Gap but also to protect ships from *Luftwaffe* attacks, which had accounted for 44 ships of 94,551 tons in the months of June, July, and August. Because early experiments with catapult-equipped merchant ships flying off expendable aircraft had been obviously makeshift, the Admiralty had been experimenting with inexpensive, easily constructed carriers especially designed for operating with convoys. At first the British converted merchant ships or naval auxiliaries; later they designed escort carriers from the keel up. The first to see action, H.M.S. *Audacity,* a converted German prize, proved herself in her short career. The *Audacity* accompanied Convoy HG-76 of 32 ships, whose escort of 12 corvettes, sloops, and destroyers, was under command of Captain Frederick John Walker, one of the Royal Navy's ablest antisubmarine tacticians.

The initial U-boat onslaught on December 17 was disrupted by several of the *Audacity's* planes, which sighted *U-131* some 20 miles ahead, homed in five escorts, and assisted them in sinking the contact keeper. Another stalker, *U-434,* was sunk by destroyers on the 18th, and although *U-574* managed to blow up H.M. destroyer *Stanley* during a midnight melee that also claimed a merchantman, H.M. sloop *Stork* finished off the U-boat by ramming. On December 21, after the *Audacity's* airmen had destroyed four German Kondor aircraft, several U-boats finally succeeded in penetrating the screen at night, sinking one ship. The *Audacity,* steaming alone, ten miles from the convoy screen, fell a victim to *U-751* some 500 miles west of Cape Finisterre. Counterattacking with disciplined coordination, Walker's escorts flushed *U-567,* sending her veteran crew to the bottom. Concurrently the convoy came within range of United Kingdom-based air escorts. The combined effect broke the back of the pack's running assault and induced BdU to break off this costly attack. Upon reviewing this nine-day operation, Dönitz recognized that the aggressive British escort tactics and particularly the use of the escort carrier, which had cost him five boats, raised serious doubts about the future of wolf pack operations in the eastern Atlantic. Renewed opportunity for successful tonnage warfare now beckoned from the west however, and by the close of 1941 the BdU was eagerly planning his first campaign in North American waters.

Phase IV: The U-Boat Offensive in American Waters

After the Japanese attack on Pearl Harbor on December 7, 1941 had brought the United States officially into the war against the Axis powers, Churchill and his Chiefs of Staff visited Washington to work out with Roosevelt and the American Chiefs of Staff the strategic direction of the war. Churchill recognized that American aid to Britain would necessarily be cut back for the time being as the United States began to grapple with her new responsibilities in the war. He recognized however the potential power of the New World and was confident of victory.

Top military direction of the war was organized at the Washington meeting. The British representatives—Admiral Sir Dudley Pound, the First Sea Lord; Air Chief Marshal Sir Charles Portal, the Chief of the Air Staff; and Field Marshal Sir John Dill, the former Chief of the Imperial General Staff—sat down with General George C. Marshall, U.S. Army Chief of Staff; Lieutenant General Henry H. Arnold, Chief of the U.S. Army Air Corps; Admiral Harold R. Stark, Chief of Naval Operations; and Admiral Ernest J. King, Commander in Chief, United States Fleet. These men constituted the first Combined Chiefs of Staff. On their shoulders rested the burden of responsibility for conducting the global war.

The United States Navy was extensively reorganized in the early months of the war. King had become Commander in Chief of the United States Fleet (Cominch), being relieved as Commander in Chief of the Atlantic Fleet (Cinclant) by Admiral Royal E. Ingersoll. Admiral Chester W. Nimitz relieved Admiral Husband E. Kimmel as Commander in Chief of the Pacific Fleet (Cincpac). In March 1942, because of confusion as to the division of function of the office of Chief of Naval Operations (CNO) and that of the Commander in Chief, U.S. Fleet, the two offices were vested in Admiral King, and Admiral Stark went to London as Commander U.S. Naval Forces in Europe (Comnaveu).

Direction of the American effort in the war fell to the Joint Chiefs of Staff—the three top American officers, Marshall, Arnold, and King. In July 1942 Admiral William D. Leahy was appointed Chief of Staff to the President and ex officio Chairman of the Joint Chiefs of Staff. To King in particular fell the earliest burden, since it was at sea that the United States could first challenge the Axis, and first was challenged.

Because the Naval District organizations were primarily administrative commands, King found it advisable to set up operational commands known as Sea Frontiers which would conduct operations in the waters they included. These commands were the Eastern Sea Frontier in the Atlantic, the Caribbean Sea Frontier, the Gulf Sea Frontier, the Panama Sea Frontier at the approaches to the Canal, and the Western, Northwestern, and Hawaiian Sea Frontiers in the Pacific.

Japan's attack on Pearl Harbor had proved a complete surprise to Germany. Hence, although Germany and Italy declared war on the United States on December 11, over a month elapsed before the U-boats could launch an attack on vulnerable American shipping. To the chagrin of Dönitz, eager for a spectacular blow, the SKL insisted on retaining a large proportion of some 64 Atlantic boats in the Mediterranean and in the heavily patrolled approaches to Gibraltar. As a result, BdU was initially able to allocate only five 1,100-ton U-boats for the impending attack on shipping between Cape Hatteras and the Gulf of the St. Lawrence. This opening thrust, designated Operation PAUKENSCHLAG, was designed to paralyze offshore traffic, thus reducing the flow of oil and other raw materials to the American East Coast industrial areas. By a gradual extension into the Gulf of Mexico and the Caribbean, BdU hoped to stretch Allied escort strength to the breaking point. Broadly speaking,

Dönitz calculated that seaborne trade in the Western Atlantic, weakly protected by inexperienced forces, might yet provide a key to tonnage victory. According to BdU estimates at this time, a sustained monthly merchant ship attrition of 700,000 tons was necessary to achieve this objective. Even if Britain could not be completely strangled, she might yet be driven to accept a negotiated peace.

The U-boat assault in North American waters temporarily stunned both United States and Canadian defense forces. Hard-hitting Group *Paukenschlag* of five boats had been closely followed across the Atlantic by six 740-ton boats which unleashed a concurrent attack in the waters off Newfoundland. Group *Paukenschlag* swiftly ambushed a score of independents between Hatteras and Cape Breton Island. From the outset, these U-boats found particularly happy hunting off the Carolina Capes, discovering many merchantmen unarmed and some still burning their running lights. In the absence of convoys *Rudeltaktik* was unnecessary. Operating individually, the Germans lay submerged offshore until dusk, then moved in with decks awash and dispatched their victims with gunfire or torpedoes. Worldwide merchant tonnage losses were greatly inflated by this mounting slaughter. From December's toll of 124,070 tons lost to U-boats, the totals climbed in January to 327,357 tons, 467,451 tons in February, and 537,980 tons in March. During March, 28 vessels aggregating 159,340 tons were sunk in the Eastern Sea Frontier alone, over half of these ships being tankers.

Against this onslaught, American shipping defense measures proved inadequate, notwithstanding the remarkable fact that Dönitz never had more than a dozen boats in the Western Atlantic. Because of demands from the Pacific and a continuing commitment of other available destroyers to North Atlantic convoys, Commander Eastern Sea Frontier, Vice Admiral Adolphus Andrews, possessed negligible surface forces and only nine patrol aircraft at the close of 1941. Although 170 army and navy aircraft were committed to offshore patrol by late March 1942, Andrews regarded his hundred-odd destroyers, Coast Guard cutters, converted yachts, and armed trawlers as insufficient for coastal convoys. Convinced that a "convoy without adequate protection is worse than none," a dictum contrary to British wartime experience, the Eastern Sea Frontier resorted to a series of emergency measures, including hunter groups, "offensive" patrols, and U-boat decoy vessels ("Q-ships") with concealed guns. The slight value of these measures can be seen not only in the destruction of 23 ships in the Eastern Sea Frontier during April, but also in the fact that not a single U-boat had been sunk in this area during the first three months of the East Coast blitz. It is small wonder that the U-boat crews referred to this period as the "Second Happy Time."

Drastic measures were required to avert a shipping catastrophe, for in March total Allied merchant ship losses had soared to over 800,000 tons for the first time in World War II. In February the British had given the United States 24 trawlers and ten corvettes, all provided with the latest asdic equipment. The first step toward providing coastal convoys was taken by the establishment of "Bucket Brigades," small convoys that ran escorted during daylight hours and put into protected anchorages at night. In mid-April the Admiralty decreased the frequency of its convoy sailings from Halifax from five to seven days, enlarging the convoys and releasing two desperately needed escort groups for service in American waters. Increasing the size of convoys cut the ratio of escorts to the ships protected, for the number of ships which can be protected depends on the *area* of the circle enclosing them, while the number of escorts depends on the *circumference* of a larger concentric circle.

It took another month to establish a convoy system on the East Coast of the United States. "Escort is not just one way of handling the submarine menace," wrote Admiral King, "it is the only way that gives any promise of success. The so-called hunting and patrol operations have time and again proved futile." That King was right can be seen from the results. U-boats had sunk 87 ships of 514,366 tons during their first four months off the East Coast, yet Dönitz promptly began shifting his boats southward on the appearance of convoys, making no effort to contest them by wolf pack tactics. The Germans found profitable hunting in the Gulf of Mexico and Caribbean where no convoy system existed, and sank 41 vessels of 219,867 tons during May, nearly half being tankers torpedoed off the Passes of the Mississippi. This onslaught was checked by the establishment of an Interlocking Convoy System which enabled ships to transfer at sea from one convoy to another. This system required extremely careful planning of convoy movements and rendezvous, but it offered the necessary flexibility for the complicated pattern of Caribbean and Gulf shipping.

Moving once again in search of unprotected ships, U-boats fell upon independent traffic off Trinidad, Rio de Janeiro, and Capetown, exploiting the logistic versatility of a handful of new 1,700-ton supply U-boats or "milch cows." Thus supported, U-boat commanders managed to double the length of their patrols off the Panama Canal and along the Guianas coast, with devastating results. In the Western Atlantic, U-boats claimed 26 merchant ships in May and averaged over 20 victims in the four ensuing months, notwithstanding the extension of convoys to Port of Spain in July. Round-the-clock air cover, as distinct from air escort, failed to deter these U-boats because they evaded radar detection by conforming to convoy course and speed during their furtive assaults. Allied escort forces succeeded in destroying three U-boats in these waters in the fall

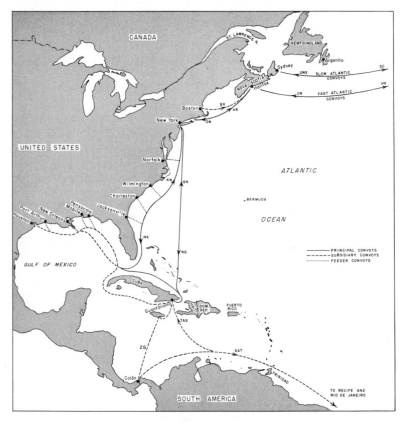

THE WESTERN ATLANTIC, SHOWING THE INTERLOCKING CONVOY
SYSTEM AS DEVELOPED IN 1942

of 1942, yet the Germans continued to exploit the Trinidad approaches
with profit to the end of the year since many independent ships continued
to use these waters.

Caribbean operations accounted for but a fraction of the 1,505,888
tons of Allied shipping lost to U-boats in the third quarter of 1942. In
mid-August ten U-boats moved into Brazilian waters for a blitz against
coastal and transatlantic shipping. Five Brazilian freighters were torpedoed by *U-507* off Bahia, provoking Brazil to declare war on Germany
and emphasizing the urgency of extending the coastal convoy system
southeast of Trinidad. Escort shortages delayed creation of this final link,
but Vice Admiral Jonas H. Ingram, commanding the U.S. South Atlantic

Fleet, scraped together sufficient forces to frustrate German hopes of reaping yet another windfall of shipping. Although dissatisfied with the meager results of this attack, Dönitz dispatched a second wave of U-boats to the Cape San Roque area during November and December. His U-boats claimed over 20 ships before the establishment of regular convoy between Trinidad and Bahia, and the destruction of *U-164* and *U-507* by Catalinas broke the back of this distant offensive.

Phase V: Return to the Mid-Atlantic

Following the adoption of convoys with air as well as surface escort in American waters, Dönitz decided to shift the burden of his attack back to the mid-Atlantic, where the U-boats would be free to attack convoys without air escort. Yet immediately he was called upon to divert a significant portion of his strength to attacking Allied convoys on the "Murmansk Run" to North Russia.

British convoys to North Russia, begun in August 1941, had suffered negligible losses to U-boat and air attack during the first three months of 1942, but with a northward shift of German surface strength, the situation changed rapidly. The new battleship *Tirpitz*, sister of the *Bismarck*, now in service, moved to Norwegian bases, as did the *Scheer, Lützow,* and *Hipper*. The next few convoys met increasingly severe air and U-boat attack. At this time, because of the Madagascar operation, American units reinforced the Home Fleet at Scapa Flow and were available for operations to protect the convoys bound for North Russia.

These convoys both Roosevelt and Churchill held to be political necessities for keeping Russia in the war. Yet increasingly severe attacks on ships making this passage led professional opinion to consider these convoys little better than suicide. Convoy PQ-16 in May lost seven out of 34 merchant ships, and casualties to the accompanying warships were heavy. The SKL planned an all-out attempt, Operation RÖSSELSPRUNG, to annihilate the next convoy to Russia, employing the *Luftwaffe,* U-boats, and heavy and light surface forces.

Fully aware of the grave risks, the Admiralty provided PQ-17 with 21 escorts and a covering force of three destroyers and four cruisers, while dispatching a distant support force of two battleships, H.M.S. *Duke of York* and U.S.S. *Washington,* three cruisers, 13 destroyers, and H.M. aircraft carrier *Victorious*. The convoy left Hvalfjordur, Iceland on June 27, 1942 with 33 merchant ships, three rescue vessels, and a fleet oiler. Routed well north of Bear Island, where the midnight sun provided continuous daylight for air attack, the convoy was subjected to three days of intensive onslaught reaching a climax on July 4. Throughout, the convoy maintained taut discipline, thereby minimizing casualties and destroying several German planes. After thwarting these attacks with the loss of only four ships, one a cripple that eventually reached port, the convoy's confidence was high. Then came a stunning series of messages from the Admiralty:

> 9:11 P.M. Most Immediate. Cruiser Force withdraw to westward at high speed.
> 9:23 P.M. Immediate. Owing to threat of surface ships, convoy is to disperse and proceed to Russian ports.
> 9:36 P.M. Most Immediate. Convoy is to scatter.

Behind this extraordinary series of messages lay the Admiralty's conviction that the *Tirpitz* would be able to engage the convoy and the cruiser force. Reconnaissance planes had lost contact with her, but the British knew that she might be in position to intercept any time after 0200 July 5. The support force of battleships and the *Victorious* was too far west to interfere, for it was protecting westbound QP-13, which was beyond Jan Mayen and thus out of serious danger. The First Sea Lord had based his decision on negative intelligence and interfered with operations 1,500 miles away where he could not know the situation. In view of the urgent tone of the Admiralty messages, Rear Admiral L. H. K. Hamilton, commanding the cruiser force, expected to see the *Tirpitz* at any moment and felt he had no alternative but to comply. The destroyers with the escort also detached themselves to support the cruisers in their anticipated desperate battle with the *Tirpitz*.

Ironically, though the *Tirpitz, Scheer,* and *Hipper* did begin to carry out Operation RÖSSELSPRUNG, as a result of confused aerial reconnaissance and of Hitler's no-risk policy, they returned to port after ten hours at sea. The British Admiralty had no way of knowing that the Germans would not attack, but they did know from past experience that German surface ships were reluctant to engage strongly escorted convoys and consistently refused action with escorts of even cruiser strength.

As a result of the order to scatter, PQ-17 lost 21 more ships. Of the 13 that reached port, 11 had joined rump convoys. Two ships were lost from the rump convoys, but 19 independents were sunk. Thus, the subsequent fate of PQ-17 indicates that even under the most difficult circumstances, convoy integrity provides the greatest chance of survival of merchant ships.

Significant consequences flowed from this operation, most notably the British decision to suspend convoy sailings to North Russia until the fall of 1942. American disappointment over the futile employment of the *Washington* and her consorts led to Admiral King's rapid transfer of these ships to the Pacific. Henceforth King viewed combined U.S.-British naval operations with disfavor. German forces in Norway had meanwhile been thoroughly roused by the success of RÖSSELSPRUNG, making a resumption of Allied convoys to North Russia additionally perilous.

When powerfully protected PQ-18 of 40 merchant ships sailed in

September, it included in its escort the British escort carrier *Avenger*, whose planes, together with the convoy's antiaircraft guns, destroyed some 40 German planes. The surface escort sank three U-boats. Although the convoy lost 13 ships, only three were sunk by U-boats. Instead of scattering, the convoy remained together, vindicating once against the wisdom of convoy integrity. For the next few months, because of the impending landings in North Africa, the British were unable to send convoys to Russia. By means of Operation TRICKLE, the dispatch of small "flights" of unescorted merchant ships in company, they managed to "pray through" only five of the 13 ships they sent, losing over 60 per cent.

In the south too U-boats became active. In mid-October, Group *Eisbaer* passed through the Atlantic narrows, and after waylaying isolated shipping, including the ill-fated British transport *Laconia*,* prepared to unleash an offensive off Capetown. One of these raiders, the *U-179*, was promptly sunk, but the remaining boats proceeded to devastate shipping east of the Cape, claiming in October and November 31 ships off Capetown and in Mozambique Channel before beginning the long return passage.

Dönitz recognized that a decisive victory could be obtained only in the mid-Atlantic. U-boat production had by July 1942 reached the rate of 30 boats a month, and this increase in strength enabled him to accept increased risks in making attacks on convoys. The risks were constantly mounting, for most Allied air and surface escorts were now equipped with radar. In addition, the availability of larger numbers of escorts permitted the Allies to form Antisubmarine Support Groups of six to eight destroyers, frigates, and corvettes. Later, escort carriers operated with the surface ships. These Support Groups, manned by highly experienced personnel, had no regular escort duties, but were available to come to the aid of convoys undergoing heavy U-boat attack.

Keenly conscious of the added danger of air escorts, Dönitz concentrated his attack in the Black Pit area. He stationed picket lines on both sides so that convoys moving in either direction could be attacked throughout its entire width while the U-boats enjoyed virtual immunity from air attack. The loss figures mounted, reaching a peak of 807,754

---

* The *Laconia* was sunk on September 12 northeast of Ascension Island by *U-156*, which discovered that the transport carried 1,800 Italian prisoners of war as well as 811 British servicemen. On orders from BdU, other *Eisbaer* boats moved to the rescue, while *U-156* broadcast a plain language appeal for assistance. The U-boats had several hundred survivors under tow on the afternoon of the 16th when an American B-24, flying from Ascension, circled and finally attacked *U-156*, even though she displayed a Red Cross flag on her bow. On receiving a report on these proceedings Dönitz forbade all attempts to rescue merchant ship survivors. During the Nuremberg Trial, Allied prosecutors attempted to prove that this "*Laconia* order" had actually constituted a veiled attempt to encourage deliberate slaughter of survivors. A full examination of relevant facts, including known cases of atrocities, destroyed this contention.

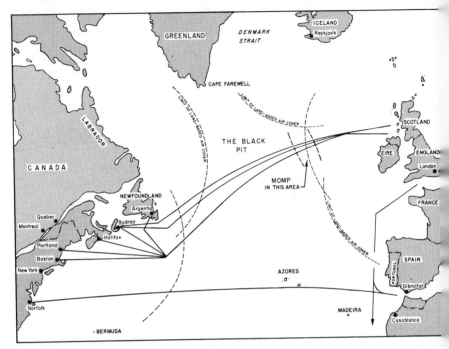

TYPICAL NORTH ATLANTIC CONVOY SYSTEM, 1942

Allied convoys were designated by a combination of letters and numbers indicating the port of origin, destination, and the particular convoy number. Principal ocean convoy routes and their destinations were: Halifax-United Kingdom, HX; United Kingdom-Halifax, ON; Sydney, Nova Scotia-United Kingdom, SC; United Kingdom-Sydney, ONS; Boston-Halifax, BX; United Kingdom-Gibraltar, OG; Gibraltar-United Kingdom, HG; United Kingdom-North Russia, PQ (later JW); United States-Gibraltar, UGS; Gibraltar-United States, GUS.

G.R.T. in November 1942, at which time Dönitz was forced to weaken the attack in a belated effort to disrupt the North African landings. Nonetheless, U-boats continued their efforts in the Black Pit area, rising to a crescendo in March 1943.

By Christmas 1942 the Allies recognized that they must devise some methods of countering the flexibility of strategic deployment enjoyed by the highly centralized U-boat command. Hence when the Allied heads of state met with the Combined Chiefs of Staff at Casablanca in January 1943, they agreed that "the defeat of the U-boat must remain a first charge on the resources of the United Nations" and ordered a staff conference to reorganize Atlantic convoy control. The consequent Washington Convoy Conference rejected politically explosive proposals for a unified Allied antisubmarine command and on March 1 adopted Admiral King's formula whereby the British and Canadians retained control of North Atlantic convoys, while the United States assumed responsibility for Central Atlantic convoys (to the Mediterranean and to the south from ports south of Halifax) as well as for the Interlocking Convoy System.

In Britain, Admiralty Operations Research scientists in analytical studies of the convoy battles of 1941–42 discovered that the number of ships sunk from convoys was completely independent of convoy size. Instead sinkings depended only on numbers of attacking U-boats and, when no air escort was present, on the number of surface escorts. Thus if the average size of convoys could be increased from 32 to 54 ships, the number of escorts would increase from six to nine, while convoy losses would be reduced 56 per cent by the enlargement of the convoy and 25 per cent by the increase in number of escorts. If air escort was present only during an average of eight hours a day, losses could be reduced 64 per cent from those obtaining during the period of 1941–42. Increasing the size of convoys would reduce their frequency, enabling the strengthened surface and air escorts to be provided without any increase in the escort forces. Also the same number of merchant ships then being employed could actually provide an increase in deliveries.

Although Allied shipping losses declined to 344,680 tons in April 1943, BdU clearly regarded this as a temporary slump, inevitably following the intensive operations of March. To offset the decreasing effectiveness of individual boats resulting from the marked improvement of Allied countermeasures, Dönitz prepared to build a new concentration of unprecedented magnitude in the North Atlantic. The showdown in the North Atlantic came on April 28, when westbound Convoy ONS-5 was intercepted by a U-boat picket line off Iceland, losing one merchantman and escaping a general attack only by heading into a fog bank. Although badly scattered by a gale off Cape Farewell, this 42-ship convoy was brilliantly rounded up by its escort commander, Commander Peter W. Gretton RN, and headed south into what proved to be a concentration of 51 U-boats. Newfoundland-based Catalina aircraft claimed the U-630 on May 4, but by nightfall U-boat Group Fink was moving in from all quarters, catching the freighters sharply etched against the northern lights. Eleven U-boats nearly swamped ONS-5's escort and sent seven ships to the bottom before dawn, adding four more victims the next morning from among the stragglers. The corvette Pink succeeded in depth charging U-192 fatally, but by dusk, as some 15 U-boats moved in, the battered convoy faced annihilation. Then the tactical situation changed completely. Nosing into another fog bank late on the evening of May 5, ONS-5 sustained no fewer than 25 separate attacks without losing a single ship. Dönitz' boats, lacking radar, were repeatedly driven off by the seven escorts. The aggressive attacks of two freshly-arrived Antisubmarine Support Groups, taking maximum advantage of radar and H/F D/F, completed the Germans' frustration and helped send four more boats to the bottom between midnight and dawn.

This action proved to be the climax of the Battle of the Atlantic. The *U-Waffe* never recovered from this unexpected reverse off Newfoundland. German wolf packs had decimated their last Halifax convoy. The intervention of Antisubmarine Support Groups, escort carriers, and long-range aircraft had provided the key to Allied success. In the three weeks following the ordeal of ONS-5, twelve convoys crossed the Black Pit, losing a total of only five ships, while air and surface escorts sank 13 U-boats. Against Dönitz' large and relatively blind wolf packs, the British tactics of bait and kill now came to fruition, forcing the U-boats to abandon the North Atlantic in May and search for less dangerous hunting grounds. Confronted by the enormous loss of 41 submarines in "Black May," Dönitz resorted once again to tonnage warfare strategy, ordering his boats south in hopes of saving the *U-Waffe* from annihilation until technological developments permitted a return to the North Atlantic. This decision permitted relatively unimpeded passage of Allied convoys in the twelve months before the invasion of Normandy. Thus, under combined pressure of vastly improved Allied antisubmarine measures and a great increase in American shipbuilding, the strategy of tonnage warfare collapsed. In July monthly Allied ship production at last exceeded worldwide shipping losses from Axis action, and by the end of the year the Atlantic Allies achieved an annual production rate of 14.4 million tons of merchant shipping, exceeding German estimates by 40 per cent.

The devastating antisubmarine offensive undertaken by Anglo-American forces late in the spring of 1943 was the product not simply of mounting warship and aircraft production but also of extensive reorganization, systematic indoctrination of personnel, and decisive advances in the science of undersea warfare. The creation of the U.S. Tenth Fleet, invested with broad supervisory control of American antisubmarine development, proved of fundamental importance in stimulating effective training, supplying scientific methods to the perfection of weapons and tactics, and coordinating operational intelligence. Established on May 1, under the personal command of Admiral King, with Rear Admiral Francis S. Low as chief of staff, this secret administrative organization provided comprehensive support for operations of the Atlantic Fleet, whose newly-activated Hunter-Killer Groups of escort carriers and destroyers or destroyer escorts were soon to distinguish themselves in the Central Atlantic.

Phase VI: The Central Atlantic and Biscay Offensives

Dönitz' decision late in May 1943 to shift pack operations southwest of the Azores presented Commander U.S. Atlantic Fleet, Admiral Ingersoll, with a long-awaited opportunity to employ his new Hunter-Killer Groups. For rapidity of tactical innovation, operations during the next three months by groups centered on the escort carriers *Bogue, Card, Core,* and *Santee* in support of Central Atlantic convoys are virtually unsurpassed in naval history. Airmen from the *Bogue,* pioneering Wildcat-Avenger team tactics, located Group *Trutz* on June 3 while escorting Convoy GUS-7A, sinking *U-217* and the milch cow *U-118* and damaging several other boats. Subsequent efforts by this 17-boat pack to locate Central Atlantic convoys were frustrated south of the Azores in mid-July by the widely-roving *Core* and *Santee* groups, which destroyed four more boats, including two supply submarines, while introducing "Fido," the U.S. Navy's new antisubmarine homing torpedo.

Driven to desperation by these aerial tactics, remaining German submariners fought back on the surface, enabling the *Bogue, Santee,* and *Core* groups in mid-summer to claim five more victims. Meanwhile the *Card*'s air group, commanded by Captain Arnold J. Isbell, had sent four more submarines, including two milch cows, to the bottom. In less than three months, Ingersoll's Hunter-Killer Groups had sunk 15 U-boats, eight operating as supply boats, with the loss of only three aircraft. This attrition of U-tankers, sharply contrasting with the sinking of one convoyed merchantman, effectively disrupted German efforts to concentrate on Central Atlantic convoys and greatly reduced the impact of U-boat operations in the Caribbean and in the South Atlantic and Indian Oceans.

Severe as were the *U-Waffe*'s losses in mid-Atlantic, they were of less concern to BdU than the concurrent slaughter of U-boats in the Bay of Biscay, where since the spring of 1942 the R.A.F. Coastal Command had been attempting a sustained offensive. Employing radar, the British aircraft had enjoyed a limited success in detecting U-boats in this transit area. This advantage disappeared when Dönitz began fitting his U-boats with a radar receiver called *Metox,* which could pick up the radar search signal at a far greater range than the reflected signal could be detected by the search receiver. Early in 1943 however planes suddenly resumed attacking surfaced U-boats while *Metox* was giving no indications. BdU interpreted this phenomenon to mean that *Metox* was emitting a signal detectable on passive radar and accordingly ordered commanders to discontinue its use. Actually the British had developed a new ultra-high-frequency radar of ten centimeter wavelength, which *Metox* could not detect. The attacks continued, aided by the aircraft Leigh Light, an 80-million candlepower attack searchlight, employed in conjunction with radar in sudden blinding night attacks from the air. Throughout March and April many of these attacks were limited in success because of the U-boats' regular practice of crash diving when attacked. While German scientists worked desperately and fruitlessly to improve *Metox,* Dönitz added antiaircraft armament to his U-boats and, reversing his previous

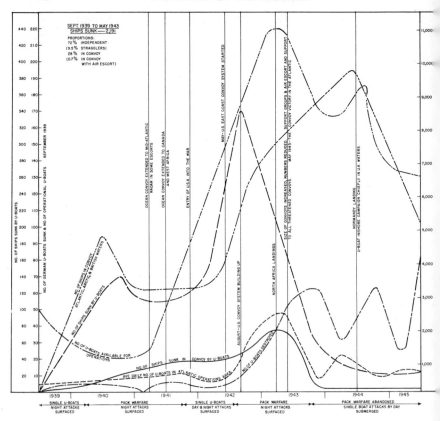

THE EFFECT OF THE CONVOY SYSTEM

instructions, ordered all Biscay transients to proceed submerged at night and surface to charge batteries only in daylight. Most significantly of all, BdU advised all commanders to fight back on the surface whenever their aerial attackers were too close to permit crash diving.

Although British bombers destroyed six submarines in the Bay of Biscay during the first three weeks of July, the "Big Bay Slaughter" did not get underway until the 28th. In the next week, American and British aircraft and the British Second Support Group sank nine U-boats. Under such relentless pressure BdU not only discontinued its group transit policy but early in August suspended all departures from Biscay bases. Thus the Bay offensive culminated in a virtual blockade of Dönitz' West France flotillas. Later BdU managed to resume sailings, routing its

U-boats along the northern coast of Spain, where they enjoyed virtual immunity from radar detection. Altogether during the campaign 28 U-boats were sunk in attempting passage of the Bay of Biscay.

Phase VII: The Final Struggle for the North Atlantic

After some three months of comparatively fruitless exploitation of tonnage warfare, Dönitz on September 19, 1943 gave orders to strike once again at the main Allied North Atlantic convoy routes. He was now prepared to employ a new weapon, the *Zaunkönig*, or acoustic torpedo, which would "home" on a ship's screws. Designed to be employed against the escorts, it was supposed to blast a hole in the screen to permit attacks on the merchant ships with conventional torpedoes. In September Group *Leuthen* struck at westbound Convoys ON-202 and ONS-18, sinking three escorts, damaging one, and sending six merchant ships to the bottom. To counter the *Zaunkönig*, British and American warships began using a noisemaking countermeasure called "Foxer," which when trailed astern drew the acoustic torpedoes harmlessly into it.

Ultimately however the German offensive in the North Atlantic was smothered by systematic day-and-night close air escort of all threatened convoys—in the old Black Pit as well as elsewhere. In this escort work, land-based planes coordinated with aircraft flying from escort carriers, which operated either with the convoys or with British Antisubmarine Surface Support Groups. The Surface Support Groups were now also able to join the land-based planes in providing night as well as day escort of convoys. These Allied countermeasures proved so effective that Dönitz withdrew his boats from the Black Pit and in October attempted a concentration south of Iceland, only to lose three U-boats to land-based aircraft. Although Dönitz recognized the extreme peril of attacking convoys in the North Atlantic, he persisted in doing so until February 1944, enduring heavy losses while inflicting only slight damage to Allied shipping. The combination of close surface escort, land-based air escort, and Antisubmarine Support Groups with escort carriers for local air support had made the North Atlantic convoys virtually immune to attack.

In mid-October the Portuguese granted the British permission to operate Coastal Command aircraft from the Azores. This acquisition of a mid-Atlantic base, combined with night air escort of threatened convoys, proved the final blow to Dönitz' hopes of organizing a renewed campaign against convoys in the North and Central Atlantic. Renewed Allied successes in the Bay of Biscay, regular air patrols from the Azores, and the relentless probing of British and American Hunter-Killer Groups in the Outer Bay effectively broke the back of this last wolf pack effort. Pending the activation of the high-speed Walter U-boat, whose production was beginning to suffer under Allied bombing raids, Dönitz candidly stated, "In the present phase of the campaign it is not victory but the survival of boats and their crews that must take priority."

Phase VIII: The Final Campaign

For several significant reasons, including the Anglo-American invasion of France, U-boat losses, which had totaled 237 during 1943, increased during the following year, while the production of the much-vaunted hydrogen-peroxide Walter U-boat continued to be delayed. Dönitz, now commander in chief of the German navy, was obliged to expend his *U-Waffe* in operations far from the vital North Atlantic.

The Royal Navy's escort carrier groups came fully into their own with the Murmansk convoys, which became the sole focus of wolf pack activity during 1944. The Admiralty, twice obliged to suspend sailings to Murmansk through the necessity of using all escorts elsewhere, had been able to reopen the North Russian route late in 1943. Northbound Convoy JW-58 provided an example of an antisubmarine task force convoy, being escorted by two escort carriers, two antiaircraft cruisers, and a close screen of nine warships, and enjoying the close cover of two Antisubmarine Support Groups. Captain F. J. Walker RN, who had commanded the *Audacity* group in December 1942, was in command of the escort. His group claimed the first shadower, *U-961*, on March 29, after which aircraft from H.M.S. *Tracker* and *Activity* teamed up with the close escort to dispose of three more boats, while the convoy proceeded without loss to Murmansk. Operating continuously within sight of the convoy, British escort carriers imposed an intolerable rate of exchange on the U-boats. Altogether British escort carriers destroyed 13 U-boats in northern waters during 1944, a period in which Murmansk convoys suffered the loss of only six ships. Increasingly heavy *Luftwaffe* attacks on subsequent convoys proved futile. Thus ended the grimly dramatic history of the North Russian convoys.

During 1944 American Hunter-Killer Groups, assigned the task of affording distant protection to North Africa- and Mediterranean-bound convoys, fulfilled their purpose chiefly by attacking U-boats refueling near the Cape Verde Islands en route to major offensives off Capetown and in the Indian Ocean. Late in February *U-709* blundered into a Hunter-Killer Group built around the escort carrier *Block Island* and was promptly finished off by two destroyer escorts, the *Bronstein* and *Thomas*. Shortly after midnight on the 29th the *Bronstein's* captain, Lieutenant Sheldon H. Kinney, detected *U-603* moving toward the *Block Island*, drove the German down, and shortly thereafter applied the *coup de grâce*. After a brief respite the group headed southwest toward an apparent concentration of U-boats off the Cape Verdes, being rewarded on

March 17 when the *Corry* and *Bronstein,* following up a series of aerial attacks, sent the *U-801* to the bottom. Two days later the *Block Island's* aircraft spotted and destroyed *U-1059,* thus concluding a highly successful cruise for this new Hunter-Killer Group.

Disturbed by growing evidence of Hunter-Killer activity, Dönitz in mid-April moved his main fueling rendezvous some 700 miles farther west, only to discover that these waters too were infested with carrier aircraft. The impossibility of continuing U-tanker operations was grimly revealed to Dönitz by the report of *U-66,* which radioed on May 5, "Mid-Atlantic worse than Bay of Biscay." Scarcely had the German completed this transmission when he was located by a plane from the *Block Island.* Lacking bombs or depth charges, the pilot homed in the destroyer escort *Buckley,* which at 0320, May 6 succeeded in closing the range to 2,100 yards before scoring a hit forward of the submarine's conning tower. During the ensuing quarter-hour engagement, the *Buckley* evaded a torpedo and then rammed the German directly across her foredeck. As the Germans hastily abandoned ship, several boarded the *Buckley* to escape drowning. The Americans, misinterpreting their intention, at first beat them off with everything from machine guns to coffee cups. Later, in a search that lasted till after sunrise, the *Buckley* rescued 36 German survivors.

German transients henceforth exercised extreme caution in surfacing off the Cape Verdes, keeping a sharp lookout for escort carriers. Late in May, *U-549* escaped several attacks by aircraft from the *Block Island* and, penetrating the screen, on the night of the 29th, sent two torpedoes into her. Amid the confusion of rescue operations and depth charge barrages, the U-boat succeeded in blowing the stern off the destroyer escort *Barr* with a *Zaunkönig,* only to be destroyed by three patterns of hedgehogs, ahead-thrown antisubmarine weapons. The *Block Island's* loss was avenged early in June when a group built around escort carrier *Guadalcanal,* Captain Daniel V. Gallery, achieved a spectacular success. On June 4, 1944 the destroyer escort *Chatelain* blasted *U-505* to the surface with assistance from the carrier's Avengers. As the Germans hurriedly abandoned ship, a boarding party from the destroyer escort *Pillsbury* plunged down the conning tower hatch, disconnected the scuttling charges, and checked the flooding. Skillfully brought in under tow by the *Guadalcanal,* the *U-505* proved an exceptionally valuable capture, for with her code books and cipher machine, naval authorities were henceforth able to decipher operational orders from BdU. She was not however the only submarine captured during the war. The Germans took two British boats; the British seized three Italian and two German submarines.

The Indian Ocean venture, though providing the *U-Waffe* with its

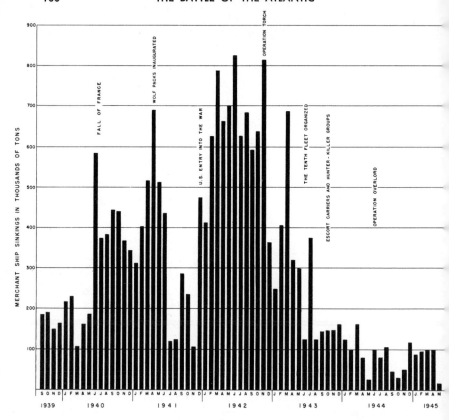

BATTLE OF THE ATLANTIC: MERCHANT VESSEL LOSSES TO U-BOATS

single area of feasible operations during 1944, tended, like patrols in the Mediterranean, to be a one-way proposition. Of the some 45 U-boats dispatched to those waters, 34 were sunk, many en route.

Belated German adoption of the snorkel (*schnorchel*), an air intake and exhaust trunk that permits a submarine to recharge batteries without fully surfacing, provided Germany with a slender hope of preserving the remnants of its *U-Waffe* long enough for the Walter boat to become operational. During the summer and fall of 1944, following the failure of his sizable anti-invasion flotilla to disrupt the Normandy landings, Dönitz dispatched several snorkel boats to the waters east of the Grand Banks with orders to operate as weather reporters. Hunter-Killer operations against these furtive boats proved relatively unrewarding, partly because the boats made no serious attempt to molest North Atlantic convoys. Amazingly enough, German submariners had sunk only half a dozen merchant ships en route from North America to the British Isles during the twelve months before Operation OVERLORD, the Normandy invasion, and their performance during the last year of the war was no more impressive. Nevertheless they managed to achieve minor success in British and American coastal waters, often lying on the bottom for hours to evade sonar detection and then cautiously launching torpedoes at their victims by means of sound bearings. These tactics were briefly effective in the Irish Sea early in 1945, but for the most part snorkel boats were as ineffective offensively as they were difficult to locate. Allied shipping losses to submarine action in the Atlantic rose from a monthly average of 30,580 tons in 1944 to some 63,270 tons during the first four months of 1945, but the pattern revealed by these sinkings indicated inshore nuisance activity rather than a threat to transatlantic convoys.

Axis U-boats destroyed 2,775 Allied merchant ships, but only some 28 per cent of these were sailing in convoy. Of over-all losses from all causes of 23,351,000 tons, U-boats accounted for 14,573,000 tons, or 62.4 per cent. All told, the Germans committed 1,175 U-boats to the war and lost 781, American forces accounting for 191. The Italians lost 85 submarines, 21 in the Atlantic. Against these figures, it can be noted that Allied merchant ships successfully completed over 300,000 voyages across the Atlantic, while hundreds of thousands more voyages were safely undertaken in the coastal waters of Britain. When Allied shipbuilding capacity reached its peak, the U-boats had no hope of winning. They lost because they dared not maintain the attack on the North Atlantic convoys which brought the material of victory to Britain. Convoy escorts proved to be a decisive task force for offensive action against attacking U-boats.

4

The Allied Offensive against North Africa

Seldom in the history of coalition warfare has there been more complete trust and loyal cooperation between allies than there was between Britain and the United States in World War II. In part this was the result of the close community of interests of the two nations, dating back half a century. In part it was the result of the intimate friendship of the two heads of government, Prime Minister Churchill and President Roosevelt. In part it was the work of General Eisenhower, who made it his special business as commander in chief to attain close concord, and who would stand for no bickering among his subordinates. In part it arose out of the willingness of all the chief officers of both nations to give and take in a friendly spirit and to drive wholeheartedly toward common objectives. Yet, despite the operational harmony that prevailed, the military and political leaders of the two allies were repeatedly at loggerheads concerning strategy.

Most of the disagreements between the British and American leaders concerned where and when to get at the enemy. In simplest terms, the Americans favored the direct approach—a drive at the heart of Germany as soon as possible. The British favored an indirect or peripheral approach, encircling and wearing down the enemy before risking a drive at his heart. Possibly the greatest British contribution to World War II strategy was keeping themselves and the Americans out of western Europe until the Germans were sufficiently weakened and the Allies were sufficiently strong to assure a quick and not-too-costly Allied victory. Perhaps the greatest strategic contribution of the Americans was at last persuading the British to join them in invading western Europe in mid-1944, before the Germans could get their new and deadly rocket warfare into high gear.

The basis for Britain's reluctance was at least partly historical, growing out of more than two centuries of British military theory and experi-ence. In the Seven Years' War (1756–63), William Pitt the Elder brought into focus with his famous War Plan the strategy toward which England had been groping since the Spanish Armada. In so doing he laid the foundations of the British Empire. Pitt's Plan was to get at France and her Spanish ally not by placing a major army on the Continent but by lending all possible material support to Britain's continental allies, while using British naval power to seal the enemy off from the seas, to support operations around the enemy's continental position, to capture the enemy's overseas trade, and to strike at the enemy's colonies beyond the seas. Thus with the use of minimum military force, Britain succeeded in containing France and Spain in Europe while establishing British claims to India, to Canada, and to the future United States as far west as the Mississippi.

In the Napoleonic Wars (1793–1815), Britain employed variations of Pitt's Plan through three coalitions, supporting allies on the Continent while using her sea power to seal off the enemy from most of the world, to blockade and destroy his fleets, and to probe for and exploit weak spots about his periphery. Thus the French, while not defeated, found themselves constantly frustrated, always threatened, and brought to the verge of bankruptcy. At length in the fourth and final coalition, Britain put a large army on the Continent and drove into France, not directly but from the south, via the Iberian Peninsula, with Portuguese and Span-ish help. At the same time, the Russians, the Prussians, and the Austrians drove in from the east. Between them, these combined forces at long last crushed the Napoleonic empire.

On the eve of World War I (1914–18) a British school of peripheral strategists proposed returning to the essential features of Pitt's Plan and the first three coalitions of the Napoleonic Wars. Warfare in the main continental theaters, said this school, should be left to the armies of Bel-gium, France, and Russia, and any other powers that could be attracted into the war against Germany. These Britain would support by subsidy, partly financed by capture of German trade, and by any other means short of actually providing large numbers of troops at the main front.

Opposing the peripheralists was a vocal school of British continental strategists who drew their inspiration from the fourth anti-Napoleonic coalition. The Kaiser, like Napoleon, was surrounded. He had no choice but to fight a two-front war. Britain's best contribution, said the conti-nental strategists, was to place her main army on the Continent. The British continental school had of course the full support of French mili-tary leaders, and French arguments were persuasive. At the outbreak of World War I in August 1914, Britain at once threw an army on the Continent. At the First Battle of the Marne, fought in early September on Paris's doorstep, a hundred thousand British regulars held the Allied left flank and helped drive a wedge between two separated German armies. The invaders were pressed back, and Paris was saved.

After the German repulse, the Western Front settled down to a four-year stalemate. Continental strategy at length won the war for the Allies, but only with American intervention and at a terrible cost in lives and treasure. The British Empire alone lost nearly a million men. To outflank the static Western Front, Winston Churchill, then First Lord of the Admiralty, had advocated peripheral strategy in the form of a campaign to seize Constantinople. The outflanking attempt failed both within the Dardanelles and among the rugged crags of Gallipoli, but in the years following World War I military analysts had concluded that Churchill's plan was strategically sound—that it failed through poor Allied planning, through a series of avoidable Allied errors, and as a result of the foresight and initiative of Liman von Sanders, German commander of the Turkish defense forces.

At the beginning of World War II, Britain again placed an army in France. Again the war in the West began with a German drive aimed at the quick defeat of France. This time the Germans succeeded. France was knocked out of the war, and the British Expeditionary Force was thrust off the Continent. Churchill, the advocate of peripheral strategy in World War I, returned to the same concept as Prime Minister and Minister of Defense in World War II. After the fall of France and the evacuation of the British army, he had no stomach for a return to western Europe—at least until Germany had been greatly weakened. And in fact Britain without allies had insufficient troops to man a new Western Front. On the other hand, Britain possessed sufficient naval power. In the circumstances, Churchill and the British Chiefs of Staff limited their offensive against the Axis powers to air attacks on German industries and communications, to attacks on German and Italian naval forces, to operations aimed at restoring British communications in the Mediterranean, to the Egyptian campaign, to distant attacks at Dakar and Madagascar, and to operations in Greece and Crete and probes at St. Nazaire and Dieppe. When Hitler invaded the Soviet Union, Churchill announced: "We shall give whatever help we can to Russia and the Russian people." Thus Britain was reviving two of the main features of Pitt's Plan: lending all possible material support to allies on the Continent, while using her naval power to support operations around the enemy's continental periphery and beyond the seas.

Soviet leaders, from the moment they found themselves in the war on the side of Britain, opposed the concept of peripheral strategy, demanding a "Second Front Now." When the United States entered the war, the American Joint Chiefs of Staff, General Marshall in particular, also insisted on an early return of Allied forces to France. What Marshall proposed was to seize a beachhead in France in the late summer of 1942,

Operation SLEDGEHAMMER. This was to be followed in 1943 by a major invasion, Operation ROUNDUP, a drive into Germany, involving a double envelopment of the Ruhr—as was actually carried out in 1944-45. In preparation for SLEDGEHAMMER and ROUNDUP, the Joint Chiefs gave top priority to the production of landing and beaching craft and began sending troops to Britain.

The British Chiefs tentatively accepted SLEDGEHAMMER, but only as an "emergency" or "opportunity" operation—in the event either the Russians or the Germans appeared on the verge of defeat—despite President Roosevelt's urging that SLEDGEHAMMER "be pushed with the utmost vigor" and without qualification. Roosevelt insisted that "it is of the highest importance that U.S. ground troops be brought into action against the enemy in 1942," but the British War Cabinet and the British Chiefs of Staff flatly refused to agree to an early invasion of the Continent on the President's terms.

Yet something had to be done in 1942. The Germans on the Russian front reconquered the territory lost during the winter and thrust toward Stalingrad on the Volga. There they could disrupt the flow of oil from the Caucasus and block American and British supplies to Russia via the Persian Gulf route. In North Africa, Rommel's tanks, forging ahead toward the Egyptian delta, appeared to have the momentum that would carry them through to Cairo and the Suez Canal.

Churchill proposed an invasion of western North Africa. There was much to commend in the proposal. Tunisia, Algeria, Morocco, and French West Africa, though loyal to the Vichy French government, were not occupied by the Germans. If the area were brought over to the Allies, Rommel could be trapped between the invading forces and the British Eighth Army, Malta could be relieved, and the Mediterranean could be reopened to Allied shipping, with a consequent saving of crucially short merchant tonnage. Moreover, bases would be secured for attacks on Italy and elsewhere in southern Europe, a French army might be mustered for action against the Axis, and phosphates and other resources would be denied the enemy.

President Roosevelt at first opposed the move into North Africa. He wished to see American forces in Europe as soon as possible—to boost the morale of the American public, to fulfill promises to Russia, and to bring a quick end to the war. The Joint Chiefs of Staff opposed the African invasion because they saw it as a strategically eccentric move that would draw more and more Allied forces away from the strategic center in western Europe and delay the invasion of France at least two years. Prime Minister Churchill insisted however that the invasion of North Africa was the best possible preparation for the invasion of France, since threatening the periphery of the Axis empire would draw German forces away from the invasion areas on the French coast.

Churchill at length convinced Roosevelt that if the Anglo-American forces were to see action against the Axis that year, there was really no alternative to his African plan. For once Roosevelt overruled his military advisers in a matter of strategy. On July 25, 1942, the Combined Chiefs of Staff committed themselves to the North African invasion, which was given the code name Operation TORCH.

Strategic and Political Plans and Preparations

The immediate objectives of the landings were three major North African ports outside the operational radius of the *Luftwaffe:* Algiers and Oran on the Mediterranean shore, and Casablanca on the Atlantic. Bizerte and Tunis, in Tunisia, and Bone, in Algeria, were rejected as too close to enemy airfields in Sicily; while Dakar, in West Africa, was too far south to be useful. The choice also reflected a compromise between American Army planners, who wished to forestall possible German counteraction through Spain, and British planners, who expected the major enemy opposition to come through Tunisia. Once the immediate target cities were secured, part of the Allied forces would have to race the Germans for occupation of the ports in Tunisia while others rushed from Casablanca to the frontier of Spanish Morocco to guard the vital communications through the Straits of Gibraltar.

Best utilization of available ships and manpower determined the various assault force assignments. American Task Force 34, called the Western Naval Task Force, was to transport 35,000 troops directly from the United States to seize the Casablanca area. A Center Naval Task Force carrying 39,000 American troops with British naval support, all staging in Britain, would invade Oran. A third contingent, the Eastern Naval Task Force, would embark from Britain 23,000 British and 10,000 American troops assigned to seize Algiers. After the ports were taken, follow-up convoys would pour in reinforcements and supplies until the conquest was complete. Because intelligence reports indicated that defending Vichy forces would resist American troops less vigorously than British, all ground commanders in the initial assaults were American. Lieutenant General Dwight D. Eisenhower USA was named Commander in Chief Allied Force, while Admiral of the Fleet Sir Andrew B. Cunningham RN assumed over-all naval command. D-day was set for November 8, 1942, the last date that year on which landings were deemed feasible across beaches exposed to the heavy ground swell usually prevalent on the Atlantic coast of North Africa during the winter season.

The venture was risky enough to satisfy the boldest. Much necessarily depended on the unpredictable reaction of the North African French. Because of the British attacks on French naval forces at Mers-el-Kebir and Dakar in 1940, the Germans had permitted the French to assemble

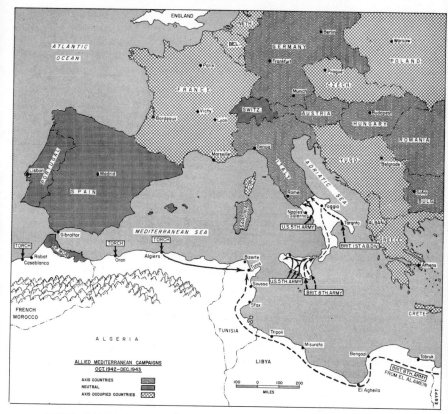

ALLIED CAMPAIGNS IN THE MEDITERRANEAN THEATER, 1942–1943

and equip a defense force of 120,000 men, 350 planes of fair quality, more than 200 tanks, a sizable amount of light artillery and mortars, and naval units which included the modern battleship *Richelieu* and a cruiser-destroyer force at Dakar. Another cruiser, the unfinished battleship *Jean Bart,* and numerous destroyers and submarines were in ports elsewhere along the coastline. If all these forces fought with determination, and if the Germans moved into Spanish and French bases to assist them, cutting the Allied supply route at Gibraltar, it appeared to many Allied staff officers that the invasion might be defeated. But it seemed more probable that the Franco government would resist a German entry into Spain, and that many of the defending French units, if they fought at all, would put up only a token resistance. Success however hinged as much on political as on military and naval factors.

Within the limits imposed by the need for secrecy concerning the operation, everything possible was done to insure a favorable French reaction to the landings. Despite strong public pressure, the Roosevelt administration had refused to break diplomatic relations with the Vichy government. In the fall of 1940, Admiral William D. Leahy had been appointed Ambassador to Vichy with his main mission to stiffen French resistance to any German domination of French Africa. Since 1941 a corps of American consular officials, led by Consul-General Robert D. Murphy, had been assiduously cultivating the good will and cooperation of leading French political and military figures in North Africa while administering U.S. economic aid. They also had been collecting intelligence concerning beach defenses, surf conditions, roads, bridges, and other information essential to the success of the landings. Two weeks before the invasion was scheduled to begin, Major General Mark W. Clark USA landed from a British submarine to meet with Murphy and pro-Allied French commanders in a secret conference near Algiers. Without being given the exact date, the French were told that the assault was coming and were urged to disrupt anti-invasion plans when the operation began. At French urging, General Henri Giraud, a widely known French senior officer who had escaped from a German prison, was spirited away from the Riviera by a submarine to Gibraltar in the hope that he could further rally Frenchmen to the Allied cause. On the eve of the attack therefore there were grounds for hope that many French army and air force units were "fixed."

There was no success in winning over the French navy beforehand however, and that was especially serious because the coastal defense batteries were manned by naval personnel. With few exceptions the Navy was tenaciously loyal to Admiral of the Fleet François Darlan, now Commander in Chief of the Armed Forces of Vichy France. As a dynamic leader who had brought the *Marine* to the peak of efficiency between wars, Darlan could both legally and morally command the allegiance of all French forces in North Africa with an authority second only to that of Pétain himself. A few weeks before the landings, Darlan sent feelers to American officials in North Africa suggesting negotiations. Murphy favored negotiating with the Admiral, but the U.S. State Department, deeply distrusting the Vichy government, feared that such contacts would lead to leaks concerning the forthcoming operation that would impel the Germans to rush troops and planes into Africa and thereby frustrate the entire scheme. Only three days before D-day however, Darlan flew to Algiers to be at the bedside of his sick son. Thus purely by chance he was well placed to exercise an immediate influence on the course of events. This totally unexpected development was to prove fortunate for the Allies.

Tactical Plans and Preparations

Because the war against the European Axis was primarily an army responsibility, it was from beginning to end commanded on the highest military level by an army officer, and naval forces were assigned to the Army as needed. As a result the Army dominated joint operations,* and the Navy deferred to the Army's desires, even in amphibious assaults. This situation contrasted with that in the Pacific Ocean Areas, where the top command was naval, and army units were assigned to the Navy as needed. As a result amphibious operations developed along somewhat different lines in the two theaters.

Planning and preparation for Operation TORCH were complicated by division of command and shortage of time. From his London headquarters General Eisenhower and his British-American staff directed the detailed planning for the assaults on Algiers and Oran. But because the forces for Morocco were to stage from the United States, plans and preparations for this phase of TORCH were left to the Joint Chiefs of Staff. General Marshall delegated the planning for the landing force to the War Department, which delegated the detailed planning to Major General George S. Patton Jr., Commander Western Task Force. Admiral King delegated the fleet-level planning for the participating naval forces to Admiral Royal E. Ingersoll, Commander in Chief Atlantic Fleet, who delegated the detailed planning to Rear Admiral Kent Hewitt, the prospective commander of the Western Naval Task Force (Task Force 34). In the preparatory phase the army and navy commanders were independent, with no common superior below the President. The command structure was thus in the tradition of joint operations from Quebec in the Seven Years' War to Norway in World War II.

In practice, planning and preparation for the Moroccan attack were closely integrated, as indeed they had to be for so organic an operation as an amphibious assault. General Patton and Admiral Hewitt conferred frequently. To coordinate naval plans with those for the landing force, Hewitt's war plans officer spent several weeks in Patton's office in Washington. Then, to achieve final coordination, Patton's planning staff moved to Hewitt's headquarters at Ocean View, near Norfolk, Virginia. Because Hewitt, prior to assuming command of the Western Naval Task Force, was Commander Amphibious Force Atlantic Fleet (Comphiblant), the amphibious training for the Moroccan landing force was directed from his headquarters.

On October 13, 1942 the Joint Chiefs issued to all commands con-

* In American terminology a *joint operation* is one carried out by elements of more than one armed service of the same nationality; a *combined operation* is one carried out by forces of two or more nations. The British use the term *combined* for both sorts of operations.

cerned with the Moroccan operation their own high-level plan, titled "Joint Army-Navy Plan for Participation in Operation Torch." It provided that, once the expedition got under way, there should in each phase be a single commander at both the theater and the local level. For the first time in modern history a large-scale joint operation was to be under unified command throughout. Command relations were set forth as follows:

(a) The Commander in Chief, Allied Force [Eisenhower], will command all forces assigned to Operation TORCH, under the principle of unity of command.

(b) The Western Naval Task Force will pass to the command of the Commander in Chief, Allied Force, upon crossing the meridian of 40° West Longitude. This command may be exercised either directly by the Commander in Chief [Eisenhower] or through the Naval Commander, Allied Force [Cunningham]. (Prior to that time these forces will remain under the command of the Commander in Chief, United States Atlantic Fleet [Ingersoll], who will arrange their movements so that they will meet the schedule of the Commander in Chief, Allied Force.)

(c) Command relations of the Subordinate Task Forces are initially set up as given in subparagraphs (d), (e), (f), and (g). They are subject to change as found necessary by the Commander in Chief, Allied Force.

(d) The command of units of the Western Task Force which are embarked in the Western Naval Task Force, will vest in the Commander, Western Naval Task Force [Hewitt], until such time as the Commanding General, Western Task Force [Patton], has established his headquarters on shore and states he is ready to assume command.

(e) When the Commanding General, Western Task Force, assumes command on shore, the naval forces designated to give further support to the occupation of FRENCH MOROCCO will pass to his control, acting through the Commander, Western Naval Task Force.

(f) Following the assault operations and when and as released by Commander in Chief, Allied Force, the United States naval forces assigned thereto will revert to the command of Commander in Chief, United States Atlantic Fleet.

(g) The United States naval forces assigned for the operation of ports and for naval local and sea frontier defenses—Sea Frontier Forces, Western Task Force, and the Naval Operating Base, Center Task Force—will be under the command of the respective commanding generals of those task forces, under the principle of unity of command.

(h) The Commander in Chief, United States Atlantic Fleet, will exercise command over all forces employed for the cover and ocean escort in the ATLANTIC of follow-up convoys between the UNITED STATES and NORTH AFRICA.

Particularly to be noted in this Joint Plan is the break with the traditional system in amphibious operations, whereby the general commanding the landing force and the admiral commanding the naval

support force remained independent and coequal throughout the operation. In the Moroccan invasion, first Admiral Hewitt and then General
Patton would be in over-all command. And there would be at any given
time only a single chain of command, via Admiral Ingersoll until the
expedition reached mid-ocean, via General Eisenhower thereafter. Though
the provision for unified local command was written only into the directive for the Western Task Force, it became the model for subsequent
directives in the European theater of operations.

Plans for the three main landings, at Algiers, at Oran, and in the
Casablanca area, while differing in such details as command relations,
were otherwise similar in purpose and outline. The objective of the
attacks was to enable the Allies to hurl a large army and air force into
a prolonged campaign against a well-equipped foe, for even if the French
put up no resistance, German and Italian reinforcements were sure to be
rushed to Africa. Since nothing like the huge volume of supplies required
to sustain the invasion forces, 600–700 tons daily per division, could be
handled across beaches, it was essential to seize well-developed ports
with ample berthing, unloading, and stowage facilities. But because direct assault inside harbors in the teeth of harbor defenses was infeasible
without prohibitive losses, plans called for units to be landed on open
beaches near the coastal cities so that their harbors could be taken from
the flanks and rear. The troops would be carried to positions off the
beaches in combat-loaded assault transports, and then transferred with
their equipment to landing craft to be put ashore in surprise night landings. Gunnery ships and naval aircraft would support the flanking drives
of the troops, while landing craft shuttled in reinforcements and supplies
until the ports were secured and readied for use. Since the best chance
for the enemy to defeat the onslaught was to deny the ports, and consequently the supplies, needed to build up large forces, it was vital to take
the harbors as quickly and with as little damage as possible. Preventing
the defenders from scuttling blockships or demolishing quays was considered so important that special units were assigned to dash in at the
start of the attacks and seize port facilities at all three objectives. Simple
in concept, complex in detail, the hastily drawn plans served as a model
for organizing further assaults in the European theater.

The training of the assault forces was beset by myriad difficulties.
Few of the land, sea, or air forces assigned to the operation were completely ready when the attack was ordered, nor did it seem likely in
the scant five months until D-day that they could be properly trained.
Responsible officers realized this, but they also knew that to delay until
all participants were fully trained might permit the Germans to move
in first, thereby making an Allied landing in Northwest Africa out of the
question.

Fortunately for the Allies, the U.S. Marine Corps and U.S. Navy entered the war with a developed amphibious doctrine and training program. And though the amphibiously trained U.S. marines were committed to the Pacific, the U.S. Army had commenced training based in part on their doctrine. During 1941 and early 1942 three American infantry divisions trained with the marines in the United States. Other infantry divisions, dispatched to Great Britain, trained amphibiously with British forces in Scotland and Northern Ireland. In the time available however, it was not possible to train sufficient U.S. Army units to undertake all three North African landings. In view of the French attitude it would have been desirable to make the invasion an all-American show, but British troops had to make up the major part of the easternmost force, operating against Algiers.

By later standards the training both for the initial landings and for subsequent combat fell far short of what was desirable, but it had to suffice. Amphibious training of crews for transports and landing craft was especially deficient. Again, there was simply not enough time. Only half its assigned transports had reached the Western Naval Task Force by August 1, 1942, fourteen weeks before D-day. There was not enough time left even for adequate indoctrination. Moreover nearly all the ships required a good deal of work on communications equipment, and they needed alterations to their interior arrangements before they could participate in exercises. Landing craft were crucial items, for until the Army could seize and ready the ports, these little vessels would comprise the sole means of bringing in ammunition and supplies. Because of a failure to enlist small craft sailors, as such, when the war began, the Navy hastily assembled some 3,000 recruits, who commenced small craft training in June 1942. While the men worked hard and enthusiastically, for all practical purposes they had only two months to train specifically for the North African venture. It was soon apparent that the techniques of amphibious assault cannot be learned in so brief a time.

German U-boat activity worsened matters by forcing the landing exercises for the Western Task Force into the sheltered waters of Chesapeake Bay at Solomons Island. As a result the landing craft crews were unable to gain needed experience in handling their craft in a heavy surf. Crews who trained in Great Britain, the majority Royal Navy, were able to practice under more realistic but still far from satisfactory conditions. The Army's historian of the North African campaign concludes: "Training for the amphibious operations in French North Africa . . . fell short of what was desired and perhaps below the requirements for victory over a well-armed and determined foe." The massive assault forces that got under way from Britain and the United States knew that the French were not particularly well armed. They had yet to find out if they were determined.

Morocco: The Approach

The Western Naval Task Force, commanded by Admiral Hewitt in the heavy cruiser *Augusta*, comprised 102 warships, transports, and auxiliaries which, when united at sea, covered more than 500 square miles of ocean. To mislead the enemy, the Northern and Southern Attack Groups sortied from Hampton Roads on October 23 and took a southerly course. The next day the Center Attack Group left Hampton Roads and took a northeasterly course as if headed for Britain. These groups later united and were joined on the 27th by a Covering Group sailing from Casco Bay, Maine; this group included the new fast battleship *Massachusetts* and two heavy cruisers. An Air Group dispatched ahead to Bermuda, comprising the aircraft carrier *Ranger*, four escort carriers newly converted from tankers, and a screen of a light cruiser and nine destroyers, joined the force on the 28th in mid-ocean.

After steering evasive courses to avoid or deceive known enemy submarine concentrations, the Western Naval Task Force neared the African coast in a strong northwest wind that raised heavy seas. Predictions from Washington were that surf on the Moroccan beaches would be too high for the landings on D-day, November 8, but Admiral Hewitt trusted the verdict of his aerological officer that the landings would be possible on the 8th but not for many days thereafter. He therefore proceeded according to plan. If impossible conditions developed, he could postpone the landings by radio and, if absolutely necessary, execute an alternate plan for landing inside the Mediterranean. As the task force approached Morocco, the men were cheered by the news that the British Eighth Army was pressing back Rommel's forces in Egypt after the great British victory at El Alamein on November 5.

On November 7 the Western Naval Task Force split apart. The Southern Attack Group turned south toward the small phosphate port of Safi, where it was to land 6,500 troops and 90 medium and light tanks to march on Casablanca from the south. The Center Attack Group headed for the small port of Fedala to land 19,500 troops and 79 light tanks to advance on Casablanca from the north. The Northern Attack Group shaped course for the coastal village of Mehdia to land 9,000 troops and 65 light tanks to capture the airfield at nearby Port Lyautey. The landings at Safi and Mehdia were expected also to tie down French units that might otherwise close in on the main landing at Fedala. The Covering Group moved toward Casablanca itself to take under fire any naval forces that tried to leave the harbor. The Air Group divided in order to support all three landings: one escort carrier to Safi, two escort carriers to Mehdia, the *Ranger* and one escort carrier to Fedala and Casablanca, only 15 miles apart.

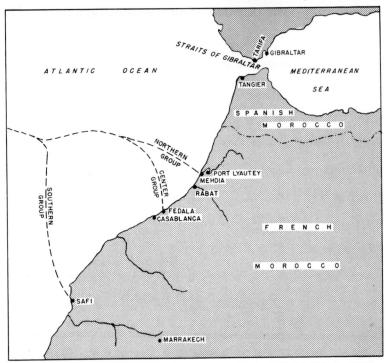

AMERICAN LANDINGS IN FRENCH MOROCCO, NOVEMBER 8, 1942

The Army had insisted upon night landings—both to achieve surprise and because army officers were not yet convinced that naval gunfire could provide adequate support for a daylight landing. But surprise would be lost if the attack groups were sighted from the Moroccan coast in the evening of November 7. To allow time for the approach, for loading of landing craft, and for the ship-to-shore movement, all in total darkness, H-hour was set at 0400, two hours before dawn.

The Army also required what the Navy regarded as an excessive amount of equipment to be carried in with the assault waves. This requirement put a strain on the supply of landing craft, which for this operation ranged from 36-foot plywood, gasoline-powered "Higgins boats" to 50-foot steel, diesel-powered LCM's (Landing Craft, Mechanized) capable of transporting a light tank. In subsequent assaults enough landing craft for army requirements would be brought to the beachhead area by LST's (Landing Ships, Tank), but for the North African invasion they were limited to the number that could be brought in by the transports.

Major General Jonathan Anderson, commanding the troops that were to land at Fedala, further complicated the landing craft situation for the Center Attack Group by a last-minute decision to increase the strength of the initial landing force by about 50 per cent. As a result, to provide enough landing craft for the assault waves, the Navy had to work out a complicated boat plan that would have been difficult for experienced coxswains to carry out on schedule even in daylight.

Morocco: The Main Assault

The assault plan for Fedala required the 15 transports of the Center Attack Group to anchor at midnight in four columns six to eight miles north of the landing beaches. The four transports of the inshore line each carried a battalion landing team. These four landing teams, comprising altogether 6,000 men, were to make the initial, pre-dawn assault. Because no transport carried enough landing craft to boat a whole team, the transports of the second, third, and fourth lines were directed to send forward additional craft to specific transports of the first line. As the craft were loaded with men and tanks, they were to advance to one of four control destroyers positioned in the rendezvous area a thousand yards nearer shore. Here they were to form "waves" of six to eight boats. When each of the loaded landing craft, numbering more than 200, had reported to its designated control destroyer, the destroyers would conduct them forward to the line of departure 4,000 yards from shore. Meanwhile four beach-marking scout boats would have advanced and anchored, each off one of the four segments of beach—designated Beaches Red 2, Red 3, Blue, and Blue 2—assigned to one of the four battalion landing teams. At 0335, the scout boats were to begin flashing flashlights seaward. At 0350, they were to ignite colored flares. At H-hour, 0400, the landing craft, on signal from the control destroyers, would head for their assigned beaches, accompanied by support boats armed with machine guns and guided by the flares in the scout boats. After putting the troops ashore, the landing craft were to retract and hurry back to the transport area for the follow-up troops. As we have seen, this elaborate and tightly scheduled plan had to be carried out in almost complete darkness.

As the Center Group transports, accompanied by the cruisers *Augusta* and *Brooklyn* and ten destroyers, headed in toward their anchorage, the Fedala assault plan began to come apart. An unexpected current carried the Center Group off course, necessitating a series of emergency turns. The first line of transports, those carrying the initial assault forces, reached the anchorage shortly before midnight, but by then the rest of the transports were straggling badly and out of position. As a result the landing craft from these vessels were late in reaching their assigned

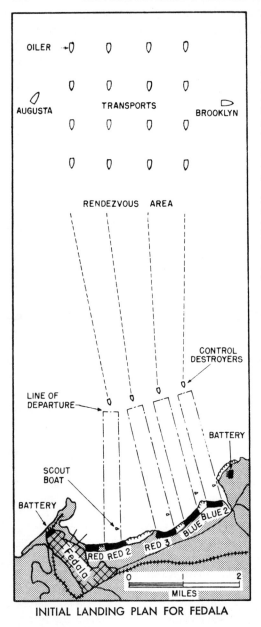

INITIAL LANDING PLAN FOR FEDALA

transports or never found them at all. The schedule was further retarded by the troops, who, overloaded with 60-pound packs, debarked very slowly down the landing nets into the pitching boats. As a result of these delays, only about half the scheduled waves of boats had reached the rendezvous area by 0400. The control destroyers however could wait no longer and began conducting their waves to the line of departure, which they reached in about 50 minutes. The beach-marking scout boats, uninformed of the delays, had for some time been showing their lights, but this only caused confusion, for two of the scout boats were out of position, one by more than two miles. At 0500, an hour late, the first waves of boats headed for the beach, followed at five to ten minute intervals by the second and third waves. The noise of the landing craft, now operating at full throttle, finally attracted the attention of shore batteries, which turned on searchlights, at first upward to look for aircraft, and then down on the water. When the support boats opened fire with machine guns, the lights went out abruptly. Meanwhile the inexperience of the coxswains was taking its toll as landing craft collided,

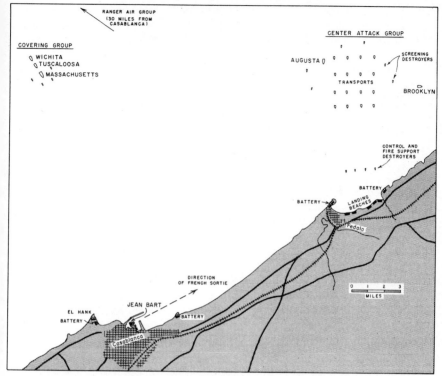

THE ASSAULT ON THE CASABLANCA AREA

crashed into rocks and reefs adjoining the designated beaches, or were caught in the surf, spun about, and broached on the beach. Some troops were spilled into the sea where they were pulled down by their heavy packs and drowned. Of the landing craft that safely made shore, many were left stranded by the receding tide and could not retract. Yet the naval crews who lost their craft were the exceptions. Most, despite their brief training, the darkness, and the difficult sea conditions, brought their troops safely ashore with their equipment and quickly returned to the transports. By dawn 3,500 troops had been landed, and the first echelons advanced and seized control of the town of Fedala. The batteries flanking the beach however were still in French hands.

Would the French fight, or would they welcome the invaders? As first light grayed the morning sky, the eyes of the fleet were on the French batteries, which would provide the answer. Friendly officers in Morocco had been tipped off that the invasion was taking place but not just where or in what strength. They had been working through the night trying to arrange for a bloodless landing. But the key French commanders, Resident General Noguès and Vice Admiral Michelier, remained unconvinced that there was a powerful American force offshore. They would not be party to a mere raid or temporary invasion. Were they to do so, Axis forces would also invade Northwest Africa, and unless the Americans had sufficient power to make good their foothold against the Axis, France would suffer reprisals without gaining offsetting advantages. Michelier therefore refused to rescind his order to the batteries to defend the coast.

Had the landing been made after dawn, as the Navy wished, or had the French batteries held their fire until the morning mists had lifted and revealed the magnitude of the American force, it is possible that General Noguès would have agreed to parley. But just as day began to break, shortly after 0600, the batteries flanking the Fedala roadstead opened fire on the landing forces and on the control destroyers. The destroyers quickly returned the fire, and were soon joined by the guns of the *Brooklyn* and the *Augusta*. The *Ranger's* aircraft, over Casablanca, now came under attack by French fighters; in a brief dogfight seven French and four American planes were shot down. Spotting planes from the Covering Group were soon being attacked by antiaircraft fire and fighter planes. At 0700 the *Massachusetts* and her consorts, the *Tuscaloosa* and the *Wichita*, turned their 5-inch batteries on the French aircraft, shooting one down. Immediately afterward the battleship *Jean Bart* in Casablanca harbor and the powerful battery at nearby Point El Hank opened fire on the Covering Group, which replied at once. The battle was on. To Admiral Michelier, putting up a fight was no longer just a matter of policy or of carrying out orders from above; it had become a requirement of honor. When later in the day a deputation from General Patton drove to Casablanca with an American flag and a flag of truce to arrange a ceasefire, they were let in through the lines and cheered in the streets, but Michelier refused even to receive them. As one of the American officers began to argue with the Admiral's aide, he was interrupted by a salvo from the El Hank battery that shook the windows of the Admiralty. Said the aide, *"Voilà votre réponse!"*

The *Jean Bart*, though uncompleted and temporarily immobilized, had an operational turret of four 15-inch guns that made her a formidable floating battery. In Casablanca harbor also were eleven submarines, eight sloops, eleven minesweepers, two super-destroyers, seven smaller destroyers, and the light cruiser *Primauguet*. The principal task of the American Covering Group was to prevent a sortie of these vessels against the Center Attack Group and the landing forces 15 miles away at Fedala. The carrying out of this task was hampered by the guns of the *Jean Bart* and by steady and accurate fire from El Hank's eight well-protected

5.3-inch and 7.6-inch guns, which had straddled the *Massachusetts* at 20,000 yards with their first salvo. The *Massachusetts* concentrated the fire of her nine 16-inch guns on the *Jean Bart*. Her fifth salvo struck the barbette of the functional turret, jamming it in train. For 45 minutes more the ships shot it out with the El Hank battery, driving the gunners temporarily to cover but not demolishing the guns. Not a ship in the Covering Group had yet been hit.

The second phase of the Naval Battle of Casablanca was initiated by Admiral Michelier, who, observing that the Covering Group had maneuvered westward, away from the transports off Fedala, seized the opportunity to send seven of his destroyers to attack the Center Group. Eight submarines also sortied. This was Michelier's best chance to break up the landing. Steaming close inshore and making expert use of smoke, the French destroyers approached the American transports and had hit one landing craft when they were intercepted and driven back by the *Augusta*, the *Brooklyn*, and two of the Center Group destroyers, which had been deployed to screen the transports against just such an attack. The cruiser *Primauguet* now sortied and led the French destroyers in a new advance. Hewitt had already summoned the Covering Group to return to the area. For two and a half hours the French ships dodged in and out of their smoke screen, exchanging salvos with the vessels of the Center and Covering Groups. Planes from the *Ranger* meanwhile made several strafing and bombing runs on the enemy force. Three of the French submarines had already been sunk in Casablanca harbor, but the remaining eight sortied and entered the confused battle. Their torpedo spreads narrowly missed several American vessels.

In the face of the immense American superiority of force, the gallant French attack, however skillfully conducted, could hardly have ended other than in disaster for the attackers. When the engagement ended just before noon, none of the American vessels had received damage of consequence. Of the French ships however, all but one had been severely damaged. Two had sunk, two others were in a sinking condition, one was dead in the water, and one had been beached to avoid sinking. Only one of the submarines returned to Casablanca harbor, and two made Dakar. Of the rest, attacked by American planes or destroyers, one was beached, one was scuttled at Cadiz, and the rest sank.

Early in the afternoon of November 8, the undamaged French destroyer and two sloops emerged from Casablanca to pick up survivors. Admiral Hewitt, taking this sortie for another attempt to attack his transports, ordered action resumed. The three French vessels made it back to the harbor under a smoke screen, but aircraft from the *Ranger* wrecked the *Primauguet*. At the end of the day the El Hank battery was still active, and workmen had completed repairs on the *Jean Bart's* damaged turret.

At Fedala the defending troops, chiefly Senegalese, quickly surrendered, and even the navy-manned shore batteries were in American hands before noon. French fighter aircraft made a few strafing runs over the beach, but bombers were chased off by aircraft from the *Ranger*. General Anderson organized his troops to meet counterattacks and prepared for the advance on Casablanca. He was severely hampered however by the increasingly behind-schedule landings of troops and supplies. There were not enough landing craft left to do the job properly, and the performance of the boat crews, exhausted after having worked all night, did not improve with the coming of daylight. Collisions and broachings continued. The numerous boats stranded and abandoned on the beach were banged together and shattered by the incoming tide and rising surf. By nightfall on D-day nearly half the 347 landing craft of the Center Attack Group had been destroyed, and only 40 per cent of the 19,500 troops embarked in the transports had been brought ashore. Unloading of supplies was even further behind schedule. It was apparent that the transports would have to remain off Fedala for several days. As they were brought in closer to the shore, a minelayer sowed a protective mine field to eastward, and the destroyers patrolled in screening areas north and west of the transport area.

Morocco: The Southern Assault

Meanwhile, 150 miles by sea southwest of Casablanca, the Southern Attack Group had scored a spectacular success at Safi. In the blackness before H-hour, despite debarking troubles caused by a heavy ground swell and the inevitable errors of inexperienced personnel, the crucial phase of the assault was conducted according to plan. First, a scout boat located the turning buoy marking the entrance to Safi's small, breakwater-protected harbor. Next, guided by a light blinking seaward from the scout boat, came two old four-stack destroyers of World War I vintage, razeed to reduce silhouette. These, carrying about 200 assault troops each, led landing craft directly into the harbor. The French had been alerted and there was a lively exchange of fire as the first "four-piper," the *Bernadou*, slowly steamed in and drove the French gunners to cover with her guns. Her consort, the *Cole*, was able to come directly alongside the quay without a single casualty. While the old battleship *New York* and the light cruiser *Philadelphia* were silencing the coastal batteries, American troops took over key positions in the town. That afternoon, after the ex-train ferry U.S.S. *Lakehurst* had brought in her load of medium tanks, all objectives of the assault were attained. Aircraft from the escort carrier supporting the Southern Group destroyed most French planes in the area on the ground. Naval gunfire stopped a half-hearted French attempt at counterattack. The entire operation had been carried out with dispatch. Though supporting landings were made on beaches flanking the harbor, only one landing craft was lost. All ships were completely unloaded in three days. By the time resistance officially ceased, an American tank force was on its way by road from Safi to Casablanca accompanied along the coast by the *Philadelphia*, several destroyers, and six gasoline-carrying landing craft.

Morocco: The Northern Assault

The primary objective of the Northern Attack Group was the Port Lyautey airfield, the only airport in Morocco with concrete, all-weather runways. Troops were to be landed on both sides of the Sebou, a narrow and winding but navigable river that connects Port Lyautey with the Atlantic. The initial attack was intended to overwhelm the seaside village of Mehdia and its ancient fortress, the Kasba, which guarded the mouth of the river. The invaders would then thrust inland to seize the airfield by double envelopment and to occupy Port Lyautey. U.S.S. *Dallas*, another razeed fourpiper, was to proceed upriver after a boom blocking access had been cut, and land a force to assist in the capture of the airfield. After the airfield was secured, an army fighter group catapulted from one of the escort carriers was to operate from the field, providing fighter cover for further operations by bombers flown in from Gibraltar.

The Northern Attack Group's assault plan was a smaller version of the one used at Fedala, except that the five landing beaches were much farther apart. Hence to the delays of debarking was added mounting confusion. Few of the troops reached the right beach. Badly scattered, they missed an early opportunity to seize the Kasba and the shore batteries near it, and were soon obliged to meet counterattacks by French colonial troops closing in from Port Lyautey. Efforts of a boat party to cut the boom blocking the river, and later efforts by the *Dallas* to ram it, failed completely under a hail of fire from the Kasba. The initial loss of landing craft was not great, but deteriorating weather and a rapidly rising surf made the build-up of supplies perilously slow. By the end of the second day only half the troops had been landed. Brigadier General Lucian K. Truscott, Jr., who commanded the landing force in this assault, did not at first make much use of naval gunfire. The light cruiser *Savannah* kept down the fire from the Kasba with her 6-inch shells, but the 14-inch shells of the old battleship *Texas*, which could have smashed the fort, were considered too dangerous to be fired at targets near where American troops were operating. Scout planes from both the cruiser and battleship however made a potent contribution in breaking up enemy tank columns by means of a novel but effective technique—dropping antisubmarine depth charges equipped with impact fuses.

On November 10, the situation took a turn for the better. In an early morning attack, the invaders broke through to the airfield against French defending troops who, expecting an early armistice, no longer offered strenuous resistance. By that time a boat party had at last cut the main cable of the river boom, enabling the *Dallas* to crash through and scrape her way up the shallow Sebou to land her troops near the airdrome. Shortly afterward the army planes from one of the escort carriers were flown in and began operating from the field. Bombers from the other escort carrier attacked the Kasba, which promptly surrendered to an American infantry team. French armored forces coming up the coast road from Rabat, the Moroccan capital, were turned back by destroyer and cruiser fire. When a column of troop-laden trucks was spotted advancing on Port Lyautey from the interior, the *Texas* reached more than eight miles inland and cratered the road with her big shells, whereupon the column quickly dispersed. That afternoon the French general in command of the area called for a cease-fire, which was granted at once. The attack had attained its main object, capturing the airfield—but too late to support the battle for Casablanca.

Morocco Secured

General Anderson's troops and armor meanwhile had advanced from Fedala to the outskirts of Casablanca. Two French corvettes, advancing at 1000 on November 10 to fire on the American troops, were chased back into Casablanca harbor by the *Augusta*. Then the *Augusta* took to her heels as shells from the repaired turret of the *Jean Bart* began to fall around her. Hewitt called for air support, and the *Ranger* sent in dive bombers that scored two hits with 1,000-pound bombs and left the French battleship settling in the harbor mud with her decks awash.

At the end of the 10th, the Americans had Casablanca surrounded. They planned an all-out attack from land, sea, and air for the next morning. Fortunately, before the attack could be launched, Admiral Michelier received orders to cease resistance, and a conference later on the 11th ended the fighting. At the conference Admiral Hewitt held out his hand to Admiral Michelier and expressed regret at having had to fire on French ships. "I had my orders and did my duty," said Michelier, taking the proffered hand; "you had yours and did your duty; now that is over, we are ready to cooperate." Soon the French and the Americans were working together to restore the port as a major rear base for supplying the prospective campaign into Tunisia.

The Axis got into the Moroccan campaign after all, causing the Americans far greater material losses than the French did. U-boats that the American task force had evaded in the Atlantic were now converging on the Casablanca area. The transports of the Center Attack Group, with no troops aboard but still unloading cargo, were obliged to remain off Fedala because a new convoy approaching from the United States would occupy all available space in Casablanca's protected harbor. In the early evening of November 11, *U-173* slipped into the unloading area and sank a transport and damaged a destroyer and an oiler with torpedoes. The following afternoon, *U-130* got into the area and sank three more transports. *U-130* got away safely, but *U-173*, after heavily damaging an American cargo ship off Fedala on the 15th, was sunk the next day by three American destroyers.

Algeria: Algiers

When the Allied forces staging from England steamed through the Straits of Gibraltar into the Mediterranean, the fact that some major move was under way could no longer be concealed from the Axis powers. The Italian naval command correctly guessed that Algeria must be the Allied target, but they were overruled by the Germans, who first estimated that the convoys were going to southern France, and then that they were headed for Crete, for Tripoli, or possibly for the relief of Malta. Axis forces—submarine, surface, and air—concentrated in the straits of Sicily, leaving the Allied transports largely unmolested. One American transport was torpedoed by a German aircraft off the African coast, but most of its personnel arrived safely, if tardily, at their destination after a long voyage in landing craft and an escort vessel. Otherwise the Eastern Naval Task Force arrived off Algiers without incident.

A massive array of naval strength supported the Mediterranean landings. The Royal Navy's Force H, based at Gibraltar, acted as a covering force. Consisting at this time of three battleships, a battle cruiser, two fleet aircraft carriers, and lighter vessels, Force H was to guard the amphibious forces from intervention by the Italian navy or by the Vichy French fleet based at Toulon. The Support Force of the Eastern Naval Attack Force consisted of three light cruisers, two escort carriers, three antiaircraft cruisers, a monitor, 13 destroyers, and 17 smaller warships. Directed from a British "headquarters ship," prototype of the later American amphibious command ship (AGC), the Support Force had the tasks of protecting the amphibious forces from air and submarine attack and from shore bombardment, and of providing tactical support for Allied troops while landing and ashore. Only 10,000 troops of the 33,000-man landing force were American, but because of the known French bias against the British, the major ground units were placed under American commanders so that the invasion would appear to be primarily American.

The plan for the capture of Algiers, capital of Algeria and best port on the Barbary Coast, called for simultaneous landings on three flanking beach areas and, as at Safi, a raid by two destroyers to seize port facilities and shipping in the harbor. In a relatively quiet and almost tideless sea, troops began to transfer to landing craft scheduled to hit the beaches at about 0100, November 8. Luckily for the invaders, there was no immediate opposition, for the troops and naval personnel assigned to this assault had had little opportunity for training in amphibious techniques. Hence the ship-to-shore movement to some of the Algerian beaches was even more confused and behind schedule than at any of the Moroccan landings. In one sector battalions were intermingled and scattered for miles along the coast. Nevertheless the landing forces managed to form up and push rapidly inland toward their objectives. Thanks to the activities of pro-Allied officers, many French troops, including the garrisons of two important airfields, surrendered without resistance. The swift Allied advance soon turned the operation into more of an occupation than a campaign, for only the coastal forts east of Algiers offered serious opposition.

Meanwhile two British destroyers had failed in their attempt to seize the port to prevent sabotage of facilities. Confused by darkness and strange waters in the early hours of November 8, the *Broke* and *Malcolm* missed the narrow harbor entrance on their first try. In their second, the *Malcolm* was so severely holed by shore batteries that she was forced to retire. The *Broke* however crashed through the boom, reached a quay, and landed her troops, who were quickly pinned down by small arms fire and captured. The *Broke* managed to escape, but she was so badly damaged that she later sank under tow.

Luckily for the Allies an early cease-fire at Algiers yielded them the port intact. Radio orders to stop resisting issued in the name of General Giraud had produced no effect. During the day however Robert Murphy succeeded in persuading Admiral Darlan to authorize the French commanding general to negotiate a truce. An oral armistice was reached at 1840, November 8, and an hour and 20 minutes later the Americans formally took over control of Algiers. Two days later Darlan, with Marshal Pétain's secret concurrence, ordered a cease-fire for all French units in Africa.*

It was well for the Anglo-Americans that the French were ready to quit. As D-day progressed, the weather worsened so rapidly that by 1800 all further support landings had to be canceled. By that time also, poor boat handling had cost the Eastern Naval Task Force 90 per cent of its landing craft. So few reinforcements and so little material had been unloaded that the situation ashore might have become desperate had French resistance continued. But Murphy's diplomatic triumph permitted the completion of the unloading of troops and supplies in the port of Algiers itself and paved the way for the launching of the Allied drive into Tunisia.

* The Marshal sent his approval by secret code. Officially and publicly however he was obliged to order French forces in Africa to continue resistance.

Algeria: Oran

The most powerful of the Allied attacks was that made at Oran by the Center Task Force. Because French feeling had been inflamed there by the British attack on the French fleet at nearby Mers-el-Kebir in July 1940, the planners allotted to this assault the best-trained American units available, the 1st Infantry Division and half of the 1st Armored Division, the latter including two armored combat teams with light and medium tanks and tank destroyers. For the same reason no British ground troops were assigned to the operation, although units of the Royal Navy screened and escorted the transports. The Center Naval Task Force included a battleship, a large carrier, two escort carriers, an antiaircraft cruiser, 13 destroyers, more than a score of smaller warships, and transports carrying a landing force of 39,000 troops, nearly all American. The plan was almost identical to that for Algiers. Simultaneous landings were to be made at two beaches west of the city, and—the major effort—on a stretch of coast east of the city adjoining and including the small port of Arzew. Two converted United States Coast Guard cutters, given to Great Britain earlier in the war, would carry raiders into the port of Oran to seize harbor facilities and prevent sabotage. Airfields behind the city were to be quickly seized so that planes could be flown in from the airstrip at Gibraltar.

At Oran the transports debarked the troops smoothly and with little confusion into their landing craft shortly before midnight of November 7–8. Coming ashore between 0100 and 0130, the troops were much less scattered than in the other landings. They moved out quickly toward their assigned objectives. Sporadic and ineffective resistance was offered at Arzew, where infantry and a naval raiding party were able to seize intact four small ships and 13 French seaplanes fueled and loaded with torpedoes. The landings west of Oran were unopposed. Three shallow-draft tankers fitted to discharge tanks on the beach, prototypes of the LST, performed brilliantly, setting ashore armored units that rushed ahead of the main attack to seize an important airfield and vital road junctions on the plateau behind the city.

Satisfaction over the success of the Oran landings was tempered by the disaster that had overtaken the ex-United States Coast Guard cutters filled with raiders attempting to enter Oran harbor. At higher command levels there had been a serious dispute over the feasibility and timing of this strike scheduled for H-hour plus two. Objectors had pointed out that the defenses were very strong and that the long, narrow harbor was a trap. The only possible hope for success was either to effect complete surprise simultaneously with the landings on the beaches, or to wait until army troops had already entered the city before closing in on the docks. By entering the harbor two hours after the first attack on the beaches, the raiders had encountered alert defenses and forfeited support from other Allied units. The *Walney*, in the lead, bulled her way through a boom blocking the harbor entrance, only to be raked by point-blank fire from two French destroyers and a torpedo boat. Staggering to the head of the harbor, she blew up and sank with 75 per cent casualties among her sailors and troops. The *Hartland* gallantly followed her sister craft with no better luck. As she attempted to round a quay, she was taken under fire at 100-foot range by a French destroyer. Losing power, the cutter drifted away, shattered and burning. Half her personnel were mowed down when, forced topside by fires raging in every deck, they were exposed to machine gun fire from all quarters. The ship was abandoned and all survivors were captured. When the city was seized by advancing army troops, they found the harbor clogged with sunken merchant shipping and small warships, the result of French demolitions. Again the French navy had offered strong resistance, upholding its honor with a tragic loss of lives and ships. The ill-fated raiding force, as at Algiers, had gallantly but totally failed in its mission. Valor could not overcome the disadvantages of a faulty plan.

Although cut off from all support, the French garrison in Oran hung on for another day. But it was unable to check the American infantry and armored units from crashing into the heart of the city on the morning of November 10. When Admiral Darlan gave orders during the afternoon for all French troops to cease fighting, organized resistance at Oran had already ended. In marked contrast to the other landings, the landing craft here had been better handled with lower losses. With the help of the port of Arzew, the supply buildup was ample to sustain the fighting. Reflecting their better training, the soldiers had shown more skill and dash than in the other African attacks.

Tunisia

With Morocco and Algeria secure, the Allies had valuable rear base areas, but Tunisia, separated from Europe by the 90-mile-wide Sicilian Channel, was their real strategic goal. The Germans moved swiftly to keep Tunisia out of Allied hands. By 1130 on D-day, November 8, the Nazis had forced the Vichy cabinet to accept their offer of air support from Sicily and Sardinia. "This caitiff decision," as Churchill branded it, "enabled the Germans to take the quick decisive action of occupying airfields in Tunisia, with all its costly consequences on our campaign." Then the Germans took over unoccupied France and attempted to gain possession of the Toulon fleet. Meanwhile Admiral Darlan, now fully committed to the Allies, was doing all he could to bring French forces and territory over from Vichy allegiance. He ordered the Toulon fleet to sortie to North Africa with the aid of British warships that stood by to offer help, but Admiral Laborde, the Vichy commander at Toulon, preferred neutrality, trusting a Hitler promise that Germany would never try to seize the ships. When the Nazis violated their word and broke into Toulon, Admiral Laborde settled the issue by scuttling his fleet.

Darlan sent orders to Admiral Estéva, senior French officer in Tunisia, for his forces to rally to the Allies, but German planes were already landing on Tunisian airfields. Except for an army contingent under General Barré that withdrew into the hills, French Tunisian forces that might have joined the Allies were quickly rounded up and disarmed. British troops joined the pro-Allied French troops on the Algeria-Tunisia border on November 12, but several thousand German paratroops landing in Tunisia the following day made it apparent that the Allies could look forward to no easy victory. There was consolation however in the information that Dakar and French West Africa had joined the Allied cause on November 23 and that Rommel was fleeing westward with the British Eighth Army in close pursuit.

Hitler's decision to hold what he could of North Africa proved foolish in the long run, for the six-month campaign that followed was far more costly to the Germans than to the Allies. But at the end of the year, heavy rains in Tunisia had mired the Allies so badly that they pulled their forces back to better defensive positions, while out in the desert the advance of Montgomery's Eighth Army was delayed until supplies could catch up with him. Despite temporary setbacks, caused largely by inexperienced personnel—the Army's counterpart of the Navy's landing craft troubles—General Eisenhower was able to get the offensive rolling again in the spring, even though by then nearly 200,000 German and Italian reinforcements and great quantities of Axis supplies had reached Africa. While the Allied forces out of Algeria drove east, with General Patton's armored divisions distinguishing themselves, the British Eighth Army fought its way north through the fortified Mareth Line. Rommel, broken in health, was ordered home by Hitler. On April 7, 1943 Eighth Army and American patrols met, having crossed 2,000 miles of Africa between them, and by May 13 the Tunisian campaign was over. Some 275,000 Axis prisoners of war were taken. Allied air, surface, and submarine forces had sunk 433,000 tons of Axis shipping. Only a few Axis troops escaped across the straits to Sicily. The first British trans-Mediterranean convoy since 1941 left Gibraltar on May 17 and reached Alexandria on May 26 without loss. Reeling back from the Russian offensive at Stalingrad and driven out of Africa, the Nazis had an early foretaste of ultimate disaster.

The Casablanca Conference

Though at the end of 1942 it was not clear that the Axis had lost its capability of retrieving the initiative, strategic planning could not wait for the military situation to clarify. It was imperative that the Allied leaders get together and coordinate plans. Stalin could not leave Russia just as the Stalingrad campaign was reaching a climax, but Roosevelt and Churchill with their chiefs of staff met at Casablanca from January 14 to 23, 1943 to review the entire strategy of the war.

The main question before the Casablanca Conference was: What next? Since there had been no firm combined planning beyond the decision to seize the North African coastline, the British and Americans had to decide what further moves, if any, should be made in the Mediterranean theater once Tunis was secured.

General Marshall and the other United States Chiefs of Staff still hoped soon to direct all resources into a single, all-out cross-Channel attack somewhere in France, preferably in Normandy. If logistic difficulties made this impossible in 1943, as many American staff planners had at length concluded, then Marshall hoped that the Allies might pin down German troops by seizing the Brittany peninsula in western France. Against this view the British planners, armed with a host of statistics, were able to put up a convincing argument. They pointed out that the Germans could have 44 divisions in France by mid-1943 to oppose an Anglo-American landing, which by that time could muster no more than 25 divisions. Until the odds could be significantly bettered in favor of the Allies, the British believed that an assault on the coast of France could lead only to defeat in that area, and another costly, humiliating ejection from the Continent.

The British were willing to invade France—but only after the German forces there had been considerably weakened. For the time being, the British planners insisted, the best way of achieving that goal, and also of assisting the Russians, was through a continuation of peripheral strategy. Diversionary attacks from the Mediterranean into Southern Europe, said they, would draw so many German units from France and from the Eastern Front that in those areas Hitler would be 55 divisions short of the total needed to defend his empire.

Continued peripheral operations in the Mediterranean theater, the planners continued, could knock Italy out of the war and possibly bring in the Turks. If all this occurred, Hitler would face defeat—even without a cross-Channel attack. But assuming that such an attack was to be carried out, the landing in France would have a far greater chance for success if the Germans were first weakened in the West by attacks elsewhere.

Though the American Joint Chiefs were not entirely convinced by the British logic, they could find no valid counter argument. They disliked seeing more Allied forces sucked into the Mediterranean, which they considered strategically eccentric to the main objective. However, one fact stood out—the British were unwilling to risk returning to France in 1943, and without full British concurrence and cooperation there could be no cross-Channel attack. After much discussion, during which Admiral

King was able to present the case for stepping up the war with Japan by a series of limited offensives, the two Allies struck a bargain. The British desired to see the war in the Pacific limited to a holding operation until Germany was defeated; then all available Allied force would be turned against Japan. They abandoned that position and consented to allocate more men and materials to the Pacific, thereby enabling the Americans to retain the initiative they had won in that theater. The Americans, for their part, consented to postpone the cross-Channel attack till 1944. Meanwhile enemy strength in Europe would be diverted and pressure maintained by means of a Mediterranean offensive in the summer of 1943. Air attacks against the heart of Germany and the *Luftwaffe* would be stepped up. Everyone agreed that the Allies must give top priority to the antisubmarine war. Otherwise no offensives anywhere could succeed.

The remainder of the conference was devoted to finding an appropriate place to strike in the Mediterranean. In the end the planners considered two possibilities, the islands of Sicily and Sardinia. Sardinia was the more weakly defended of the two and would provide bomber bases for raids on the industrial centers of northern Italy, but the island lacked a harbor adequate to mount a major amphibious assault. On the other hand, capture of Sicily, although much more difficult, would more directly threaten Italy, possibly forcing her out of the war, would definitely secure the Sicilian Channel, and would offer the prospect of destroying more enemy forces. Sicily was therefore named the target, D-day being fixed for an appropriate time in July 1943. On this note of resolve and harmony the Casablanca Conference ended.

The day following the close of the Casablanca Conference, President Roosevelt startled statesmen and military leaders around the world by announcing to the press a policy that he himself had formulated, with the concurrence of Prime Minister Churchill. This was the decision that the United States and Britain would accept nothing short of "unconditional surrender" of Germany, Italy, and Japan. Terms would neither be offered nor considered. Not even Napoleon at the height of his conquests ever so completely closed the door to negotiation. To adopt such an inflexible policy was bad enough; to announce it publicly was worse.

The policy of Unconditional Surrender ran counter to the earlier insistence of British and American leaders that they were fighting not the people but the leaders who had misled them. The policy was the sort of mistake that statesmen of the 17th and 18th centuries never made. They understood better than some of their successors that today's enemy might be needed as tomorrow's ally. And a war pushed to the point of complete victory might ruin victor as well as vanquished.

5

Operations against Sicily and Italy

Following the successful landings in French Morocco and Algeria, United States warships withdrew from the Mediterranean, leaving Allied operations in those waters to the Royal Navy. Vice Admiral Hewitt returned to the United States to resume his regular duty as Commander Amphibious Force Atlantic Fleet (Comphiblant). The U.S. Navy remained responsible in North Africa only for the Moroccan Sea Frontier, including the port of Casablanca and the air base at Port Lyautey, and the port of Oran, including Mers-el-Kebir.

With the Allied decision to invade Sicily it became necessary for United States naval forces, personnel, and material to return to the North African theater of operations. In February 1943 Admiral Hewitt was relieved as Comphiblant by Rear Admiral Alan G. Kirk and proceeded to North Africa to assume command of all U.S. naval forces and operations in that area as Commander United States Naval Forces Northwest African Waters. In mid-March Hewitt's command was designated U.S. Eighth Fleet. For the rest of the war the Eighth Fleet included all United States naval forces in the Mediterranean. Operationally it was subordinate to Lieutenant General Dwight D. Eisenhower, the Supreme Allied Commander, through Admiral of the Fleet Sir Andrew B. Cunningham, Commander in Chief Mediterranean. Administratively, it was directly under Admiral King as Commander in Chief U.S. Fleet. In other words, Hewitt received his military orders from Eisenhower but drew his ships, men, and material from King. It was the immediate responsibility of Hewitt and his staff to carry out the naval planning for the American phase of the invasion of Sicily.

Code-named Operation HUSKY, the Sicilian invasion was planned and executed as an operation in itself, a limited objective. The Allied chiefs proposed to invade Sicily and then see what happened before assigning further Mediterranean targets. Several benefits were expected to result, stated by Churchill as: (1) making Mediterranean communications more secure, (2) diverting German pressure from the Russian front, and (3) intensifying the pressure on Italy.

Churchill and the British Chiefs of Staff hoped that the fall of Sicily would lead to the collapse of the Mussolini government and the withdrawal of Italy from the war, thus opening the way to the Allies for further Mediterranean ventures. They also anticipated that the ensuing disaster to Axis arms might cause the Turks to abandon neutrality and enter the conflict against the Axis. Though the American Joint Chiefs of Staff were less enthusiastic, they admitted that Allied forces assigned to the European theater could not be kept idle until an invasion of France became possible in 1944, and that Sicily was the obvious target. All Allied leaders agreed that seizing a foothold on national territory of the Axis would bring a tremendous morale boost to the western Allies.

The military leaders who successfully concluded the Tunisian campaign continued in command of the Sicilian expedition. Eisenhower received four-star rank to assume over-all command of Operation HUSKY. His deputy, General Sir Harold R. Alexander, controlled all ground troops; naval forces again served under Fleet Admiral Cunningham; and Air Chief Marshal Sir Arthur W. Tedder commanded the Allied air forces. Ground forces assigned to the assault included the American Seventh Army (Lieutenant General Patton) and the British Eighth Army (Lieutenant General Montgomery). The naval assault forces were the Western Naval Task Force (Vice Admiral Hewitt) and the Eastern Naval Task Force (Vice Admiral Sir Bertram Ramsay). Under Vice Admiral Sir Algernon V. Willis, an all-British Covering Force of 6 battleships, 2 fleet carriers, 6 light cruisers, and 24 destroyers would protect both landing forces against possible incursions of the Italian fleet.

Sicily: Planning and Preparations

Planning the Sicilian landings proved a long and complicated process. There was little opportunity for Eisenhower's top commanders to confer in order to iron out snarls. Headquarters of the commands were scattered across North Africa, far distant from each other. Moreover Alexander, Patton, Montgomery, and other senior officers were preoccupied with concluding the Tunisian campaign and could at first give Sicily scant attention.

Reconciling the strategic and tactical requirements of the various service arms vexed planning even worse. Everybody agreed that the ultimate tactical object was to seize the Straits of Messina as soon as possible. The main enemy supply artery would then be cut and Italo-German forces trapped before they could withdraw to the Italian mainland. But simply sailing in to land within the Straits was not considered feasible, because beaches therein lay beyond the range of effective Allied fighter cover. The only landing sites where adequate land-based air support could be provided lay in the southeast corner of Sicily between the cities of Licata and Syracuse. In this area Allied fighters from Malta, Gozo, Pantelleria, and the Cape Bon peninsula could effectively break up Axis air attacks. Yet this conclusion far from settled the matter. In the Licata-Syracuse region there were but three ports, of which only Syracuse had any considerable tonnage capacity. Both army and navy planners feared that the quantity of supplies that might be handled through these ports and across the beaches could not sustain the number of divisions necessary to defeat the enemy's garrison in Sicily. The best compromise appeared to be to seize beachheads in the part of Sicily that could be covered by fighters, developing airfields to extend fighter cover, and then to land a few days later on beaches near the major ports of Palermo and Catania.

No one really liked this complicated plan of successive assaults. Generals Alexander and Montgomery flatly rejected it on the ground that enemy reinforcements might penetrate between the widely dispersed Allied armies. Army commanders demanded a single, massed assault in the region of Sicily that could be covered by Allied fighters, a requirement that naval commanders considered impossible to fulfill logistically.

In the nick of time two developments in amphibious technology broke the deadlock in planning. With the arrival of numerous newly built LST's and hundreds of DUKW's (amphibious cargo-carrying trucks, known also as ducks or amtrucks), naval staff planners concluded that the army attack could just barely be supplied across the southeast Sicilian beaches with the help of the few available ports. Early in May General Eisenhower approved the new plan for a mass assault.

D-day was set for July 10, 1943, H-hour at 0245. The date and hour were selected to provide moonlight for paratroop drops, with the moon setting in time for the assault waves to close the beaches in total darkness. Because the selected H-hour exposed the fleet to a moonlight approach, navy planners suggested a later approach with landings after dawn, preceded by naval gunfire to neutralize beach defenses. The army planners discarded the suggestion, holding that ship-to-shore movement in darkness was necessary for surprise and insisting that naval gunfire would be ineffective because it was "not designed for land bombardment."

Admiral Hewitt's Western Naval Task Force, organized into three components codenamed *Joss, Dime,* and *Cent,* was to seize a beachhead incorporating the small ports of Licata and Gela and the fishing village of Scoglitti, along a 37-mile front on the Gulf of Gela. Subdividing into four groups, Admiral Ramsay's Eastern Naval Task Force was to seize the Pachino peninsula and an area along the Gulf of Noto just outside the coastal defenses of Syracuse. The landing front was tremendously wide, nearly 100 miles—the most extensive landing of any in World War

II. In numbers also the actual assault phase was the most powerful of the war, not equaled even by the assault on Normandy a year later. More than 470,000 troops, about half American and half British, were assigned to the initial landings. Staging through every available North African port from Bizerte westward, American forces embarked in a vast armada of 580 ships and beaching craft, carrying 1,124 landing craft. Staging from the Eastern Mediterranean and Tunisia, the British used 818 ships and beaching craft, including the vessels of the Covering Force, and 715 landing craft.

A serious defect in the preparations resulted from lack of cooperation of the Allied Air Forces because of a then irreconcilable difference of opinion regarding the employment of tactical air power. The Air Forces were addicted to their doctrine of "sealing off the beachhead" by blasting enemy communications so that there could be little or no movement into or out of the beachhead areas. Meanwhile attacks would be made on enemy airfields to ensure that air interference with the landings would be slight. The Air Forces believed that their technique would obviate the necessity of close tactical support available on call from ground observers on ships or shore. Hence they did not participate in the joint planning and forbade pilots to answer calls for support from ship-based or ground stations other than those approved by Air Force Headquarters in North Africa.

The Allied armies and navies mistrusted the effectiveness of this air doctrine. They wanted the kind of support that had been furnished off Casablanca by U.S. aircraft carrier *Ranger* and that was to become routine in Pacific operations. But Air Marshal Tedder had his way. Although a tactical air force was assigned to support the landings, it was to be controlled from North Africa with no assurance of priority to army-navy requests for aid. To fill the gap General Patton wanted aircraft carriers assigned to the assault forces to fly immediate strikes on call. But Admiral Hewitt felt that this could not really be justified in view of the great demand for carriers elsewhere and the presence of abundant land-based Allied air power from bases within easy range of the beachheads. The attack therefore proceeded without a firm air plan known to all the commanders. At best, air support would be slow; at worst, nonexistent.

Since no one wished to risk repeating the disasters that followed the attacks within the ports of Oran and Algiers, no forces were earmarked to land directly within enemy harbors. But British Commandos and American Rangers were to neutralize key enemy installations, and elements of two divisions of paratroops were to land before H-hour to seize vital airfields and bridges.

Because Sicily was such an obvious Allied objective, extensive efforts were made to convince the enemy that the main attack would come in Greece, with a secondary assault on Sardinia. The most dramatic was the dropping of a carefully prepared corpse into the sea off the Spanish coast to wash ashore near Cadiz. "Major William Martin," as the corpse was called, had a briefcase filled with choice misinformation that quickly fell into the hands of German agents. Local German and Italian commanders were not fooled, but Hitler and the German High Command were, with the result that German armored divisions and Axis mine and torpedo craft were moved to both Sardinia and Greece, where they contributed nothing to the defenses of Sicily. Slow Italian minelayers, left to mine Sicilian waters, did not lay enough mines to prove any serious obstacle.

Training for the Sicilian campaign was much more thorough than had been possible for the North African operation. As the new LST's, LCT's, and LCI's arrived in the theater, they were rushed into training maneuvers in virtually all ports, large and small, on the North African coastline.°
While troops exercised with the crews of the new LCVP's in landing through the surf, shore parties practiced forwarding supplies, evacuating wounded, directing gunfire, and the myriad other tasks that are part of an amphibious assault. Most of the assault divisions managed to stage reasonably realistic rehearsals with their task forces on a divisional or near-divisional scale. While possibly no commander thought his particular unit had received enough training, by prior standards Hewitt's and Ramsay's task forces were well prepared.

A combination of beach gradient and surf in the tideless Mediterranean had caused the formation along the coasts of Sicily and elsewhere of "false beaches," sand bars a hundred yards or so offshore over which water shoaled too much to permit the passage of such large beaching craft as LST's.

The landing craft and bases command, under Rear Admiral Richard L. Conolly usn, resolved this problem during training in Africa by developing pontoon causeways, standard pontoon units shackled together to form a bridge to shore. It also proved feasible to "marry" LCT's to the larger LST's so that a sort of ferry service could be run between the LST's anchored offshore and the beach. Both methods worked; both were vital to the successful supplying of the Seventh and Eighth armies after the initial landings.

While the Allied forces prepared, so did the Axis. The Italian fleet remained the best weapon against the landings, for if it could evade the powerful British Covering Force it might play havoc with the assault convoys. But since Axis commanders could not know where or when the Allied blow would fall, their chance of achieving the necessary surprise

---

° The LST (Landing Ship, Tank), the LCT (Landing Craft, Tank), and the LCI (Landing Craft, Infantry) were *beaching craft,* permitting a shore-to-shore expedition by transporting men, vehicles, and supplies from one beach to another. The LCVP (Landing Craft, Vehicle and Personnel) and the LCM (Landing Craft, Mechanized) were smaller *landing craft,* generally carried aboard transports to make ship-to-ship landings.

for a successful naval counterattack was slight. Moreover the Italian *Supermarina,* citing lack of adequate fighter cover, forbade fleet operations within easy Allied air attack range in the waters around Sicily. The defending Axis commanders accordingly pinned their hopes on a successful ground and air defense. Air attacks and resistance by seven Italian coastal divisions were expected to pin the Allies to the beaches, while counterattacks by four Italian and two German mobile divisions were supposed to fling the attackers into the sea. Unwisely Mussolini refused Hitler's offer of three more German divisions. While coastal defenses around all the major ports were strengthened, anti-invasion exercises were held at Gela, for here both the Germans and the Italians expected an Allied landing. Mobile forces were billeted in strategic locations, and some 350,000 troops, including more than 50,000 Germans, awaited attack by the 470,000 Allied invaders.

To participants in the concurrent Pacific war, the odds, considering numbers only, would have appeared to favor the defenders overwhelmingly. In the New Georgia campaign, which roughly coincided with the Sicilian campaign, nearly 34,000 Americans spent six weeks wresting a small corner of New Georgia Island from about 8,000 Japanese defenders. In the Pacific, the Allies rarely undertook an assault without at least a 3-to-1 numerical superiority, and often the odds were far in excess of that. Yet, though air and surface support for Allied assaults against defended positions in the Pacific theater became increasingly powerful, the invaders could generally expect stout resistance. The Japanese would retreat only from an utterly hopeless situation. Few would surrender. If the retreat were cut off, they usually fought to the last man. To military men acquainted with that sort of war, the Allied plan to invade Sicily with only a slight numerical advantage over the defenders would have seemed an invitation to disaster.

But Sicily was a hollow shell. Poor deployment of defense forces, with little provision for defense in depth, was one reason. The main reason however lay in the attitude of the Italians. The Sicilian reservists, to whom Mussolini had entrusted the defense of their homeland, detested the Germans and were far from being ardent Fascists. The Sicilians, together with most of their compatriots on the Italian mainland, saw clearly that the war into which their government had led them was not likely to serve Italian interests. They regarded their military situation as hopeless and rather welcomed an Allied invasion that would take them out of the war and the hated Germans out of Italy.

As D-day approached, Air Chief Marshal Tedder's Mediterranean Allied Air Forces launched a series of raids that put all but a few airfields in Sicily out of operation and forced the Germans and Italians to base their remaining planes on the Italian mainland. And, though Tedder's planes failed to win complete control of the air over the target area, they badly disrupted the Sicilian transport system, and further reduced the already low morale of the Italian forces.

To the last, Mussolini and Field Marshal Albert Kesselring, the German army commander in Italy, remained confident that the invaders would be destroyed "at the water's edge," but General Guzzoni, the Italian commander in Sicily, knew his men and was less optimistic.

Sicily: Assault and Follow-Up

On July 8, 1943, the jam-packed North African harbors emptied as the huge Allied invasion fleet stood out to sea. Routed so as to make it appear that Greece and Sardinia rather than Sicily were the targets, the convoys passed safely through the extensive Allied mine fields, and in due course turned toward their departure points off Malta.

The weather was calm, and there had been no enemy air attacks. By the morning of July 9 however, the confidence that reigned in the Malta headquarters of General Eisenhower and Admiral Cunningham changed to anxiety as the seas made up steeply in a howling wind. Soon the beaching craft were plunging heavily through rough seas, and even the large transports were taking green water over their bows. Trusting to the aerologist's reports that the wind would die down by the morning of D-day, Admirals Hewitt and Ramsay decided to let their task forces continue. After painful reflection, the commanders at Malta decided not to interfere. Navigation became intensely difficult as lighter craft, especially the LCT's, were slowed by the storm. Nevertheless the general pattern of the approach was maintained. Remarkably close to schedule the assault ships closed their assigned beaches, marked by British beacon submarines that blinked signals seaward.

Admiral Hewitt's Western Task Force concentrated its attacks on three groups of beaches in the Gulf of Gela. The western flank at Licata was assigned to the *Joss* force, the center at Gela to the *Dime* force, and the eastern flank at Scoglitti to the *Cent* force. All was quiet as the transports and the troop-carrying LST's anchored in position. Ashore, fires blazed here and there from Allied bombings, and occasional distant gunfire marked areas where paratroops, dropped earlier in the night, were harassing the enemy. Scout boats stealthily closed the shore, some putting men on the beach to determine exact landing points for the infantry. This proved no easy matter, for the smoke-shrouded hills looming in the darkness offered poor landmarks. Yet it was crucially important to place the troops on the right beaches lest the entire pattern of the attack be disrupted.

On the transports, organized confusion reigned as the ships rolled heavily in the aftermath of the storm. Rail loading the LCVP's that were to carry in the first assault waves was difficult, even impossible for some

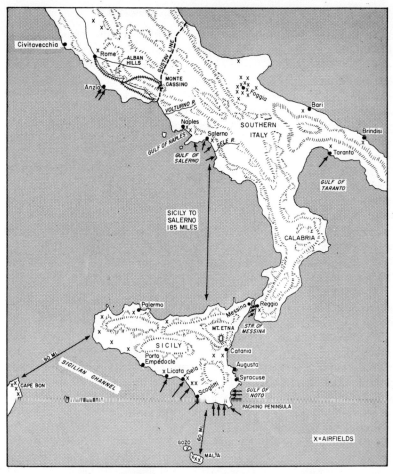

ALLIED OPERATIONS AGAINST SICILY AND ITALY

transports, so that for the most part the troops were obliged to clamber down the spray-drenched nets into the pitching small craft. Rocket-firing support boats suffered heavily; many were too damaged in launching to be able to participate. At Scoglitti, to which *Cent* force was lifted entirely in large transports that had steamed from Chesapeake Bay, the rolling of the ships so delayed launching that H-hour had to be postponed an hour. But from the *Joss* and *Dime* forces, waves of LCVP's circled until all their numbers had joined up and then, guided by minesweepers and submarine chasers, moved to the line of departure about 2,000 yards offshore.

Quiet still reigned as the first waves, on signal and guided by blinking lights from the scout boats, began the run from the line of departure to the shore. Admiral Hewitt, supporting the suggestion of the navy planners, had pleaded with the army to be allowed to deliver a dawn pre-invasion bombardment before the infantry hit the beach. But the army commanders, hoping to slip the men ashore in darkness before the enemy realized what was happening, refused. The best Hewitt could get was permission for supporting destroyers, gunboats, and rocket-firing craft to open fire if reaction from the shore indicated that the assault waves had been discovered.

It soon became obvious that tactical surprise was lost. Searchlights flashed across the water from the dark shore, picking up the LCVP's. With a distant crackle enemy machine guns opened up. When artillery shells began to raise geysers in the water, the supporting craft at last opened fire. Meanwhile the infantrymen, tense, seasick in the pitching assault boats, awaited the end of their seagoing ordeal. As the boats touched down and the bow ramps fell, they hesitated momentarily, then rushed ashore, forgetting nausea, scurrying inland to locate and consolidate their assigned positions.

Enemy fire was heaviest at Licata. Here a group of LCI's, scheduled to land behind a first wave of LCVP's that were to clear the beach defenses ahead of them, instead found themselves the lead wave. In the darkness, the smaller craft had headed for another part of the beach. The LCI's, pressing in despite fierce enemy fire from automatic weapons, established fire ascendancy with their own guns and landed their troops.

Enemy fire gradually lessened on all beaches as the invaders rapidly overran enemy pill boxes and gun emplacements, or as supporting destroyers and gunboats blasted hostile positions one by one. For several hours enemy shells fell sporadically on the various American landing areas, but by 0800 most enemy artillery was silent. The Americans climbed the hills toward their D-day initial lines well ahead of schedule. United States Rangers rushed into Licata and Gela—too late at the latter to prevent the dynamiting of an important pier earmarked for unloading. Except for some delays and scattering of troops on the wrong beaches as a result of difficulties of night navigation in landing craft, the landing had proceeded smoothly and more or less according to plan. Ground resistance was light, the Italians defenders happily surrendering at every opportunity.

With the initial beachhead secured, air attacks and unloading problems became Admiral Hewitt's principal worries. Of these, the air attacks proved the easier to deal with. A heavy volume of antiaircraft fire greeted the numerous flights that the Axis air forces placed over the ships, forcing the aviators to bomb inaccurately and indiscriminately. Use for the first time in the theater of proximity-fused (VT) antiaircraft shells greatly increased the effectiveness of defensive fire. Hewitt's ship losses were a destroyer, an LST loaded with badly needed anti-tank artillery, and an ammunition ship in a follow-up convoy.

The false beaches badly hampered off-loading supplies on D-day, preventing LST's from landing vehicles directly on shore. Pontoon causeways proved hard to rig in the heavy weather, and the number of available components was scanty. Clearing of supplies from smaller craft, LCT's, LCVP's, and LCM's, while more efficiently done than in North Africa, remained a troublesome bottleneck at Gela and Scoglitti. Poor beach exits through soft sand and the inefficiency of the army shore engineers caused material to pile up at the water's edge. Loaded landing craft frequently had to return to their ships.

Fortunately for the invaders, the use of DUKW's mitigated D-day supply difficulties. Launched from LST's or transports, these ingenious vehicles could carry ashore the army's standard 105 mm. artillery piece or three tons of other supplies. Several hundred DUKW's expedited unloading and rushed supplies inland to army dumps. But the DUKW could not carry a tank or heavy truck. Getting these ashore continued to plague landing officers until sufficient causeways and LCT's were available to clear transports and LST's of heavy equipment. After D-day, matters vastly improved as Hewitt's forces shifted unloading to better beaches—those at Scoglitti were abandoned altogether—and the ports of Gela and Licata finally became available for the use of LST's.

The temporary shortage of tanks, anti-tank guns, and tank destroyers on D-day and the morning following enabled the navy to make its most spectacular contribution to the success of the Sicilian operations—and incidentally to convince some skeptical army commanders of the value of naval gunfire against shore targets. General Guzzoni, as soon as he received news of the Allied landings, ordered counterattacks on Gela by armored forces. These attacks proved the most serious threat the Seventh Army encountered in Sicily. Patton, and the army in general, now learned in dramatic fashion the value of coordinated, carefully directed naval gunfire. At about 0900 on D-day U.S. cruiser *Boise* and two destroyers, aided by seaplane spotting, checked and turned back a group of Italian tanks closing in on Gela. The next day the *Boise* gave a front-row repeat performance for General Patton. Going ashore that morning, Patton found the beachhead menaced by an advance of about 60 tanks spearheading the German section of Guzzoni's attack. From the top of a building in Gela, Patton could clearly see the 30-ton Panther tanks advancing across the flat plain, with no anti-tank artillery between them and the beaches. A young naval ensign nearby with a walkie-talkie radio inquired of Patton if he could help, and received an emphatic "Sure!" whereupon the ensign radioed *Boise* the location of the enemy. The resulting shower of 38 six-inch shells, together with fire from newly-arrived divisional artillery, halted the German advance. Throughout the rest of the day, Hewitt's ships continued to batter retreating enemy tanks, infantry, and targets of opportunity.

Naval gunfire might have been even more effective had it been possible to have better air spotting. As the fighting progressed, ground observers were sometimes blinded by smoke from burning wheatfields and buildings and were always limited in their fields of observation. SOC float planes from the cruisers, sitting ducks for Messerschmitt fighters that the Nazis sent over the beachhead, were all too quickly shot down, though while they lasted they performed well in spotting targets. Fast fighters of the type used by Tedder's air forces, though clearly needed, were not available in Sicily.

The failure of the Air Forces to participate in joint planning now resulted in the most publicized disaster of the campaign. American paratroops had dropped behind Gela before the landings. Another drop from 144 transport planes was scheduled for the night of July 11–12. No one in the Western Task Force learned of this in time to get the flight routed away from the ships or to notify all antiaircraft crews. When the planes came over, their arrival coincided with the tail end of an enemy air raid. Through faulty identification, 23 of the Allied transports were shot down by antiaircraft guns on shore and in the task force. Two nights later another flight of transports was similarly handled over the British task force when eleven planes were downed by friendly fire.

Admiral Ramsay's Eastern Task Force, landing British troops on the Pachino Peninsula and in the Gulf of Noto in order to capture Syracuse, experienced conditions similar to those at the American landings. Rough seas hampered the swinging out and launching of assault boats. And although the British were somewhat more protected from the gale than the Americans, the problems of boat handling at the eastern beaches were formidable, and the waves of landing craft were mostly behind schedule. Fortunately for the invaders, enemy fire here was light, and in one area surprise, on which the Allied armies placed such high value, was so complete that Montgomery's troops caught the crew of an Italian fieldpiece fast asleep. Such batteries as opened fire were quickly silenced by Allied warships or by the rapidly advancing assault forces. Large numbers of Italian coastal troops actually stampeded in their eagerness to surrender. By the end of D-day the Eighth Army had not only made up lost time but was well ahead of schedule.

The British, because they were closer to enemy airfields in southern Italy than the Americans, suffered more severely from air attack. But the relatively new technique of ground-based fighter-director control of covering aircraft proved itself in this area, helping break up numerous raids. Admiral Cunningham, vividly recalling the savage bombing of his fleet at Crete two years earlier, found it little short of incredible that Allied naval forces could now remain off the enemy coast with near impunity.

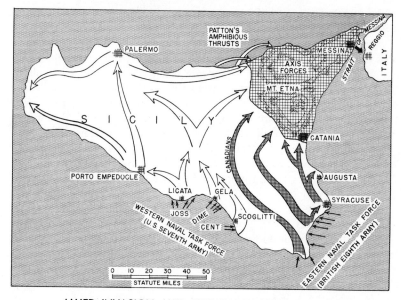

ALLIED INVASION AND AXIS EVACUATION OF SICILY

The most spectacular success of the Eighth Army attack was the speedy capture of Syracuse. A company of Montgomery's paratroopers jumped to seize a key bridge by which the port is approached from the south, and held it against everything the defenders could send against them during D-day. That evening the 19 survivors of the heroic 73 who held the bridge were relieved by the vanguard of Montgomery's army coming up from the south. That night the British occupied Syracuse without a struggle. When nearby Augusta fell a few days later, the Allies possessed two of Sicily's best ports. Though many beaching craft were still employed in running supply shuttles from Africa, they of course found it much easier to discharge in captured ports. In Sicily, more than in most places, the worst port proved better for bringing in supplies than the best beach.

Sicily: The Axis Evacuation

The Allies hoped to capture most of the Axis forces in Sicily by entrapping them somewhere west of Mt. Etna in a great pincers movement. While Patton's Seventh Army swept northward across the interior of the island and then advanced eastward along the north coast, Montgomery's Eighth Army was to drive north along the east coast to capture Messina and cut the escape route to Italy across the Straits of Messina.

The Seventh Army carried out its part of the double envelopment

with breathtaking speed. Two regiments advanced west along the southern coast and on July 16 captured Porto Empédocle, thereby acquiring
a good port for supplying an advance to the north. In the Empédocle
area the Americans at last found Italians who would fight, but nevertheless captured 6,000 of them. Advancing north across Sicily, elements of
the Seventh Army in four days marched more than a hundred miles by
road to enter Palermo on the north coast on July 22. Here they were
greeted by crowds shouting "Down with Mussolini!" and "Long live
America!" By the 24th all western Sicily was in American hands, and
Patton was advancing along the north coast toward Messina, accompanied
by U.S. light cruisers *Savannah, Philadelphia,* and *Boise* and several destroyers to provide gunfire support and by beaching and landing craft to
bring forward supplies.

Meanwhile the other arm of the pincers, Montgomery's Eighth Army,
was stalled short of Catania on the east coast. To avoid having to make
a costly frontal assault on this enemy strong point, Montgomery decided
to leave the coast and strike inland, around west of Mt. Etna. Redeploy-
ing his forces for this change of front took until August 1. When the
Eighth Army again began moving, it made slow progress in the rugged
terrain at the base of the mountain, where minor defense forces could
harass and delay much stronger attacking columns. Patton's Seventh
Army, advancing in the interior and along the north coast, had by this
time also lost momentum. The Allied armies were now in fact in line
abreast on a front stretching from the north coast across the northeast
tip of Sicily to Catania on the east coast. Patton three times employed
his accompanying naval forces to land troops behind the enemy lines.
No enemy troops were entrapped by these amphibious thrusts, but the
first two, each in battalion strength, expedited the Axis withdrawal. The
third, in regimental strength, fell short of the now rapidly retreating
enemy. Admiral Cunningham, in a complimentary message to Admiral
Hewitt, characterized the naval support that Patton had received as "a
model of the effective application of sea power in the support of land
operations."

On the other hand, Cunningham complained that "No use was made
by the Eighth Army of amphibious opportunities." Certainly Montgomery
failed in his assigned task of cutting off the Axis at Messina. Patton
actually got there ahead of him, but not in time. On July 17 the Axis
forces in Sicily had received orders to fight a delaying action and then
to evacuate the island. Because the Eighth Army was nearer Messina
than the Seventh, elite Axis units, mostly German, had been sent to the
Etna area to hold Montgomery, while the rest of the Axis forces in Sicily
headed north and east for the Straits of Messina, rotating clockwise like
a swinging door with its hinge on Mt. Etna. The Seventh Army's early
advance, for all its speed, was not so swift as the Axis withdrawal. By

August 3 the German and Italian forces were in the northeast tip of Sicily holding back the Allied attack, and the Axis evacuation across the Straits of Messina had begun.

High level bombing by the Allied Air Force did little damage to the ferries, motor rafts, motor barges, and other Axis craft crossing and re-crossing the three-mile-wide Straits loaded with troops and equipment. Dive bombing was suicidal in the face of massed Axis antiaircraft fire. A few British motor torpedo boats penetrated the Straits but achieved little. The Allies were unwilling to risk larger naval craft against the formidable shore batteries that the enemy had assembled. By August 17 about 45,000 German and more than 60,000 Italian troops had made good their escape with most of their equipment.

Sicily: Conclusions

Some postwar military commentators, particularly among the Germans, have expressed the opinion that an initial assault in or near the Straits of Messina would have been feasible. A successful landing here, while the defenders were deployed to contest a landing elsewhere, would have bottled up Axis forces in Sicily as they had been bottled up in Tunisia. But after the landings in Northwest Africa, Allied commanders in the European theater made it a set policy never to stage an amphibious assault beyond the radius of land-based fighter support—a wise decision, as experience proved. Carrier air, which in the Pacific proved fully able to fill the gap, was not in sufficient quantity in the Mediterranean. American fleet carriers were all in the Pacific. Escort carriers, still in short supply, were busy in the Atlantic combating the U-boat. There were never enough British fleet carriers, and these carried so few planes and of such inferior quality that they could do little more than provide air cover for the naval forces to which they were attached.

Despite the successful Axis evacuation, the Sicilian campaign was a major triumph for the Allies. Even before the campaign was over, the Axis coalition had begun to fall apart. In Italy the discouraging news from Sicily, climaxed by a 560-plane raid on Rome itself, finally prompted the King to make the popular move of deposing Mussolini and taking him into "protective custody." Marshal Pietro Badoglio, the new head of government, announced that he would continue the war against the Allies, a pronouncement that nobody took very seriously. Hitler considered rushing in enough German troops from Russia to seize Italy with an immediate *coup d'état*, but conditions on the Russian front forbade it. The most he could do for the time being was to accept the change of government, while moving additional German divisions into Italy from France and Germany.

With less than five per cent Allied casualties (7,800 killed, 14,000 wounded), Operation Husky in just over a month's time had achieved most of the objectives set forth at the Casablanca Conference. Allied Mediterranean communications were now completely secure. Italy seemed certain to collapse. Italian troops, no longer reliable, would have to be replaced in Italy, France, Yugoslavia, Greece, and elsewhere by German troops. On the Russian front, German pressure, especially from the *Luftwaffe,* was somewhat relieved. The way was laid open for further Allied attacks against which the Nazis had to prepare by further deploying their forces. British hopes that Turkey would enter the conflict were not realized, for the Turks insisted that they were not yet ready. But the Sicilian success greatly reinforced the Allied position in the eyes of neutral nations. Soon Germany would be fighting alone against heavy odds.

Italy: Planning and Preparations

In May 1943, just as the Tunisian campaign was ending, Roosevelt and Churchill and the Combined Chiefs of Staff had met again, this time in Washington. Here they once more threshed over differences of opinion regarding the proper strategy for defeating Germany. The British advocated the invasion of Italy as the inevitable next step after Sicily. Their planners estimated that an Allied cross-Channel attack could succeed only if German forces in France were reduced to no more than 12 divisions. The surest way of attaining such a reduction, they argued, was to eliminate Italy from the war, for then the Nazis would have to send their own troops to replace 24 Italian divisions in the Balkans. An invasion of Italy moreover would enable the Allies to seize the complex of airfields about Foggia to strengthen the coming bombing offensive against Germany.

The Americans acknowledged the cogency of the British argument but reaffirmed their opinion that Germany could be defeated only by an invasion of western Europe. A campaign in Italy, they pointed out, would tie up Allied as well as German forces and thus might further delay the cross-Channel attack. General Sir Alan Brooke, Chief of the Imperial General Staff, then expressed the opinion that the invasion of France in any event would not be feasible before 1945 or 1946. If so, replied General Marshall, the Allies ought to stop planning for an operation that was continually being postponed, and the Americans should shift their main force to the Pacific, where it could be used at once.

Evidently, if the Allies were to adhere to their plan of putting the primary emphasis upon defeating Germany, they would have to reach another compromise. Being reasonable men, they succeeded—though the details were not all spelled out until some time after the actual conference had ended. The Americans agreed to the invasion of Italy, with the important proviso that only the forces already in the Mediterranean should be used—less seven divisions that were to be withdrawn to the United Kingdom as a nucleus for building up the cross-Channel attack force, and a portion of the assault shipping for operations against Burma. The British, for their part, committed themselves definitely to an invasion of France, with May 1, 1944 as the target date. They agreed that the general conduct of the war in the Pacific should be left to the American Joint Chiefs of Staff. They also accepted in principle the Joint Chiefs' "Strategic Plan for the Defeat of Japan," a remarkable document which we shall consider in a later chapter. They insisted however that the "Strategic Plan" be carried out with forces already assigned to the Pacific theater. Thus Allied operations against both Italy and Japan were to be limited in order to build up forces in the United Kingdom to 29 divisions for operations against Western Europe.

Since the team of Eisenhower, Alexander, Cunningham, and Tedder was to be retained, it fell upon their staffs to begin planning the invasion of Italy on the eve of the Sicilian assault. Despite pressure from Churchill, Eisenhower refused to make a firm commitment regarding the Italian operation until he had tested the strength of the enemy in Sicily. However, within a week after the launching of Operation HUSKY, Allied prospects were sufficiently bright for Eisenhower's planners to begin considering when and where Italy should be invaded.

The success of HUSKY shocked Kesselring and other German continental strategists out of their conviction that the Mediterranean was a moat to their fortress. Viewing it now as a highway open to Allied exploitation by the use of sea power, they fully anticipated an early Allied invasion of Italy. Some German planners estimated that the Anglo-American forces might land as far north as Rome, possibly even at Leghorn or Spezia. In anticipation of a northern landing, the Germans made provisions to withdraw their forces rapidly beyond the Apennines to avoid having them trapped in the Italian boot.

But the Allied military leaders had no intention of invading beyond the range of their land-based fighter support. Original plans called only for an invasion via the toe of the boot. The final plan, authorized July 26, was for Montgomery's Eighth Army to cross the Messina Strait to Reggio as soon as feasible after the end of the Sicilian campaign. The invasion of the Italian toe was however to be now considered chiefly a diversionary attack, to draw the Germans away from the main assault. This was to be in the Gulf of Salerno, at the extreme attack radius of Sicily-based Spitfire fighters equipped with extra, droppable fuel tanks. Landing at Salerno on September 9, 1943, the newly formed Fifth Army under Lieutenant General Mark W. Clark USA was to drive for Naples 35 miles away.

What the Badoglio government wanted was merely to shift sides, to join Britain and the United States in an alliance against Germany without the humiliation of a formal surrender. But Roosevelt and Churchill, recalling the disapproving public reaction in their countries to the "Darlan deal" in North Africa, did not care to treat the Italians like returning prodigals. Besides, the President and the Prime Minister were inhibited by their own formula of "unconditional surrender." After lengthy and melodramatic secret negotiations reminiscent of spy fiction, a bargain was struck. Italy would surrender and get out of the war, the effective date to coincide with the landing at Salerno. From that date Italian troops who followed the Badoglio government would fight the Germans rather than the Allies. The Italian Fleet and Air Force were to proceed to designated points and place themselves under Allied control. Thus a major purpose of the Salerno and Reggio landings was fulfilled before the attacks began.

Because German troops continued to pour into Italy, Badoglio requested that the main Allied landing be made north of Rome, with an airborne division to be dropped on Rome itself. He promised to have Italian troops in place to join the Allied forces both near the beachhead and near Rome. Eisenhower favored the Badoglio plan, but uncertainty, shortage of forces, and lack of trust between the negotiating parties brought the project to nought. The Allies continued with their plan to land at Salerno, and did not risk informing an erstwhile enemy where the landing was to be. Hence the Italians were unable to assist the invaders in any way.

Meanwhile preparations for the Salerno operation were proceeding under circumstances even more trying than those for Sicily. For this assault Admiral Hewitt was to command all the Allied amphibious forces. These were divided into a primarily British Northern Attack Force carrying two divisions, and an American Southern Attack Force of equal strength. Two more divisions in floating reserve would follow up. Twenty-six transports, 120 LST's, and 90 LCT's prepared to land troops on two groups of beaches about eight miles apart in the Gulf of Salerno. The landings were to be supported by seven cruisers (including three American), two monitors, and 35 destroyers and a Support Carrier Force of five escort carriers and ten destroyers. The Royal Navy provided a Covering Force of four battleships, the fleet carriers *Illustrious* and *Formidable,* and 20 destroyers. The Covering Force, in addition to fending off surface attack, was assigned the task of providing combat air patrol for the Support Carrier Force.

The immediate targets were the port and town of Salerno, the Montecorvino airfield, and the passes through the hills leading to Naples. These objectives were assigned to British forces and to United States Rangers. American forces, to the south, would cover their flank, add depth and body to the beachhead, and link up with Montgomery's Eighth Army coming up from Reggio. The chances of the Eighth Army's being able to join hands with the Salerno beachhead were considerably lessened however by Montgomery's demands for massive artillery support to cover his crossing of the Straits of Messina. Fulfilling his demands took until September 3, and then the Eighth Army finally crossed virtually unopposed.

As the landing site, Salerno had both good and bad features. Readily identifiable mountain peaks behind the beaches offered excellent guides to the assault forces, but the mountains also provided superb sites for observation, defensive gun emplacements, and staging areas for counterattacks. The beaches, with better gradients and fewer offshore bars than those at Sicily, were suitable in some places for LST's to beach directly at the shore. On the other hand, the Gulf of Salerno was readily mined, and Allied intelligence learned belatedly that mines were sown there in abundance. Hence extensive minesweeping would have to precede the ship-to-shore movement. That meant that the transports were obliged initially to put their troops into landing craft nine to twelve miles from the beaches, and it required a complete rescheduling of the intricate landing plan.

Arrangements for air support over Salerno were superior to those for Sicily. The presence of the escort carriers in direct support would prove an immense advantage. Moreover Eisenhower demanded that the air forces cooperate more closely with the army and the navy. Admiral Hewitt now had his flag in the *Ancon*, an amphibious command ship (AGC), converted from a passenger-cargo vessel and equipped with elaborate radio and radar gear. Aboard the *Ancon* an air force general headed a fighter-director team, and there were two standby fighter-director ships. Air spotting for naval gunfire support was improved by the use of high performance army P-51's flown by pilots trained by naval aviators.

In other respects the planning for Salerno was less efficient than that for Sicily. Because the planners had great difficulty getting from the high command firm commitments for men and material, changes were being made on the landing plan even after the departure for the beachhead. Such apparent indecision was exasperating to the force commanders, who could not know that an important reason was the highly-secret peace negotiations, of which no more than a dozen men were informed. There were other reasons for last-minute changes. Priority for certain equipment had to be given to the Eighth Army, slowly working its way up the toe of the Italian boot. And while the Salerno task force was en route, several gunfire support cruisers, including U.S.S. *Boise*, were detached to join a force under Admiral Cunningham that would occupy the great naval base at Taranto when the Italian fleet steamed out to surrender under the terms of the armistice.

Again, as before Husky, the Army insisted that the landing be made in darkness and without pre-landing naval bombardment. Admiral Hewitt once more argued in vain against this plan. Complete surprise, he contended, was impossible, and in darkness confusion was inevitable. The *Luftwaffe* had already twice raided Bizerte, and these were no mere blind stabs, for Bizerte was the chief assembly point for beaching craft. Enemy reconnaissance planes would undoubtedly detect the assault forces en route to the beachhead. In any event, the Axis high command must have noted Salerno as a likely invasion point, for it was the key to Naples, Italy's finest port, and it was just within extreme operational radius of fighter planes based on Sicily. The army commanders remained unmoved, arguing that though the enemy might suspect Salerno, a little surprise was better than no surprise at all. A bombardment, they said, would be a dead giveaway, attracting additional German forces to the beachhead without achieving important destruction of enemy defenses. As a result of the Army's decision, there was no gunfire preparation at Salerno, and, in the American sector, not even any supporting fire as the assault waves closed the beach.

The Germans were in fact already at Salerno in division strength. As we have seen, when the German high command suspected that the Badoglio government was negotiating with the Allies, they lost no time dispatching divisions to take over Italy. By the time of the Salerno assault there were eight German divisions in northern Italy under Field Marshal Erwin Rommel, and eight in central and southern Italy under Field Marshal Albert Kesselring. Kesselring had organized southern Italy for defense against Allied landings. Lacking the strength to check Montgomery's advance from Reggio, he settled for a delaying action by two of his divisions, distributing the rest to protect Rome and the Naples area. Suspecting that the Allies would land at Salerno, for the reasons adduced by Hewitt, he ordered thither the bulk of the 16th Panzer Division and a regiment of paratroops to dig in at and behind the landing areas. The Germans arrived at Salerno in time to mine and wire the beaches, to mine the Gulf, to emplace guns in positions from the hills right down to the water, and to deploy tanks for counterattack. Kesselring also drew up plans for moving other German divisions rapidly to Salerno. Everything possible was done to make the region a hornet's nest for the Allied invaders. There was a real possibility that the Germans might be able to throw the Allied forces into the sea at the outset, or at least that they might reinforce their troops more rapidly than the Allies and thus be able to counterattack effectively a few days later.

Only one serious flaw marred Kesselring's preparations. His superiors declined to commit additional forces near Naples. Influenced by Rommel, Hitler originally intended to withdraw German forces north of Rome. It was only through Kesselring's persuasion that he agreed to make any stand at all in the south. Rommel, who understood sea warfare better than most of Hitler's generals, saw clearly enough that the Mediterranean was no barrier to naval power. The Italian coasts were standing invitations to the Allies to outflank and cut off any German forces in the Italian boot. The Apennines, on the contrary, as they swing across northern Italy from the Adriatic Sea to the Gulf of Genoa, form a barrier where relatively few defenders can hold the line against strong attacking forces. Hitler, taking the advice of both Rommel and Kesselring, but the full advice of neither, straddled the issue. He ordered Kesselring to make a stand in southern Italy but gave him insufficient troops to defend Salerno and Naples.

Various elements of the Salerno assault forces departed Oran, Algiers, Bizerte, and Tripoli between September 3 and 6. These joined other elements from Palermo and Termini north of Sicily, and on September 8 (D minus 1) shaped course for the Gulf of Salerno. During the approach, the task force came under attack by German aircraft that sank an LCT and damaged several other vessels.

At 1830 on September 8, as the Allied attack forces were approaching the Gulf, General Eisenhower broadcast a radio announcement of the Italian armistice. Badoglio confirmed the news in a broadcast from Rome. Then he and the King fled to Brindisi, leaving no one in authority in the capital. To the Germans the announcement was the signal to execute their carefully planned Operation ACHSE for disarming the Italians and taking over control of all Italian administration and communications. This they speedily accomplished against weak resistance. Only the Italian fleet and some of the air force units were able to escape. Most of the disarmed Italian troops simply vanished, blending into the civilian population. Mussolini, rescued by the Germans, was put at the head of a puppet government in northern Italy.

The Salerno-bound Fifth Army greeted Eisenhower's announcement with jubilation—and the conviction that the war was over. Senior officers found it difficult to convince the troops that, although the Italians had quit fighting, there were plenty of Germans to offer resistance.

Salerno: Assault and Follow-Up

For once the approaching Allied assault forces were enjoying perfect weather. There would be no problems of heavy surf at Salerno. Aboard the transports and beaching craft the troops stirred restlessly in the heat, but lulled by the erroneous belief that only surrendering Italians would greet them, they displayed little of the anxiety that had been prevalent at Sicily.

At midnight the transports carrying American forces were in position off the southern sector of the Gulf of Salerno, and minesweepers advanced to clear channels to the shore. Scout boats, using radar fixes from extinct volcanoes looming dimly in the distance, closed the shore, located their assigned beaches, and blinked signals seaward. Rail-loaded LCVP's

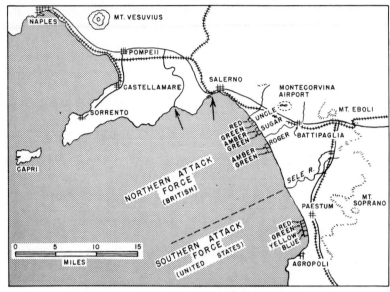

INVASION OF ITALY (SALERNO), SEPTEMBER 9, 1943

splashed into the water, then cast off to begin seemingly interminable circling until their waves had joined. That completed, they opened throttles and raced through darkness to the line of departure 6,000 yards offshore. From here, on signal, they headed for the beach. Tension grew as seasickness overcame many of the troops. Crews in the scout boats heard clanking and clattering and saw headlights ashore as German motorized troops moved to the water's edge to contest the landing. In this sector however the defenders chose to withhold their fire. Suddenly at H-hour, 0330, as the first wave of landing craft neared the beach, a loudspeaker ashore blared in English, "Come on in and give up! We have you covered!"

Despite the shock of realizing that they had a fight on their hands, the assault troops rushed resolutely ashore as, just at first light, the ramps of the landing craft slammed down. At that moment the quiet was succeeded by pandemonium. The German defenders at last opened up with rifle, machine gun, mortar, cannon, and tank fire, and German aircraft came sweeping over the beaches bombing and strafing. The troops of the first assault waves by-passed enemy strong points to gather in prearranged assembly areas. Then came DUKW's bringing ashore howitzers and ammunition. Thus armed, the invaders dueled German tanks and infantry at point-blank ranges. Landing and beaching craft pressed through heavy fire to land reinforcements. Sailors, struggling with pontoons, managed to rig causeways for landing tanks while shells slapped the water around them. By afternoon, though some individual beaches were completely interdicted by enemy fire, the Americans had seized a precarious hold on their sector of the beachhead.

In the British sector, to the north, the Germans inadvertently did the invaders a favor by opening fire on LST's before they could anchor in position to launch their LCVP's. That automatically canceled the Army's restriction against pre-landing naval fire support. Rear Admiral Richard L. Conolly USN, commanding an amphibious group in this sector, had forehandedly prepared for such an opportunity by ordering three destroyers into position a mile off the beach. These now opened fire against shore installations. Rocket-firing beaching craft supported the first assault wave as it headed for the beach. Despite this support, the first wave, landing precisely at 0330, met strong resistance, and beaching craft advancing to land ammunition and equipment suffered heavy damage from shell hits. Except on the extreme left flank, where American Rangers and British Commandos landed against little or no opposition and quickly pushed to the defiles in the hills, the pattern of combat was much the same in the northern sector as in the southern. Though by the end of D-day the Fifth Army had occupied all the designated beaches, the beachhead area in both sectors was still dangerously thin.

The beachhead, such as it was, had been saved by supporting warships. On call from shore fire control parties or using spotting aircraft, the light cruisers *Philadelphia* and *Savannah,* a British monitor, and four destroyers off the American beaches repeatedly silenced mobile enemy batteries, knocked out machine gun positions, and dispersed concentrations of enemy infantry and tanks. Three British cruisers and a monitor off the northern beaches, unable to establish dependable communication with their shore fire control parties, achieved little on D-day; but six destroyers and three beaching craft successfully took over the whole support role in this area, at times approaching so close to the shore as to come under enemy rifle fire. By the end of the day, Hewitt's ships had expended many hundreds of rounds on dozens of call-fire missions, and not a few rounds without benefit of ground or air spot.

As soon as the Germans realized the crucial role played by the supporting warships, they shifted the weight of their air attack to these vessels. Although their sorties were fewer than at Sicily, they were more effective. High altitude bombers introduced a radio-controlled glide bomb, released from great heights when German fighter-bombers had drawn down the Allied air cover. On September 11 one of the glide bombs ripped through the *Savannah,* blowing out a section of her bottom and forcing her to retire for repairs. Two days later the British cruiser *Uganda* suffered a similar fate. But U.S.S. *Boise,* having completed her part in the Taranto operation, was en route to Salerno, and Admiral Cunningham ordered two more British light cruisers up from Malta.

Meanwhile the *Philadelphia* was proving not only the most effective but the luckiest gunnery ship in Hewitt's force. Repeatedly near-missed by both conventional and glide bombs, sometimes by a matter of feet, she escaped severe damage and expended almost all of her ammunition on shore targets. The best defense against the glide bomb proved to be smoke. Even a fairly light smoke haze over the roadstead served to confuse the German radio operators who controlled the bombs.

By September 12 Clark's Fifth Army had somewhat enlarged its beachhead, but at the center it had not yet reached its assigned D-day line. On the 12th the supporting escort carriers were forced to retire to Palermo for refueling, first sending their aircraft ashore—not to the Montecorvino airport, which though in Allied hands was still under enemy fire, but to emergency airstrips hastily constructed within the beachhead. By now elements of five German divisions had reached the Salerno area and had massed 600 tanks and mobile guns for an all-out attack down the Sele River, the dividing line between the Allied sectors. The German strategy was to split the Fifth Army, concentrating first on one sector and then on the other.

This crisis came on September 13–14. As the German attack gained momentum, the Allied situation became so critical that General Clark asked Admiral Hewitt to prepare plans for evacuating either the northern or the southern Allied force and relanding it with the other. At Clark's request a division of paratroops was flown up from Sicily and dropped at Salerno at night. To avoid a repetition of the tragedy over Sicily, when paratroops were shot down by friendly fire, all antiaircraft guns in the Allied fleet and army were silenced. Meanwhile General Eisenhower ordered Marshal Tedder to support the Fifth Army with every available plane.

The German attempt to break through to the beach was defeated primarily by naval gunfire support, but also by the Fifth Army's hard fighting, by improved Allied air support, and by two faulty German decisions—one tactical, the other strategic. In the afternoon of the 13th, the local German commander ordered his main body of tanks to drive down the Sele toward a fork in the river and gain access to the beach across a bridge shown on German maps. But the bridge had already been destroyed, and the road that led to it was flanked by drainage ditches that prevented the tanks from deploying. When the absence of the bridge stopped the German tank column, the Americans, having noted the German movement, were ready with infantry and two battalions of well-sited artillery. The tank force, trapped in the narrow road, was destroyed. This setback ended the most promising attack the Germans were able to make. The fact was that Kesselring lacked the means to match the Allied rate of reinforcement. Two more German divisions during the first week of the invasion might well have thrown the Allies into the sea. But

Rommel, regarding the southern campaign as useless, refused to release any troops from northern Italy.

As Kesselring's forces renewed their attack on the 14th, the Allied cruisers and destroyers closed in to hammer tank columns and assembly points. The *Philadelphia* and *Boise* each expended several hundred rounds of 6-inch shell on all types of targets. As other ships, including the British battleships *Valiant* and *Warspite,* rushed to the Salerno area to assist, it became apparent that the tide had turned—though the venerable *Warspite* soon became the third victim of German glide bombs and had to be towed away.

On September 16, advance elements of the Eighth Army at last made contact with the Fifth Army. That same day Kesselring, concluding that his attempt to recapture the beachhead was proving too costly, decided to abandon Salerno and Naples and withdraw to a prepared defense line behind the Volturno River. "On 16 September," he afterward wrote, "in order to evade the effective shelling from warships I authorized a disengagement from the coastal front. . . ."

As the Nazis withdrew, they demolished the harbor of Naples and did what they could to wreck the city—not only to delay the Allies and add to their logistic problems but also to wreak vengeance on the turncoat Italians. But the Allied navies, by opening the port of Salerno and performing near-miracles in supplying the army across the Salerno beaches, enabled Clark's Fifth Army to enter Naples on October 1, 1943. That concluded the Salerno operation, which had cost the Allies 2,100 killed, 4,100 missing, and 7,400 wounded.

Montgomery's Eighth Army meanwhile had occupied the Foggia airdrome near the Adriatic coast and pushed on to the northwest. On October 6 the two Allied armies abreast reached the Volturno. There the new battle line formed while both sides brought up reinforcements for the next round. The Navy's salvage experts, who had cleared the wreckage from harbors in North Africa and Sicily, had already set to work to restore Naples as the principal Allied port in Italy. Despite the German demolitions, Naples was soon receiving tonnage in excess of its peacetime capacity.

Most of the Italian fleet was now in Allied hands. On September 9 three new battleships, six cruisers, and ten destroyers had fled from Genoa and Spezia to give themselves up, as required by the terms of the armistice. Pounced upon off Sardinia by German bombers, the battleship *Roma,* fleet flagship, was sunk by a glide bomb with the loss of 1,400 lives. The rest of the force, and the older battleships from Taranto, proceeded to their destinations without being further molested. On September 11 Admiral Cunningham signaled the British Admiralty, "Be pleased to inform Their Lordships that the Italian Battle Fleet now lies under the guns of the fortress of Malta."

Stalemate at Anzio

The invasion of the Italian mainland yielded disappointingly small dividends to the British and Americans. A few extra German divisions were tied down, and the Allies had gained additional combat experience, but even the value of the bomber base at Foggia proved to be largely negated by the barrier of the Alps. The Allies found themselves engaged in a major land campaign of minor strategic importance in a secondary theater of operations. Further advances would have to be conducted through terrain and weather that heavily favored the defense.

For the Germans the Volturno line was only a temporary stand, to be held while they prepared still stronger defenses farther up the Italian boot. Through October and the first two weeks of November, they fought rear-guard actions as they backed off to their Winter Line, 40 miles northwest of Naples. This line, a system of carefully prepared defense positions on the mountain slopes, they intended to hold as long as possible. Northern and central Italy were now securely under Nazi domination, and Marshal Kesselring, left in command of all German forces in Italy by Rommel's departure for France, could count on 19 German divisions to hold the 14 that the Allied Fifth and Eighth Armies assembled for an all-out attack on the Winter Line.

In seeking a means of breaking the Nazi defense barrier, Generals Eisenhower, Alexander, and Clark had already initiated planning for an end-run landing behind the Winter Line in the vicinity of Rome. Their purpose was to cut the enemy's main lines of communication and to threaten his rear. Much the best beaches for attaining the first of these objectives were at Anzio. Anzio was 37 miles southeast of Rome and 20 miles south of the Alban Hills (*Colli Laziali*), which dominated roads and railroads leading from Rome down to the German defense line.

But beaching craft and landing craft were now leaving the Mediterranean for Britain in such numbers that only a single-division assault on the Italian coast could be mounted. Hence the Anzio assault was planned to follow the opening of the drive against the main German defenses. Only if this drive were sufficiently successful for the Fifth Army and the landing force to be mutually supporting would the landing be undertaken. Eisenhower in fact stipulated that the Allied armies advancing up the boot must have reached a position where they could expect to join the Anzio amphibious force within 48 hours after the landing, for with the shipping now at his disposal he could not be certain of supplying the beachhead much beyond that length of time.

Montgomery's Eighth Army began its advance against the Winter Line on November 28, 1943. Clark's Fifth Army started two days later. Both quickly bogged down in the face of stiff German resistance and almost continual rain that sapped the strength of the invaders and turned dirt roads into quagmires. Three weeks after the opening of the drive, the Allied armies had not advanced ten miles, and the right flank of the new German Gustav Line was firmly anchored on Monte Cassino, nearly 75 miles from Anzio. The end-run project was clearly infeasible. On December 22, Alexander, on Clark's recommendation and with Eisenhower's concurrence, canceled the Anzio operation.

At this point Churchill intervened personally. Meeting with the leading Allied commanders at Tunis on Christmas Day 1943, the Prime Minister insisted that the Anzio project be revived. The end-run must be made moreover without waiting to see if a renewed attack on the German line would succeed. Whether or not the Anzio attack was successful in cutting the German supply lines, it could not fail, said Churchill, to divert strength from the Gustav Line. He conceded however that in the circumstances a one-division assault would be too risky. But cancellation of a planned operation against the Andaman Islands in the Bay of Bengal had released 15 LSI's (Landing Ships, Infantry) for use in the Mediterranean. And at Churchill's request President Roosevelt permitted 56 LST's to remain a little longer in the Mediterranean, with two important provisos: that the cross-Channel attack remain the paramount operation, and that Churchill drop his insistence upon further peripheral operations to be directed against Rhodes and the Aegean Islands.* Enough beaching craft and their associated landing craft were thus made available for a two-division assault on Anzio. That was enough for Churchill. He brushed aside objections by Eisenhower and others that even two divisions were insufficient for what would amount to an independent attack. Eisenhower in any event was about to leave the theater to prepare for the cross-Channel assault, which he was to command. His successor as Supreme Allied Commander Mediterranean, Sir Henry Maitland Wilson, accepted the risk of a two-division landing at Anzio. So did General Alexander. D-day was set at January 20, 1944. Drawn from the Fifth Army and earmarked for the assault were the United States 3rd Division, the British 1st Infantry Division, three battalions of Rangers, two battalions of Commandos, and a regiment of paratroops.

Ground forces for the Anzio attack were to be commanded by Major General John P. Lucas USA, naval forces by Rear Admiral Frank J. Lowry USN, Commander VIII Amphibious Force, U.S. Eighth Fleet. To meet

---

* At the Teheran Conference the preceding November Churchill had stated that a major purpose of the operations he proposed against the German-held islands in the Aegean area was to open up a shorter, more easily defensible supply line to Russia—the main objective, be it noted, of his Dardanelles-Gallipoli campaign of World War I. Another purpose, said he, was to provide Turkey with air support as a further inducement to enter the war on the Allied side. Churchill hoped that the Turks might be influenced to attack German forces in the Balkans. If not, the Allies would at least be able to operate from airfields in Turkey, whence, among other targets, they could strike at the Ploesti oil fields in Romania, on which the Germans were heavily dependent.

the early invasion date, army and naval staffs immediately went to work and by all-out effort had plans completed and approved by January 12, ten days before D-day, which at General Lucas's request had been postponed to January 22. Meanwhile the Eighth Army prepared to apply pressure on its sector of the Gustav Line in order to keep the Germans from transferring any of the defending troops elsewhere, and on January 17 the Fifth Army renewed its attack on Cassino both in order to attract German reserves that might be used against Anzio and in the hope of breaking the Gustav Line loose from its anchor. The Allied Air Forces began "sealing off the beachhead" by means of intensive raids on roads, railroads, bridges, and enemy airfields, and on January 19 reported that they had succeeded in their mission.

With misgivings about the strength of the coming assault heightened by a dismayingly poor landing rehearsal in the Gulf of Salerno, the Anzio forces left Naples on January 21, advancing by a roundabout 110-mile route to deceive the enemy. LST's, LCI's and LCT's formed the bulk of the troop lift, with numerous LCVP's aboard to boat the first assault waves. Careful reconnaissance revealed that only weak enemy forces manned the beach defenses. Rocket-firing beaching craft were to lay down a barrage a few minutes before the LCVP's touched down, primarily to detonate the mines on the beaches.

In contrast to the disorderly rehearsal, there followed one of the smoothest landings of the entire war. Lowry's forces hit the beaches exactly at H-hour, 0200, and quickly solved the problems caused by enemy mines and the confusion inevitable in night landings. Enemy resistance at the beach was slight. For once Allied assault forces had attained real surprise, and a night landing without preparatory naval fire had paid off. For three nights before the assault, Kesselring, vaguely aware that something was afoot, had ordered an alert against enemy landings at any of several points, including Anzio. But on the night of January 21–22 he had let his staff persuade him to discontinue the alert in order to rest the men. Once aware of his error, he rushed mobile guns and numerous battalions of troops toward Anzio over roads, railroads, and bridges that had been quickly repaired following the Allied air attack. The beachhead had not been "sealed off" after all. Nor had the Fifth Army attack on Cassino succeeded; there the Germans still held. Nevertheless the end of D-day saw 36,000 Allied troops ashore at Anzio, with fewer than 150 casualties. Despite a severe storm on D-day plus 4, nearly 70,000 men, more than 25,000 tons of supplies, 500 guns, and 237 tanks crossed the beaches in the first week of the attack. Lucas and Lowry's task was to keep them there; Kesselring's was to contain them and push them out.

General Lucas had two choices: to advance before consolidating, or to consolidate before advancing. If he advanced at once to the Alban Hills, his guns could block traffic to the Gustav Line before the Germans could bring up their forces in strength. Such a move would carry out the main intent of the original Anzio plan, but it would invite a German counterthrust that might cut Lucas's communications with the coast. General Clark, recognizing this danger, had ordered General Lucas only to seize and secure a beachhead and to "advance on" the Alban Hills, deliberately ambiguous phrasing that left Lucas considerable freedom of action. Interpreting his orders conservatively, Lucas chose to pause and consolidate his beachhead, throwing up strong defenses before pressing inland.

The Anzio landings had thrown the Germans into panic, causing them temporarily to evacuate Rome. But Lucas's cautious course enabled them to re-estimate the situation, and allowed Kesselring time to augment the German defenses. The delayed Allied attack failed to break through to the Alban Hills, but the German counterattack stalled in the face of Allied defenses, reinforcements, and naval gunfire. The end result was a stalemate. "I had hoped," said Churchill, "that we were hurling a wildcat onto the shore, but all we got was a stranded whale." The initial assault, as Eisenhower and other officers had foreseen, was too weak to carry out its mission, and the reinforcements came too late to do anything but save the beachhead. Lucas cannot be blamed for making the choice he did. The basic cause of failure was shortage of beaching and landing craft.

The saving of the beachhead was in itself something of a miracle. With naval forces and shipping at first considered barely adequate to lift, supply, and support the original two divisions, Admiral Lowry managed to evacuate most of the civilian population and ultimately to keep seven divisions supplied. The solution to the supply problem was the introduction of a system first worked out by the U.S. Seventh Fleet in the Pacific. Trucks and DUKW's were preloaded in Naples, driven aboard LST's, carried overnight to Anzio, and there driven directly to supply dumps. Through this means an LST that usually required a full day to unload could be emptied in an hour. By early February a regular ferry service had been established. Each day a convoy of six LST's left Naples carrying 1,500 tons of supplies preloaded in 300 trucks. Each week 15 LCT's made the run from Naples to Anzio. Every ten days four Liberty ships arrived at the beachhead with supplies from Naples or North Africa. Meanwhile the fleet, despite bad weather, fire from heavy German guns that rimmed the beachhead, enemy dive and glide bombs, and U-boat attacks, continued to support the forces ashore and to maintain their overwater line of supply. In the process it suffered its roughest handling up to that time in the Mediterranean. The British lost two cruisers, three destroyers, four beaching craft, and a hospital ship; the Americans, a minesweeper, a minecraft, six beaching craft, and two Liberty ships. Damage to vessels, particularly from aircraft, was widespread.

The miserable Italian stalemate lasted until mid-May 1944. Nothing much was accomplished by either opponent on either front. It soon became clear that the Fifth Army, instead of achieving a double envelopment of the enemy, had merely split into two segments, while the Germans, enjoying the advantages of the interior position, were able to shift forces rapidly as needed between the Anzio beachhead and the Gustav Line. In March 90,200 Americans and 35,500 British were packed into a beachhead surrounded by 135,000 Germans with well-sited guns up to 280 mm. that were able to reach every part of the beachhead and the roadstead. German shelling, sporadic by day, was stepped up after dark. During the night the invaders could also expect from one to half a dozen air raids. Allied headquarters at Anzio were established underground in a wine cellar. Wherever possible the troops also sought underground shelter, but the continual rains so raised the ground water level that most foxholes and dugouts soon filled. Hundreds of thousands of sandbags were used to build crude shelters on the surface. In such conditions the men passed week after week, constant targets for enemy fire. It is not surprising that of the 59,000 casualties suffered by the Allied forces at Anzio, nearly a third were from disease, exhaustion, and neuroses. Of the rest, 5,000 were killed in action and 17,000 wounded.

As the rains ceased and the roads hardened with the advance of spring, the Allies prepared to infuse new vigor into their attacks on the Gustav Line. By May they had 27 divisions in action in Italy—seven at Anzio, the rest opposite the main German line. To oppose these, Kesselring now had 26 divisions. On May 11, the Allies began an all-out offensive, aimed at breaking through the German right flank. On the 13th, a French corps of the Fifth Army finally breached the enemy line and advanced rapidly, accompanied by the Americans. Thus outflanked, the Germans gave way at Monte Cassino under determined attacks by British and Poles of the Eighth Army. Allied troops now surged up the peninsula. On the 25th the Americans made contact with a patrol out of Anzio. On the night of June 2-3, the Germans broke off contact all along the front and hastily withdrew to the north. On June 4, the triumphant Allies entered Rome, where they were joyfully received by the inhabitants. On June 6, Allied forces in England crossed the Channel and invaded Normandy, thereby reducing the Italian front to a mere backwater of the European war.

6

The Defeat of Germany

Following the Casablanca Conference in January 1943, Lieutenant General Sir Frederick Morgan of the British Army had been
directed to set up a Combined Planning Staff to prepare for the coming
Allied invasion of western Europe. Shortening his title, Chief of Staff to
the Supreme Allied Commander (designate) to Cossac, General Morgan
built up a large and efficient organization that surveyed possible landing
beaches from Norway to Portugal, with special attention to those on the
English Channel, for the Channel beaches offered the shortest routes
across water and hence the quickest turnabout of Allied shipping in the
assault. The Cossac staff considered and dealt with problems as diverse
as the tactical control of the Strategic Air Command in Britain and the
availability of landing craft. On the solid foundation of General Morgan's
work rested a great deal of the success of Operation OVERLORD, as the
cross-Channel invasion came ultimately to be called.

By the time of the Teheran Conference in November 1943, Cossac
had done all he could pending the appointment of the actual commander.
At Teheran, Roosevelt, Churchill, and Stalin all agreed to the target date
for OVERLORD of May 1, 1944, yet the supreme commander had still not
been selected. When the cross-Channel attack was tentatively being
planned for 1942 or 1943, the Combined Chiefs of Staff had reached an
understanding that the commander of any large operation would be of
the same nationality as the majority of the troops. Since at the earlier
date British forces would necessarily predominate, Churchill had promised the command to Field Marshal Sir Alan Brooke; but as it became
obvious that by May 1944 American troops would outnumber the British,
Roosevelt and Churchill agreed that the supreme commander should be
an American. At first the President planned to give the command to
General Marshall, but Admiral King and others protested this selection,
insisting that Marshall could not be spared from the Joint and Combined

Chiefs of Staff. In early December 1943 Roosevelt at last made his decision, appointing General Eisenhower to command Operation OVERLORD. The officers appointed to head the naval, ground, and air forces under Eisenhower were all British: Admiral Sir Bertram H. Ramsay, General Sir Bernard Montgomery, and Air Chief Marshal Sir Trafford Leigh-Mallory.

For his task Eisenhower was given the broadest of directives:

> You will enter the Continent of Europe, and, in conjunction with the other United Nations, undertake operations aimed at the heart of Germany and the destruction of her armed forces. The date for entering the Continent is the month of May, 1944. After adequate channel ports have been secured, exploitation will be directed towards securing an area that will facilitate both ground and air operations against the enemy.

The significant thing about this directive is that it provided for nothing less than ending the war. All previous British and American operations in Europe had had more limited objectives, for Allied commanders realized that decisive results could be attained only by means of a drive on Germany from the west. Operation OVERLORD however was conceived on a scale that would permit attaining the ultimate objective. Unlike the landings in Sicily, where the assault forces included most of the combat troops available, the divisions that were to seize a beachhead in western Europe were merely an advance force. Plans called for pouring in more than 50 divisions before the coming of winter.

Planning for OVERLORD was perhaps the most complex problem in the history of warfare. The problem had to be attacked from both ends at once, from the standpoint of strategic desirability and from the standpoint of logistic feasibility. Under the first consideration the planners of Supreme Headquarters, Allied Expeditionary Force (called Shaef for short) had to consider when and where to invade; under the latter, whether supplies, equipment, and personnel could be provided and transported to attain specific aims.

The choice of the landing area was a basic consideration. General Morgan had recommended a stretch of Normandy coast between the mouth of the Orne River and the Cotentin (Cherbourg) Peninsula, a selection accepted by Shaef and the Combined Chiefs. As Shaef planners recognized from the beginning, the chosen landing area was not ideal. An assault directly across the Strait of Dover to the Pas-de-Calais area offered the shortest sea route and hence the quickest turnabout of assault shipping. The Pas-de-Calais also offered the best natural beach conditions and was closest to the Dutch and Belgian ports and to the Ruhr, the industrial center of Germany. But it was obvious to Allied intelligence officers that the Germans expected the landing to come in that area and had made elaborate preparations to throw it back into the sea. Moreover the Pas-de-Calais beach area that could be quickly exploited was too narrow to support operations on the scale planned after the initial assault phase.

The Normandy coast had good beach conditions for part of its length, was somewhat sheltered by the natural breakwater of the Cotentin Peninsula, and was within operational radius of fighter planes based on England. And though the terrain behind the beaches offered special difficulties, it provided good possibilities for a breakout on both flanks. A thrust to the sea on the right flank would isolate German forces in the Brittany (Brest) Peninsula; a wheeling movement on the left flank would provide opportunity for capture of important French ports, notably Le Havre. (See map page 179.) Recognizing that capturing ports from the rear would take time and that the Germans would destroy the port facilities before abandoning them, the Allies decided to construct artificial harbors off the beachhead to expedite unloading of the deluge of supplies that would be required.

General Morgan had recommended a diversionary attack on the southern coast of France, to be carried out simultaneously with the Normandy landings. This proposal the Combined Chiefs of Staff at first accepted, seeing in an invasion of France from the Mediterranean not only a diversion but a means of cutting off German troops in Southwestern France and of securing the port of Marseille for supplying and reinforcing the southern flank of the Allied advance into Germany. The southern project was initially given the code name ANVIL.

General Morgan also recommended that if the necessary landing and beaching craft could be made available the Normandy assault should be broadened to include landings on the east coast of the Cotentin Peninsula. Landings here would permit the early isolation and capture of the port of Cherbourg at the tip of the Peninsula. One of Eisenhower's earliest official acts in assuming command of OVERLORD was to accept Morgan's concept of a broadened front in Normandy and to send Montgomery ahead to London to demand that the strength of the initial cross-Channel assault be increased from three to five divisions. Since the only place the landing and beaching craft for a broadened OVERLORD could come from was ANVIL, Operation ANVIL had to be postponed until the middle of August so that craft assigned to it could first be used in OVERLORD. This expedient together with the reallocation of one month's production intended for the Pacific brought the number of beaching craft for OVERLORD to the just-acceptable minimum. So short was the supply that the loss of three LST's to German motor torpedo boats during an invasion rehearsal brought the reserve force of LST's down to zero. Landing and beaching craft, given top priority by the American Joint Chiefs in anticipation of a 1942 or 1943 cross-Channel attack, had been cut back both to step up construction of antisubmarine craft for the

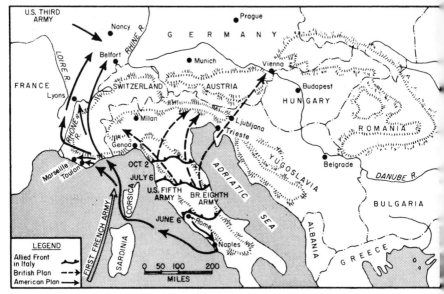

AMERICAN AND BRITISH STRATEGIES IN THE MEDITERRANEAN,
SUMMER 1944

Battle of the Atlantic and as a consequence of uncertainty as to when,
if ever, the Americans would overcome British reluctance to go ahead
with the invasion of western Europe. The postponement of ANVIL meant
of course that it could not serve as a diversion for OVERLORD, but to
Eisenhower the advantage of securing a major Mediterranean port on his
right flank made the southern invasion nevertheless eminently desirable.

Because troops for southern France would have to come from Italy,
Operation ANVIL was nearly canceled when the Allied drive stalled at
Anzio and before the German Gustav Line. Even after the Fifth and
Eighth Armies broke the German line in the spring of 1944 and then
went surging up the Italian boot, Churchill and the British generals insisted that ANVIL should be canceled. They wanted to exploit the momentum of the advance in Italy with a landing at Trieste on the Adriatic,
followed by a drive through the Ljubljana Gap to Austria. The Ljubljana
project was aimed as much at political as at military objectives, but it is
questionable whether Allied forces attempting to penetrate the rugged
Gap with its narrow, winding road could have overcome resistance by
the 25 German divisions in the area in time to reach the Danube ahead
of the Russians. Eisenhower kept insisting on ANVIL, which for security

reasons was renamed Operation DRAGOON. Backed by Roosevelt, who regarded the Ljubljana project as militarily eccentric, Eisenhower finally had his way.

As plans for Operation OVERLORD finally crystallized, they called for three paratroop divisions to be dropped the night before D-day. Then after sunrise on D-day, two American and three British divisions would make nearly simultaneous assaults from the sea. Five beach areas were selected: Utah and Omaha for the American assault; Gold, Juno, and Sword for the British. Preceding the landings, the beaches and their defenses would be subjected to heavy aerial and naval bombardment. By now not even the most skeptical Allied army officer opposed daylight landings and naval gunfire support.

Even though OVERLORD, including the follow-up forces, was the largest amphibious assault ever mounted, it was only part of the over-all strategy against Germany in the spring of 1944. The Fifth and Eighth Army had 25 German divisions tied down in Italy, making them un-available for use elsewhere. On the Eastern Front, where the beaten German armies were being driven back toward the Fatherland, 212 di-visions faced the Soviets. Although Allied forces in Italy and Russia far outnumbered those that would be used in the invasion of western France, they had the strategic effect of a holding force as far as OVERLORD was concerned, enabling the invaders at Normandy to exert their full power against a fraction of the total German strength.

German Defense Plans

Estimating that the Allies would at length attempt to re-enter the Continent from the west, Hitler ordered his western armies to prepare to throw the invaders into the sea. He also directed their commander in chief, Marshal Gerd von Rundstedt, to build an "Atlantic Wall" of case-mated artillery to sweep every possible landing beach from Spain to Norway. But Hitler, his attention focused on Russia, could give only sporadic thought to the situation in the west. The Atlantic front remained the stepchild of the *Wehrmacht*.

Though the Germans agreed that the Allied assault on western Eu-rope would come not later than the spring of 1944, they were not at all agreed as to *where* it would come. The army identified the Pas-de-Calais as the most probable target, both because it was nearest England and because here installations were being built for launching Hitler's V-weapons—pilotless aircraft and long-range rockets. As soon as the Allies detected these installations and recognized the peril they posed for Eng-land, they would doubtless drive at all costs for the launching sites. German army intelligence argued further that the Allies would avoid the Normandy beaches because these were backed by terrain that favored the defense—the difficult *bocage* country of small fields separated by earthen walls topped by trees and thick hedgerows. German naval intelligence officers however reached quite different conclusions. Studying the pattern of Allied bombing, minesweeping, and minelaying, and noting the degree of activity in various British ports, they concluded that the landings would come west of the Pas-de-Calais. And Hitler, in one of his intuitive insights, pointed out the Cotentin and Brittany peninsulas as likely Allied targets. As a result of these varying estimates, though the Pas-de-Calais beaches were the most strongly defended, the Normandy beaches were by no means neglected.

Rundstedt meanwhile had come to distrust the Atlantic Wall concept of static defense. Studying the Salerno assault, he reached the conclusion that his armies had little chance of defeating the invaders at the water's edge in the face of naval gunfire support. Hence he came more and more to rely on mobile infantry and armored divisions placed in strategic positions well inland, whence they could be rushed to the coast to prevent the Allies from exploiting any beachhead they might succeed in seizing.

In early 1944 Hitler placed Field Marshal Rommel under Rundstedt's command with the specific responsibility of defending the Atlantic coast from the Scheldt to the Loire, using the German Seventh and Fifteenth Armies. This appointment led to confusion and divided objectives, for Rommel, basing his estimate on his experiences in North Africa, concluded that Allied air power would prevent Rundstedt's mobile reserves from reaching the coast in time to achieve decisive results. He insisted that the armored defense forces must be placed within five miles of the coast. The decision, he argued, would have to be reached on the beach, and unless the invaders were thrown back into the sea within 24 hours, Germany faced defeat. Hitler, called upon to resolve the conflict between the theories of Rommel and Rundstedt, straddled the issue. He placed some of the armored forces under the former, but not enough to carry out Rommel's plan. The bulk of the reserves Rundstedt retained in the hinterland.

Denied the forces he believed he needed, Rommel concentrated upon static defense. He even neglected training, using his troops as laborers. He energetically set about strengthening the Atlantic Wall, with emphasis upon concrete casemates. He set great store by mines, both sea and land, and planned to sow them thickly on all the beaches and in the beach approaches, but German factories could supply only four per cent of the hundred million mines he wanted. He planned several rows of beach obstacles on which landing craft would impale themselves. Fortunately for the Allies, the two rows that would have been effective at low tide were not installed in time. All the obstacles were intended to be mined, but the mining was far from complete at D-day. As a

DISTRIBUTION OF GERMAN DIVISIONS, JUNE 6, 1944

second line of defense, behind the coastal gun sites, Rommel had the lowlands flooded wherever possible. For obstacles against paratroop and glider landings, he had stakes set close together into the ground ("Rommel's asparagus") in likely stretches of open country. For lack of mines, he planned to install specially rigged artillery shells atop the stakes and join the detonators together with barbed wire that would set off explosions on contact. This plan was largely foiled because the shells arrived too late to be installed.

Rommel, the master of mobility and maneuver, did not rely entirely on static defense. He did what he could to provide for the swift movement of his infantry forces and of the panzer divisions that Rundstedt retained in the rear area. But he lacked sufficient motorized vehicles and, as a result of Allied air supremacy and of previous bombing and sabotage of railroads and bridges, what he had were all but useless for transporting troops at the time of the landings. It is ironic that the inventors of the Blitzkrieg were obliged to proceed to the battle area largely on foot and on bicycles.

Selecting D-Day and H-Hour

The target date for the invasion of France had been set for May 1, 1944, with the understanding that the actual date would be determined by the physical conditions of tide, visibility, weather, and availability of equipment. In order to get an additional month's production of landing and beaching craft, General Eisenhower, with the concurrence of the Combined Chiefs of Staff, postponed the target date to June 1. This was about as late as the invasion could well take place, for the Allies needed all the summer campaigning weather they could get in order to consolidate their conquest of France. With the June 1 target date in mind, the Shaef staff began to look for the combination of natural conditions most favorable for the landing. They desired a moonlit night preceding D-day so that the airborne divisions would be able to organize and reach their assigned objectives before sunrise. They wanted the naval forces and convoys to cross the English Channel during the hours of darkness and to have 30 to 90 minutes of daylight before the landings so that preparatory bombing and naval bombardment of defenses would be effective. The crucial requirement, to which the others would have to be geared, was the tide. It must be rising at the time of the initial landings so that the landing craft could unload and retract without danger of stranding. Reefs and foul ground off the British objectives made a landing at low tide infeasible. Yet the tide had to be low enough that underwater obstacles could be exposed for demolition parties. The final choice was one hour after low tide for the initial landings. Follow-up waves would then have less and less beach to cross as the tide came in. All the required conditions could be met over a three-day period once each month. A fortnight after the three-day period they would be met again except for the moon, which would then be in its new phase. The earliest date after June 1 when the conditions would be fulfilled was June 5, with June 6 and June 7 also suitable. Eisenhower accordingly selected June 5 for D-day, with H-hours ranging from 0630 to 0755 to meet the varying tidal conditions at the five assault beaches.

The Naval Plan

The naval forces, predominantly British, bore large responsibilities for the Normandy invasion. They had to transport the assault troops to the beaches and land them with their equipment. They had to provide shipping to handle the enormous flow of supplies across the Channel— 600 to 700 tons a day per division, in addition to mechanized equipment. They had to act as floating artillery until the guns could be put ashore. They had to provide for the orderly and timely arrival of reinforcement troops and their supplies and equipment, and they had to make provision for the evacuation of casualties. They had to keep German naval forces out of the Channel. They had to sweep lanes through the mine fields and clear the beaches of obstacles that would impede the landing and deployment of troops ashore.

Under Admiral Ramsay's over-all command, the 2,700 vessels (including beaching craft) of the Normandy attack force were divided into the mainly American Western Naval Task Force under the command of Rear Admiral Alan G. Kirk usn and the mainly British Eastern Naval Task Force under Rear Admiral Sir Philip Vian. The Western Naval Attack Force was further subdivided into Task Forces U and O to support Utah and Omaha Beaches respectively, and the Eastern Naval Task Force comprised Task Forces G, J, and S, which held the responsibility for Gold, Juno, and Sword Beaches. The Navy participated in training activities beginning in December 1943 and culminating in April and May, 1944 with full-scale rehearsals by each of the lettered task forces, including realistic landings on the south coast of England. These exercises simulated Operation NEPTUNE, as the naval phase of OVERLORD was called, in every respect except actually crossing the Channel. Even so, when the real NEPTUNE got under way, the meshing of the various task forces had to be extemporized from operational plans which until then existed only on paper. This was no small achievement, for the vessels came from points as widely separated as the Thames Estuary and Northern Ireland. Intricate timing was required to bring all the component parts of the invasion to the beaches on schedule; any disruption could prove disastrous.

Bombing the Railroads

The Combined Chiefs of Staff at the Casablanca Conference of January 1943 had ordered American and British strategic air forces based on Britain to join in a combined bomber offensive for the "progressive disruption of the German military, industrial and economic systems, and the undermining of the morale of the German people to the point where their capacity for armed resistance is fatally weakened." The Allied air forces in short were to make an all-out attempt to defeat Germany by air attack alone. The combined air forces selected as their primary targets submarine construction yards, followed by the aircraft industry, transportation, oil plants, and other war industry, in descending order of priority. The Americans attacked by day in order to attain precision bombing; the British, regarding daylight bombing as too hazardous, preferred night area bombing that laid waste to industrial and military centers.

Whether this "strategic bombing" could actually force a determined foe to surrender was never really put to the test. The requirements of the Mediterranean theater delayed the offensive until the late spring of 1943. By then the *Luftwaffe* had acquired enough fighter aircraft to make the strategic bombing plan too costly. The drive to burn out German industry quickly shifted into a battle for air supremacy as the Allies concentrated their attacks on enemy planes, aircraft storage parks, and aircraft repair depots and on German aircraft and associated industries. Menwhile the Germans were busily shifting their key manufacturing facilities to the southeast, beyond effective attack from the Britain-based bombers. At the end of 1943, when Allied victory in the air appeared to be in sight, photographic reconnaissance detected the V-weapon launching sites in the Pas-de-Calais area and elsewhere—all pointed ominously at England. Destruction of these was then given overriding priority.

General Eisenhower, on assuming command of the Allied Expeditionary Force, was determined to avert the lack of cooperation that had marked Allied air force operations in the Mediterranean theater. Hence he demanded and obtained control of the U.S. Army Strategic Air Force and the British Bomber Command, both based on the United Kingdom. On attaining control, he shocked the strategic air command by adopting Air Chief Marshal Leigh-Mallory's plan for diverting a portion of the Allied air power to the destruction of railroads in France and Belgium. No one denied the necessity of disrupting and delaying German ground movements by any means whatever, because for OVERLORD to succeed, the Allies would have to follow up their relatively light assault with reinforcements at a much faster rate than the enemy could move defense forces to the invasion area. But the strategic air command believed that bombing the railroads would have little lasting effect, that the attempt would be a waste of bombs and bombers that could be used more profitably on other missions. The air command's objections were backed by Churchill and the British War Cabinet, who feared that too many French and Belgian civilians would be killed; having burned their fingers at Mers-el-Kebir and at Dakar, they had no desire again to risk turning potential allies into potential foes.

Despite resistance and counter-arguments, Eisenhower put Leigh-Mallory's "transportation plan" into effect in mid-April 1944. The Allied bombers first systematically worked over the railroad marshaling yards.

Early in May they also began hitting bridges, with such success that before the end of the month not a single bridge spanned the Seine between Paris and the English Channel. On May 21, which the air forces called "Chattanooga Day," fighter-bombers began bombing and strafing tracks, rail facilities, and trains, putting more than a hundred locomotives out of commission the first day. The French and Belgians, far from resenting these Allied attacks on their own soil, recognized their value and gleefully entered into the spirit of the thing with wholesale sabotage. Many a piece of rolling equipment was found useless because some essential part had vanished or a wheel had been mysteriously cracked. Missing railroad spikes caused numerous wrecks.

The Leigh-Mallory plan proved more effective than its stanchest adherents had anticipated. By D-day rail traffic that could have served the German defenses in the invasion zone had declined by about 50 per cent. German attempts to make good the shortage by greater use of road transportation were largely defeated by lack of sufficient trucks or enough gasoline. The preponderance of the Allied build-up in their Normandy bridgehead was assured, particularly since the Allied air forces, despite the diversion of many of their planes, had by D-day won nearly complete command of the air.

On the Brink

Weeks before D-day the entire southern part of England became an armed camp, sealed off from the rest of the country. No one was allowed to cross the line in either direction without a special pass. Stores of all kinds crowded the depots, offering tempting targets to German bombers that never came. As early as May 30, troops began to embark in the transports and beaching craft that would carry them across the Channel. The next day the movement toward France began as 54 blockships, to be sunk as breakwaters off the beaches, left western Scotland. A hundred and fifty minesweepers next advanced into the Channel to begin sweeping a clear passage for the convoys. By Saturday, June 3, all troops were embarked, the fire support ships had put to sea from Scapa Flow, Belfast, and the Clyde, and the convoys were beginning to form off the ports of southern England. NEPTUNE-OVERLORD, the most complex and most minutely planned military operation in history, was under way. Nothing that could be anticipated had been left to chance. There was nevertheless one element of uncertainty—the weather, and on that everything else depended.

Beginning on June 1, at Admiral Ramsay's headquarters in a country mansion near Portsmouth, General Eisenhower met twice daily with the top army and navy commanders of NEPTUNE-OVERLORD to hear the weather forecasts. On the morning of the 3rd the forecasts began to be

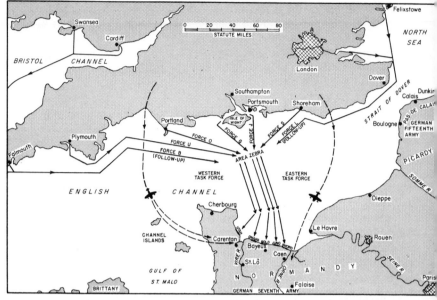

ROUTES OF THE INVASION CONVOYS, OPERATION OVERLORD,
JUNE 6, 1944

discouraging, and grew more alarming through the day. At a special
meeting at 0400 on Sunday, June 4, the meteorologists reported hopeless
prospects for the 5th. High winds, low clouds, and high waves would
combine in the target area. Air support would be impossible, landing
of troops most hazardous, and naval gunfire undependable as a result
of the storm conditions. When Eisenhower had considered all factors, he
made the decision to postpone the invasion 24 hours.

A mighty coiled spring already unwinding had to be stopped, wound
up again, and readied for release the next day. That this was done without serious consequence is a tribute to the skill and adaptability of everyone who played a part in the operation. Sunday evening, as the wind
howled outside and the rain came down in squalls, the commanders met
again at Ramsay's headquarters. Faces were gloomy. It seemed incon-
ceivable that the weather could clear by the morning of Tuesday, June 6,
the new D-day. If there had to be another postponement, it would have
to be for at least two weeks. June 7 was out, for some of the warships
and convoys that had been marking time at sea were running low in
fuel. In two weeks security would be lost, morale would suffer severely,
the whole world would know that something had gone wrong.

To the relief of the commanders, the weather experts now reported prospects for a break in the weather. On this slender hope, Eisenhower set the invasion forces again into operation, but at Leigh-Mallory's request he called another meeting to be held a few hours later for the final decision. When Eisenhower left his mobile trailer camp headquarters to attend the last weather conference, it was still blowing and raining, but by the time the commanders had again assembled, the night sky had begun to clear. The meteorologists now brought in the word that the clearing weather would last at least until the afternoon of the 6th. On the basis of this report Eisenhower at 0415 made his irrevocable decision: "O.K. We'll go."

Across the Channel later that morning, Marshal Rommel left his headquarters in his command car and headed for his home in Germany, where he planned to spend June 6, his wife's birthday. He and the other top German commanders in the West had been warned by their intelligence organization that the Allied invasion was about to be launched, but the commanders had received so many false alarms that they failed to take the accurate warning seriously.* At any rate, they considered a landing unlikely under the weather conditions then prevailing. For lack of meteorological stations west of Europe they had no intimation of the clearing weather on the way.

Once Eisenhower had made his decision, Operation NEPTUNE gathered momentum. From all ports along the south coast of England, from ports on the east and west coasts, from Northern Ireland, from Scotland, and from the Orkneys elements of the armada put to sea. Most headed for Area Zebra, the assembly area southeast of the Isle of Wight. Remarkably enough, despite blowing weather, the thousands of ships involved came together at Area Zebra and moved across the Channel in darkness on almost perfect schedule. Halfway across, each of the swept lanes divided into two—one for fast, the other for slow convoys. While fighter aircraft provided a protective umbrella overhead, minesweepers led the way for the advancing forces, marking the swept lanes with lighted dan buoys. Because Allied bombers had destroyed most of the German coastal radar stations, and Allied jamming made the rest ineffective, the Germans did not detect the assault convoys during the crossing. The Allied fire support ships reached their assigned anchorages off Normandy around 0200, June 6. The attack transport *Bayfield*, head-

---

* German agents had penetrated Resistance groups on the Continent and learned the signal by which the underground would be alerted by BBC from London. It consisted of the first two lines of Verlaine's *Chanson d'Automne*. The first line, "*Les sanglots longs des violons de l'automne,*" was broadcast on June 1; the second, "*Blessent cœur Blessent mon cœur d'une langueur monotone,*" was broadcast in the evening of June 5. German radio monitors heard and recorded both signals, but the practical-minded German commanders scoffed at the notion that the Allies would alert the underground by means of lines of romantic poetry inserted into a public broadcast.

quarters ship for Task Force U, dropped anchor off Utah Beach at 0230. The amphibious command ship *Ancon*, flagship of Task Force O, anchored off Omaha Beach 20 minutes later.

The Normandy Landings

The first troops to land in Normandy were the three airborne divisions, which were dropped about 0130 in the morning of June 6. The British 6th Airborne Division landed between Caen and Cabourg with the mission of seizing bridges over the Orne River and the adjacent Caen canal in order to prevent German reinforcements from moving in from the northeast. (See map page 170.) The American 82nd and 101st Airborne Divisions were approaching their objectives, and the 82nd was seize control of the causeways leading inland from the beaches over meadows that the Germans had flooded, and to capture bridges in the vicinity of Sainte Mère-Eglise and Carenten. The paratroops at first met only limited resistance because the Germans, convinced that the main assault would be directed against the Pas-de-Calais area, regarded the Normandy drops as a mere diversion. By dawn, the 6th and 101st Airborne Divisions were approaching their objectives, and the 81st was containing a German infantry division near Sainte Mère-Eglise.

Off the Normandy beaches, the Allied transports had begun lowering landing craft promptly after dropping anchor, and at 0400 they began debarking the assault troops. These were to advance in a series of waves along boat lanes to the line of departure, where the landing craft were to circle until signaled to advance to the beach. Between the transport area and the beach the fire support vessels were at anchor flanking the boat lanes—the battleships and cruisers 11,000 yards offshore, the destroyers 5,000 yards. Fire support for the American beaches was furnished by the old U.S. battleships *Texas, Nevada,* and *Arkansas,* which were to engage the heavy defenses with their 12- and 14-inch guns, while U.S. heavy cruisers *Tuscaloosa, Quincy,* and *Augusta,* five British and two French light cruisers, a Dutch gunboat, and 22 destroyers took on the lighter beach targets. In the British sector H.M. battleships *Warspite, Nelson,* and *Ramillies* provided the big guns, and were assisted by five British cruisers and numerous destroyers to blast smaller targets. As the leading boat waves headed in from the line of departure, they were to be accompanied by gunboats and rocket-equipped LCT's, which were to blanket the beaches with fire just before the troops stepped ashore.

A little after 0300 a German search radar station had at long last detected and reported "large craft" off the Normandy coast. The shore batteries thereupon were manned in full strength and readied for action. A little past 0500, when first light dimly outlined the silhouettes of the nearer fire support vessels, the batteries opened fire. A few of the vessels replied at once, and by 0600 the pre-landing naval bombardment of the beaches was under way in full fury.

At Utah Beach the support ships checked fire as 276 B-26 medium bombers from England swept over the beaches and dropped 4,400 bombs. Bombing visually through an overcast, many of the B-26's dropped their bombs harmlessly into the water. Nevertheless the American 4th Infantry Division went ashore at Utah in 26 waves against little opposition, the first wave hitting the beach right on schedule at 0630. Here lack of reference points ashore and a southerly tidal set caused the landing to be made three quarters of a mile south of the intended beaches. As it turned out, this accident proved fortunate for the Americans, because the beach obstacles were lighter in the actual landing area than in that designated in the NEPTUNE plan. Beaches in the Utah sector moreover were not protected by formidable obstacles, and here the coastal defense troops were from a "static" division of green reservists and foreign conscripts who were not inclined to fight past hope. By the end of D-day 21,300 troops, 1,700 vehicles, and 1,700 tons of supplies had been landed at Utah beach, and the invaders had suffered fewer than 200 casualties. The 4th Division had established a beachhead six miles deep and six miles wide, had made contact with the 101st Airborne Division, and was ready to press across the base of the peninsula and to link up with the V Corps in the vicinity of the Vire Estuary. As it turned out, the Americans took their heaviest material losses of the day in the waters off the beach, where undetected mines sank a destroyer, two LCI's, and three LCT's.

In sharp contrast to Utah, Omaha proved the most heavily armed and fortified beach that the Americans or their allies were to assault during the entire war.[*] Rommel had given this area special attention, and the defenders had armed the coast here to a strength approaching that of the Pas-de-Calais beaches. The Omaha defenses began 300 feet inshore of the low-water line with a row of 7-by-10-foot steel frames planted upright like gates. Behind these were sharpened, half-buried stakes pointed seaward. Next came a row of "hedgehogs," each composed of three six-foot iron bars crossed at right angles. Many of these obstacles were connected by wires and mined. Just inshore of the high-water line was a sea wall, partly concrete and partly piling, backed by a heavy coil of barbed wire. Behind this was a level shelf from 100 to 300 yards wide, thickly mined and crisscrossed by anti-tank ditches. On the far side of the shelf rose a line of bluffs, too steep even for tracked vehicles. Four deep ravines, breaks in the bluffs through each of which ran a narrow road, gave access to the interior. Guns were everywhere, some mobile, some

---

[*] This does not mean that Omaha Beach was necessarily the most formidably defended, for not even the hard-fighting Germans ever fought virtually to the last man, as the Japanese did on many an island in the Pacific.

casemated. Abandoned stone and brick villas at the foot of the bluffs had been converted into strong points. Trenches for riflemen ran along the top of the bluffs, and here also were machine-gun emplacements, artillery up to 88-mm. caliber, and mortars up to 90-mm. Other gun emplacements were dug into the bluffs so as to enfilade the beach and dominate the four exit ravines. Some of the defenses were manned by soldiers from a static division, such as guarded Utah Beach, but most of the defenders were first-line German troops of the 352nd Division. These had been moved from the interior to the coast at Rommel's insistence the preceding March.

At Omaha Beach shore batteries opened fire on the *Arkansas* at 0530. Some gunnery vessels replied at once, and at 0550 all began the scheduled bombardment of assigned targets. This beach was supposed to be bombed from high altitude by 480 B-24 heavy bombers. But the B-24's, obliged to bomb by instrument because of cloud cover, delayed releasing several seconds to avoid hitting ships or boats. As a result they scattered their 1,285 tons of bombs as much as three miles inland. At Omaha not a single bomb hit the beach or coastal defenses, and indeed the invasion forces did not know that the B-24's had passed overhead. But though bombers contributed little in breaching the Atlantic Wall, Allied fighter planes were entirely successful in keeping the *Luftwaffe* away from the American beaches throughout D-day.

The preparatory naval bombardment of Omaha Beach lasted only 35 minutes. Then all ships lifted fire as the first wave of landing craft headed in from the line of departure. The time allowed was obviously too brief, particularly since numerous targets had not been spotted in advance by aerial reconnaissance, and a good many of the known targets were invisible to spotter planes circling over the beaches. Despite the handicaps however, the ships had knocked out about half the enemy's guns.

The first infantry assault wave was preceded by LCT's carrying standard tanks and by amphibious tanks, some boated, some going in under their own power. Most of the non-boated amphibious tanks were swamped by the choppy sea and went down. The tanks that reached the beach came under heavy shelling, and several were stopped and set afire. LCVP's, coming in next, began taking hits while still 500 yards off shore. By the time they dropped ramps, at 0630 or thereabouts, the fire from the bluffs was intense. Through a hail of bullets and shells, the troops had to wade some 75 yards to the beach and then work their way 250 yards more through the obstacles to the dubious protection of the sea wall. A great many failed to make it.

While the first wave of assault troops huddled against the sea wall, 16 underwater demolition teams landed and proceeded to blast channels through the beach obstacles so that later waves could be brought in ever closer to the sea wall on the rising tide. The teams succeeded in blasting five broad channels, at the cost of more than half their number killed or wounded. Waves of infantry, coming in at ten-minute intervals after 0700, at first merely fed men into the growing mass of prone figures carpeting the beach behind the sea wall. A little after 0800 LCI's, LCM's, and DUKW's headed for the beach with artillery. Nearly all of the DUKW's were swamped or turned back by the choppy seas, and three of the LCI's were hit by shells, set afire, and sunk. Little artillery in fact reached Omaha Beach on D-day. But army engineers managed to blow gaps in the barbed wire behind the sea wall, machine guns were set up, and under the leadership of surviving officers, small groups of men began rushing across the shelf and scaling the bluffs. By noon the Americans had begun to penetrate inland.

What enabled the invaders, with almost no artillery, to advance against the fearsome defenses of Omaha Beach? Sheer courage played its part and tanks helped, but the principal answer is naval gunfire. The *Texas,* the *Arkansas,* and two British and two French cruisers, using air spot by Spitfires based on England, sealed off the beachhead with a ring of fire, preventing the Germans from either reinforcing or shifting their defense forces. But the direct support that cleared the way for the assault forces was provided by nine American and three British destroyers. Closing the shore to within 1,000 yards, actually scraping bottom, these delivered call fire as requested by shore fire control parties or fired at targets of opportunity. The bluffs, which proved an obstacle to vehicles, were a shooting gallery for the destroyers, which could supplement call fire by means of visual observation of enemy positions in the rising ground. During D-day U.S.S. *Carmick* alone expended 1,127 rounds of 5-inch shell, and other destroyers fired almost as many. Thus supported, by nightfall on June 6 some 34,000 troops, nearly five regiments of the 1st and 29th U.S. Divisions, had gone ashore at Omaha. Here they had overrun the bluffs, seized the exit ravines, and established a line more than a mile inland. The price had been high: casualties among the invaders amounted to about 2,000 killed, wounded, and missing.

The landings on the British beaches were easy compared to those at Omaha. In the British sector obstructions were less formidable and less thickly sown, and here the coast defenses were manned by troops of a static division including numerous Poles and Ukrainians. Here too the beaches got a far more extended preparatory naval bombardment than at either Utah or Omaha, for the British landings had to be delayed from an hour to an hour and a half to allow the rising tide to cover the reefs and foul ground in this area. By the end of D-day the 50th British, the 3rd Canadian, and the 3rd British Division, which had landed respectively at Gold, Juno, and Sword Beaches, had penetrated four miles inland, and the 3rd British Division had made contact with the 6th Airborne

Division. Though the British D-day penetration was much deeper than that attained by the Americans at Omaha, it fell short of plans, which included the occupation of Caen. The British were in fact to enter Caen only after weeks of hard fighting.

The Allied invasion could hardly have caught the Germans more off guard. Because of the bad weather preceding D-day, the German Seventh Army, defending Normandy and Brittany, had been taken off alert. Rommel, muttering, "How stupid of me! How stupid of me!" hastened back to France, reaching his headquarters on the 6th a little before midnight. After he had heard the reports of the day's fighting, he said to his aide, "If I were commander of the Allied forces right now, I could finish off the war in 14 days."

Hitler's headquarters, still convinced that the Normandy landings were a diversion and that the main Allied attack would come against the Pas-de-Calais, retained the bulk of the German Fifteenth Army in Flanders, holding back two panzer divisions that might have been rushed to the beachhead early on June 6. It was one of these divisions, belatedly committed, that initially kept the British out of Caen. Hitler now saw that an Allied drive south from Caen would isolate his Seventh Army from his Fifteenth, which continued to guard the Pas-de-Calais. He therefore ordered Rommel and Rundstedt to pour their available reserve strength into the Caen area, making it their focal point for the defense of the Continent. Hitler thus played neatly into Marshal Montgomery's hands. For it was Montgomery's plan to contain as many Germans as possible at Caen, while the Americans first captured the port of Cherbourg in order to assure an adequate inflow of supplies and then thrust south and east in the vicinity of St. Lô. The Allied forces would thus pivot on their left, using Caen as the hinge, and face east on a strong front—both to defend the lodgment area and for an advance toward Germany.

In the evening of June 6 perhaps the strangest fleet ever to sail from any harbor anywhere had got under way from British ports. Included were tired old merchant ships (code name: Gooseberries) on their last voyage, huge concrete caissons (Phoenixes), enormous cruciform steel floats (Bombardons) with their heads visible above the surface, and quantities of tugs and other auxiliaries. This was Operation MULBERRY, which was to provide harbors where none existed—one off Omaha Beach, the other off Gold Beach.

Mulberry A arrived off Omaha Beach at dawn on the 7th after a 5-knot crossing. Construction began that afternoon with the sinking of a line of Gooseberries off shore. To extend the line of Gooseberries, Phoenixes next were sunk with their flat upper surfaces protruding above the water. Outside the artificial harbor, or Mulberry, thus formed was moored a row of Bombardons to act as a floating breakwater. Inside, extending

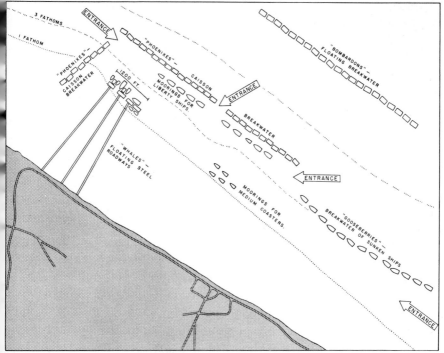

"MULBERRY A," OMAHA BEACH

from the beach, were pontoon piers ending in pierheads constructed to rise and fall with the tide.

By June 17 Mulberry A was ready to receive ships. Here and at Mulberry B in the British sector, which was ready at about the same time, unloading proceeded rapidly. Two days later the worst storm in the English Channel in half a century roared down from the northeast, so battering Mulberry A that it had to be abandoned. Mulberry B, somewhat protected by reefs and better sheltered under the lee of the cape north of Le Havre, survived the storm with comparatively minor damage. Before the invasion, many would have predicted that the loss of one of the artificial harbors would have meant disaster for the Allies. But while awaiting their construction the Navy had found it possible to beach LST's shortly after high tide and unload them when the tide receded. By such means unloading after the destruction of Mulberry A was actually stepped up. At the end of June, 15,000 tons of supplies and 15,000 troops were being landed daily over Omaha Beach alone.

The Battle of Normandy

By June 18 a corps of the U.S. First Army had driven across to the Gulf of St. Malo, thereby sealing off the Cotentin Peninsula. The Americans then wheeled to the right and by the 24th had pushed the 40,000 German defenders to the northern tip of the peninsula and had surrounded Cherbourg. The Army now called upon the Navy to knock out the heavy coastal batteries guarding the waterfront and flanking the city. These batteries, up to 280-mm. (11-inch) caliber, and with a range up to 40,000 yards, were for the most part heavily casemated. Some were in revolving steel turrets capable of being trained inland as well as to sea. For naval vessels to attack such ordnance was contrary to established doctrine that warships should not expose themselves to coastal guns of caliber approaching their own. Nevertheless a naval force under Rear Admiral Morton L. Deyo USN complied with the Army's request. From 1200 till after 1500 on June 25, the *Nevada, Texas,* and *Arkansas,* U.S. heavy cruisers *Tuscaloosa* and *Quincy,* two British cruisers, and eleven destroyers stood up to the shore guns, pounding them from the sea while the American troops stormed Cherbourg from the landward side. The ships, directing their fire chiefly by means of shore fire control parties and spotter aircraft, did much to weaken the city's defenses. By use of smoke and violent maneuver, most of the vessels avoided anything worse than near misses. Two of the destroyers were hit however, and the *Texas* had her bridge wrecked by a 280-mm. shell. The next day the attacking troops received the surrender of the German defending general, and by July 1 the entire peninsula was in American hands. The Germans as usual had done their best to render the port unusable, but the destruction had been carried out so inexpertly that British and American salvage engineers had the harbor in partial use within two weeks.

During the drive for Cherbourg, the Allied forces in Normandy had established a continuous front and had attained an 18-mile southward penetration at the center. Aircraft based on England virtually isolated this beachhead area from the rest of France. German troops advancing from the interior had to move by night and in small formations. Highways leading to the Allied lodgment, under repeated attack from the air, became choked with dead men, dead horses, and shattered equipment. Meanwhile in the first 30 days 929,000 men, 586,000 tons of supplies, 177,000 vehicles, and vast quantities of armament poured into the beachhead from the Channel. The invaders thus attained over the enemy a two-to-one local superiority in manpower and a three-to-one superiority in tanks and guns. The time had come for the long-planned breakout on the western flank.

The British, continuing their pressure on Caen, opposite the eastern flank, entered the city on July 8, after it had been pulverized by artillery

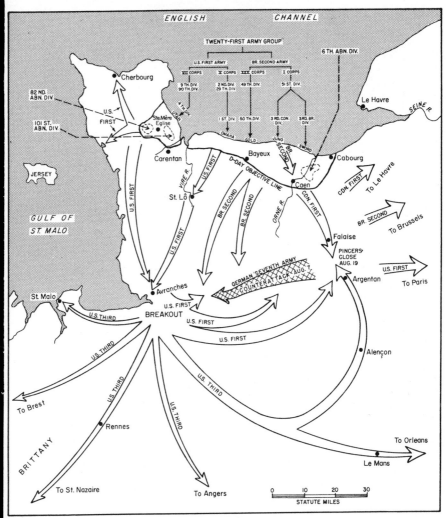

INVASION AND BATTLE OF NORMANDY

and 2,500 tons of aerial bombs. German-held St. Lô, after receiving a similar treatment, was occupied by the U.S. First Army on the 18th. The First Army then pressed southward, flanked on the left by elements of the British Second Army, and worked its way around the western flank of the German Seventh Army. This pressure on the Germans enabled the newly formed U.S. Third Army under General Patton to break through at Avranches and fan out south, east, and west. The effect was to seal off the Brittany Peninsula and to establish a broad front for an eastward advance in the direction of the Rhine, toward which Patton with his usual dash now directed the bulk of his army. Patton's drive to the east left the German Seventh Army nearly surrounded. Common sense now dictated that the Germans retire eastward with all possible speed to avoid being entrapped, but Hitler decreed that they should drive to the west in a futile attempt to penetrate the U.S. First Army and cut Patton's communications at Avranches. This move enabled the American First and Third Armies to complete the encirclement of the enemy on August 19, advancing northward to meet the newly formed Canadian First Army driving down from Caen. Though the Germans entrapped within this "Avranches-Falaise pocket" were subjected to merciless pounding by aircraft and artillery, they managed on the 20th to break through the Canadians and hold open a corridor long enough for 40,000 troops to escape to the east. But 50,000 Germans that did not get out were captured and another 10,000 were killed. The Allies, now 1,500,000 strong, were already moving on Paris and toward Germany.

Most senior German army officers had long since reached the conclusion that Germany was defeated and that further resistance could only result in the ruin of the Fatherland. On July 1, when the British began their successful drive on Caen, Field Marshal Keitel, chief of the *Wehrmacht* staff, telephoned from Hitler's headquarters to Headquarters West and asked despairingly, "What shall we do?" "Make peace, you fools!" replied Rundstedt. "What else can you do?" Hitler thereupon relieved Rundstedt, replacing him with Field Marshal Gunther von Kluge. On arriving in France, Kluge soon agreed with Rommel that further resistance was hopeless, and that if Hitler could not be brought to reason, they should seek a local armistice with Eisenhower and thus force the Führer's hand. On July 15, while directing operations in the vicinity of Caen, Rommel made a final attempt to convince Hitler before taking independent action. "The armies are fighting heroically everywhere," he reported, "but the unequal combat is nearing its end. It is in my opinion necessary to draw the appropriate conclusion from the situation. I feel it is my duty as Commander-in-Chief of the Army Group to express this clearly." Two days later Rommel was severely injured when a strafing fighter plane killed his driver, and his car crashed into a tree.

Meanwhile, officers nearer German headquarters, noting that Hitler seemed determined to pull Germany down in the ashes of his own funeral pyre, had decided that the Führer must be assassinated. On July 20 the attempt was made. A time bomb in a brief case was placed under a table at which Hitler was standing studying maps with his staff. The bomb exploded, killing four officers, but Hitler himself was only slightly hurt.